TO GET RICH IS GLORIOUS

To Get Rich Is Glorious

Challenges Facing China's Economic Reform and Opening at Forty

EDITED BY

Jacques deLisle
Avery Goldstein

BROOKINGS INSTITUTION PRESS
Washington, D.C.

The Brookings Institution is a private nonprofit organization devoted to research, education, and publication on important issues of domestic and foreign policy. Its principal purpose is to bring the highest-quality independent research and analysis to bear on current and emerging policy problems. Interpretations or conclusions in Brookings publications should be understood to be solely those of the authors.

Library of Congress Cataloging-in-Publication Data.
Names: deLisle, Jacques, 1961– editor. | Goldstein, Avery,
    1954– editor.
Title: To get rich is glorious : challenges facing China's economic
    reform and opening at forty / edited by Jacques deLisle and Avery
    Goldstein.
Description: Washington, D.C. : Brookings Institution, [2019] |
    Includes bibliographical references and index.
Identifiers: LCCN 2019012060 (print) | LCCN 2019014026 (ebook)
    | ISBN 9780815737261 (epub) | ISBN 9780815737254 (pbk.)
Subjects: LCSH: China—Economic policy—2000– | China—
    Economic policy—1976–2000. | China—Economic
    conditions—2000– | China—Economic conditions—1976–2000.
    | China—Foreign economic relations.
Classification: LCC HC427.95 (ebook) | LCC HC427.95 .T62 2019
    (print) | DDC 330.951—dc23
LC record available at https://lccn.loc.gov/2019012060

9 8 7 6 5 4 3 2 1

Typeset in Adobe Caslon Pro

Composition by Elliott Beard

CONTENTS

TO GET RICH IS GLORIOUS

China's Economic Reform and Opening at Forty

Past Accomplishments and Emerging Challenges

JACQUES DELISLE | AVERY GOLDSTEIN

In 2018, China marked the fortieth anniversary of its reform era and the beginning of Xi Jinping's second five-year term as China's top leader. Xi had begun his first term by identifying serious challenges that confronted the country after a generation of mostly highly successful reforms, and promising dramatic changes to ensure the continuation of economic progress. Xi sought to reframe the modernization effort that had been at the center of "reform and opening" as an agenda of "national rejuvenation" to realize the "China dream."[1]

When Xi delivered his key speeches at the national meetings that confirmed his continued leadership (as Chinese Communist Party general secretary at the Nineteenth Party Congress in October 2017 and as president at the Thirteenth National People's Congress the following March), he both reiterated his commitment to a bold new round of reforms and articulated ambitious benchmarks for success in the coming decades. Xi moved beyond vague references to "rejuvenation," the "China dream," and the importance of making great progress in time for the twin centennials (of the CCP's founding in 1921 and the PRC's founding in 1949). He called for China to become a fully modernized, advanced society by 2035 and a country in the front rank of the world's great powers measured by economic development and military power by 2049.[2] Xi's implicit comparator was the United States, and he thus suggested that in terms of wealth and power China should expect to be a true peer of the United States on the world stage by mid-century. Publicly stating these goals encouraged expectations of the Chinese people about improvement in the quality of their lives and raised eyebrows abroad as many wondered whether China was announcing its intention to use its greater clout—rooted in its long run of economic success—to reshape a post–World War II international system, including its economic institutions and norms, that has reflected the preponderant position of the United States.

Although Xi's pronouncements in 2012–2013 promised decisive action on China's mounting economic and economics-related problems, the record during Xi's first term was unspectacular, in part because China has encountered large and intractable obstacles. Much of the difficulty that the Xi-era agenda for economic reform has faced reflects the consequences of four decades of remarkable accomplishments under the policy of "reform and opening" (*gaige kaifang*). In December 1978, China was barely two years into the post–Mao Zedong era. The chaos of the Cultural Revolution was still a fresh memory. The rural economy was based on collectivized farming, with mandatory sales of agricultural output to state procurement agencies. Urban industry and commerce were largely state-owned and subject to state economic planning (albeit in a less pervasive form than in Soviet-style economies). China's per capita GDP was around $200 (in current U.S. dollar terms as measured by the World Bank), ranking it among the poorest countries in Asia and around the tenth percentile globally.[3] China's foreign economic policy was one of near-autarky. Exports were seen as merely a way to acquire foreign currency necessary to pay for imports, and trade was conducted through a handful of state monopoly companies. International trade was less than 10 percent of China's GDP, and foreign investment was negligible.[4]

All of this began to change in December 1978, with the Third Plenum of the Eleventh Central Committee of the Chinese Communist Party—the cumbersome name for the foundational moment of the reform era. The meeting marked the consolidation of power by Deng Xiaoping, who had returned from a second period of political oblivion following his purge at the instigation of the radical Gang of Four after the death of Deng's sometime patron, Premier Zhou Enlai. Partly building on the Four Modernizations associated with Zhou and adopted by Mao's short-lived successor

Hua Guofeng, Deng and his leadership cohort launched the policies of "reform" (meaning market-oriented economic reform at home) and "opening" (to economic—and broader—engagement with the outside world).

The first decades of reform brought striking results, largely due to a fundamental political choice to eliminate obstacles rooted in the planned economy and Mao-era policies, and to permit formerly prohibited activities that seemed sure to boost production and productivity by tapping into labor reserves, human capital, and entrepreneurial talent at home, and capital and technology from eager investors abroad. Mao had repeatedly rejected economic policies of this sort. He did so not because he did not think they would produce economic growth but because they did not align with his ideological preferences. Mao implicitly acknowledged as much when he temporarily tolerated partial returns to basic market economic principles to overcome difficulties his policies produced. In periods of retrenchment from collectivization during the middle 1950s and after the Cultural Revolution, but most spectacularly in the aftermath of the depression and famine the Great Leap Forward produced, Mao entrusted economic policy to pragmatists to find ways to promote an economic recovery. What worked in each instance was an embrace of market norms (especially relying on material incentives and responsibility for profits and losses) that became the kernel of the reform and opening program adopted at the end of 1978. Notably, when Deng led the break with the Maoist past, he echoed his own pragmatic approach to policy from the post–Great Leap retrenchment—one that had been anathema to Maoist economic policy: "It doesn't matter whether the cat is black or white; if it catches mice, it's a good cat."

Once in charge, Deng and those around him permitted bottom-up initiatives that enlivened the domestic economy. The first big breakthrough and fundamental key to success was the decollectivization of agriculture, which amounted to a return to family farming under the production responsibility system.[5] Although the land itself remained collectively owned, land use rights were allocated to individual households. Rising state procurement prices and free markets for the sale of agricultural products reconnected labor and investment with material rewards. The regime thus essentially followed a program of land reform that had fostered productive agriculture elsewhere—including in the PRC before collectivization in the 1950s.

Early in the reform era, the regime also began to tolerate small-scale private entrepreneurs and altered the economic incentives for larger enterprises in the urban industrial and commercial sectors. Here, too, the logic of relying on material incentives, the relaxation of price controls, and the freeing of markets were defining features of reform policies. Enterprises gained new freedoms to choose suppliers, customers, and employees, often using contracts to structure those relationships and create legal rights and obligations.

Key policy changes for established enterprises included the granting of greater autonomy to managers and the assignment of responsibility for profits and losses to production units and their leaders. State-owned and collectively owned enterprises faced a hardening of the typically soft budget constraints of socialism that had undermined enterprise efficiency, and entered a more arm's-length fiscal relationship with the state, which increasingly substituted tax payments for profit remissions and shifted access to capital from state allocations to bank loans, bonds, and other financial instruments. Especially as the reform era moved deep into its second decade, many state and collectively owned enterprises were privatized or at least corporatized. Such enterprises coexisted and competed with newer firms that always had faced more market-oriented incentives and constraints. These new enterprises took increasingly varied ownership forms, including single-owner private firms, limited liability companies, joint ventures, foreign-invested firms, and stock exchange–listed companies.

Reform in the urban industrial and commercial economy came later and proved to be more difficult than in rural China. There was no clear precedent in the PRC's own history, or in the experience of other communist countries, for urban reform that was comparable to the template China's initiatives on rural reform drew upon. The political clout of the bureaucratic patrons of state-owned industry, and more pointed ideological objections to dismantling the pillars of socialism in the industrial economy, slowed and diluted reforms. Success instead turned on "outgrowing" the inherited, planning-era economy with new sectors and types of firms emerging from below, and on the top-down decision to step up the opening of the country to the outside world.

The decision to end the self-imposed international isolation of Mao's economic development model had, from the beginning of the reform era, envisioned a role for foreign economic engagement to boost the country's modernization. At first, the regime was relatively cautious about encouraging trade and foreign investment, but the "opening" side of "reform and opening" soon accelerated. Rights to engage in foreign trade were gradually extended to more numerous and diverse enterprises, and eventually were made universal. China began to lower its high tariffs and remove nontariff barriers, especially as Beijing intensified its push to enter the WTO in the 1990s, with its accession finally taking place in 2001.

Increasingly open and liberal rules for foreign investment developed over the course of the reform era. Geographically, foreign investment–friendly legal regimes began with four Special Economic Zones on the southeast coast at the dawn of the reform era, then expanded to more than a dozen coastal cities, to larger special zones, and even to far-inland areas (under the Jiang Zemin policy of the "great opening of the West"). A policy initiative for still-more-liberal enclaves began in 2013 with a free-trade zone in Shanghai. Policies and rules tested in such special zones often became models for nationwide changes.

Permissible forms of foreign investment proliferated and became more flexible over time. What began as a limited regime that allowed only for majority Chinese-owned joint ventures in 1979 expanded to include more flexible contractual joint ventures, wholly foreign-owned enterprises, a revised and more adaptable equity joint-venture form, companies that could sell shares to foreign individuals and, later, institutional foreign investors, and finally foreign acquisition of Chinese firms. Ever wider sectors of the Chinese economy were opened to foreign investment. Laws and policies shifted from requiring that projects generate foreign exchange or bring in needed technology, and that they receive probing case-by-case approval, to much more permissive rules that generally allowed foreign investment, except in a shrinking range of specifically prohibited sectors or cases where authorities determined that national security concerns (vaguely and broadly defined) weighed decisively against allowing foreign ownership.

These developments reflected an early and growing recognition of the benefits to China and investors of combining foreign capital and technology with China's plentiful, able, comparatively docile—and, in the early decades, inexpensive—labor supply. From the beginning of the reform era through the dramatic impact of China's accession to the WTO, foreign investment has been closely bound up with China's burgeoning export sector—which was also assisted by currency policies that gave Chinese goods an enhanced price advantage in global markets.

For China's leaders and policy-makers, the international opening also served to advance domestic reform. They recognized the usefulness of international competition in catalyzing change. The torturous negotiations that led to China's WTO entry at the turn of the century provided leverage to push through policy reforms to improve the efficiency of domestic industry and subjected Chinese firms operating within China and in international markets to the discipline of competition with formidable foreign rivals.

After forty years of interlinked reform at home and opening abroad, China has been profoundly transformed. It has the world's second largest economy by GDP measures, and the largest by purchasing-power parity measures.[6] Its per-capita GDP has reached nearly $9,000, placing China among the group of upper-middle-income countries. Agriculture has been decollectivized and commercialized and has shrunk to less than 8 percent of GDP (from nearly 30 percent at the start of the reform era) as the countryside has industrialized and the population has urbanized, with more than half of Chinese citizens now living in cities.[7] Although the definitions of state-owned, collective, and private enterprises are murky and contested, private firms, including foreign-invested ones, now account for most of China's economic output. China has become the world's largest trading economy (with a trade to GDP ratio of 38 percent, down from a 2006 peak of nearly two-thirds), ranks among the top destinations for foreign investment, and has emerged as a significant and rapidly growing source of outbound foreign investment, which is slated to expand as Beijing implements its Belt and Road Initiative.[8] China has assumed a much more prominent role in international economic regimes, taking the lead in founding the Asian Infrastructure Investment Bank (a multilateral development bank) and promoting the Regional Comprehensive Economic Partnership (a mega-regional trade-plus pact), casting itself as a principal proponent of economic globalization in a time of U.S. retreat, and seeking to make the renminbi a major international currency.

The improvement in the standard of living among the vast majority of China's citizens during the era of reform and opening has contributed to high levels of support for the regime and its policies. Despite disagreements among researchers about the accuracy of public-opinion surveys measuring support for China's government, there is consensus on the general portrait the data present: A clear majority of China's people (often an overwhelming majority) express satisfaction with the regime's policies, are optimistic about the direction of the country, and indicate that they expect their children to have a better life than they do.[9] In recent years, the regime has moved more forcefully to address some of the problems that have been sources of significant public discontent, through policies that aim to improve the social safety net, tackle the environmental costs of focusing solely on rapid economic expansion, and reduce corruption.

Notwithstanding this impressive record, the regime also has faced mounting challenges in sustaining the economic success that has legitimated its rule. Although GDP growth was very high over the first decades of reform, averaging near double-digits, more recently the pace has slowed. In China's larger and more mature economy during the 2010s, the leaders in Beijing have acknowledged this reality and adjusted the goals for GDP growth rates to a "new normal" of 6 percent to 7 percent annually.[10]

Structural issues and deep-seated problems make the challenge of sustaining growth and economic transformation more daunting as the reform era enters its fifth decade. While the accomplishments of the first four decades of reform have been remarkable by any measure, the gains reaped during this period (and especially its early phases) were relatively low-hanging fruit. With much progress already achieved by abandoning Mao-era policies, following a fairly clear path toward initial market-oriented reforms, and exploiting China's existing comparative advantage in engaging with the international economy, the tasks of reform have become more complex and difficult. China's economic success since 1978 has brought it to a level of per-capita income that, in many developing countries, has been associated with a "middle-income trap"—that is, a stagnation of growth rates and a stalling out of hitherto rapid progress.[11]

Rapid growth has been accompanied by severe environmental degradation, and China increasingly must bear the deferred costs of cleaning up its air, water, and soil, and the public-health consequences of not having done so. Demographic trends compound the difficulties: China faces the flattening of the Lewis curve as the relatively easy productivity gains of moving a vast agrarian population into the monetized industrial (and post-industrial) economy are exhausted.[12] Partly thanks to the restrictive population-control policies in place from the mid-1980s through the mid-2010s, China is confronting the waning of what had been a huge demographic dividend, with a rapid transition from a ratio of the old and very young to working-age population that was abnormally low by international standards to one that will be unusually high for a middle-income country.

In rural China, increases in agricultural production and incomes had already slowed by the mid-1980s, although the negative effects were offset in part by a boom in "township and village enterprises," which accounted for a growing fraction of rural residents' incomes.[13] But the TVEs themselves soon ran into serious financial difficulties, and shut down or were sold off in large numbers. Meanwhile, the movement of hundreds of millions of Chinese to cities, which was a major factor in national economic growth and transformation, stripped parts of the countryside of young, productive agricultural workers. By the 2000s, rural China, especially areas near fast-growing cities, faced additional stresses rooted in broader economic development as local officials seized and transferred land from rights-holding rural residents for meager—and often legally inadequate—compensation.

In urban areas as well, economic problems became difficult and complex. State-owned enterprises, which remained a significant factor in the economy, especially as sources of jobs and recipients of capital, continued to exhibit the productivity problems that made them a perennial target of policies seeking to advance still-incomplete reforms. Mechanisms for allocating capital were a source and a reflection of problems as well: stock markets have been notoriously volatile and occasionally crisis-prone; non-performing loans, partly the product of politically influenced or policy-driven lending to state-linked enterprises or local governments, have burdened China's banks and required government measures to recapitalize them; and large, unmet demand for capital has led to the rise of extensive shadow banking and informal, sometimes illegal, lending practices that could pose systemic risks. Like their rural cousins, city dwellers have faced undercompensated expropriation of their residences and businesses by local governments acting in collaboration with real-estate developers.

Moreover, while overall incomes in both urban and rural China have risen dramatically during the reform era, the distribution of wealth has become more skewed. Wide disparities have emerged between prosperous coastal regions and a lagging interior, between cities and the countryside, and within urban areas that are home to the world's first or second largest group of billionaires as well as recent migrants from the countryside who work in the informal economy and lack full access to China's modest social safety net and other publicly provided goods.[14]

Although the CCP regime has enjoyed, and enforced, remarkable social and political stability, it faces significant and likely growing challenges in these areas. The incomplete nature of economic reform in a one-party state where officials are not reliably held accountable for unlawful activities has made corruption an endemic condition. Officials and the politically connected have engaged in arbitrage between state-controlled assets and new opportunities for enrichment that markets have presented.[15] Public anger directed at local officials who may be blamed for various forms of corruption, environmental disasters, economic difficulties, abuses of power to expropriate property, and failures to deliver government services has produced tens of thousands of mass protests annually. Slowing growth, increasing inequality, and perceived unfairness in the distribution of opportunity mean that the regime faces a persistent risk of more significant, economically disruptive upheaval.[16]

At the same time, China's policy of opening to the outside world has been fading as a driver of growth and development. China's international economic engagement expanded dramatically and did much to build China's wealth and power during the first decades of the reform era. But by the twenty-first century, troubles were brewing. For an economy as large as China's, export-led growth was no longer a realistic option. Foreign markets that had helped drive China's growth during the first decades of reform were a limited and potentially unreliable source of demand, as became painfully clear with the global financial crisis of 2007–2008 and as China's exporting prowess began to produce a backlash from its trading partners.

Countries and companies that saw their market shares or profitability falling, their industries relocating (many to China), their workers losing jobs, and their trade deficits with China swelling increasingly asserted that China was winning unfairly.[17] China's trading partners complained of tariff and nontariff barriers that limited access to China's markets and impeded competition with local firms as China's domestic consumption expanded. They also charged that Beijing improperly aided exporters, enabling them to sell their goods at below-market prices abroad, and that China manipulated exchange rates, keeping the renminbi's value artificially low to advantage Chinese goods in foreign markets. As the reform era neared its fortieth anniversary, concerns about China's industrial policies—especially the Made in China 2025 program and other efforts to move China to the global forefront of emerging, technology-intensive sectors—became a focus of urgent foreign worry and ire about Chinese policies that affect other states' economies and the global economy. Bright spots for China's trading partners—including high commodity prices driven by China's booming imports—were not enough to offset these growing sources of friction.

China's trade-related issues became salient in the electoral politics of major trading partners, especially the United States. Although trade liberalization had a generally positive effect on U.S. employment (especially in high-skilled service sectors), prices for consumers and intermediate goods users and overall growth, the lowering of barriers to Chinese goods and the resulting surge in imports from China did have a significant negative impact on jobs and wages in some manufacturing sectors and the localities where they are concentrated.[18] Those unevenly distributed economic losses had political consequences. In the 2016 presidential election, candidates critical of liberal trading regimes, especially with China, fared well in primaries, with Donald Trump winning the Republican nomination and Bernie Sanders finishing a strong second to Hillary Clinton in the Democratic contest. In the general election, both major-party candidates condemned the Trans-Pacific Partnership—a sweeping trade-plus agreement with countries that had a less negative reputation among the U.S. public than China did. Assessments of the impact on voting of high exposure to Chinese import competition variously found that it drove support for more right-leaning Republican and left-leaning Democratic candidates, candidates opposed to trade liberalization, and Trump.[19]

Although China has remained a top-tier recipient of foreign capital throughout the reform era, foreign investors have had chronic and, in some respects, worsening grievances about China's policies and behavior. International companies doing business in China have consistently and stridently complained of a tilted playing field that benefits Chinese competitors at their expense through a variety of mechanisms that include selective and uneven enforcement of laws and regulations, favoritism toward well-connected Chinese firms, and preferential treatment obtained through corruption that multinational firms must forego because of home-country legal requirements, internal corporate rules, or concerns about public image and shareholder reaction.

In recent years, more charges have been added to the mix. Foreign acquirers of Chinese firms have been thwarted by China's anti-monopoly regulators, in what frustrated would-be buyers see as instances of protectionism. The advent of broad authority for national security review of foreign investments has raised the prospect of additional forms of disguised protectionism. While weak protection of foreigners' intellectual property rights has been a major focus of criticism throughout the reform era, in recent years E.U. and U.S. companies, and government agencies that hear

their complaints, increasingly have asserted that Beijing is leveraging foreign companies' interest in access to Chinese markets to require sharing
or transferring of technology and intellectual property, or simply stealing
it in the course of business operations. Espionage by allegedly state-linked
actors targeting United States and other foreign companies' valuable commercial information and technology exacerbated this area of friction in
China's external economic relations.

Additional concerns emerging in the mid-2000s included the impact
on national security of rising Chinese investment in significant or sensitive
sectors of other countries' economies. The response has been tougher laws,
regulations, and practices that expand and tighten the process of oversight
to limit Chinese investment in or acquisition of companies whose location
near sensitive government or military installations, role in the domestic
economy or defense industries, or advanced technologies might have implications for national security.[20]

After an election campaign that included much condemnation of
China's economic policies and their alleged effect on the United States,
the Trump administration increased pressure on China and insisted that
China accept demands that addressed a long-standing litany of U.S.
complaints. With China not acquiescing to the U.S.'s agenda, Washington announced escalating and expanding tariffs on Chinese goods, and
Beijing responded in kind. Under both presidents Obama and Trump,
U.S. authorities indicted Chinese nationals accused of state-linked
cyber-spying.

In U.S. policy discussions, the economic conflicts with China were one
part of a larger dispute over a range of American grievances that linked
political and economic concerns about China and that had been deepening
for at least a decade. Major issues included state-sponsored cyber-attacks,
the vulnerability inherent in relying on supply chains in which China
played a central role, and the potential security risks of relying on Chinese
technology in vital American infrastructure, especially telecommunications. The economic and related political and security issues contributed to
a bipartisan reassessment of American policy toward China. The decades-
long consensus on the wisdom of engagement, broadly understood—
seeking areas of cooperation and managing conflicts with a rising China
whose role could be shaped so that it would be a constructive participant
in global affairs—had begun to erode during the Obama administration
and declined further after Trump became president. In its place, a view of

China as a rising threat that had to be countered, and whose rise should not be facilitated, became the mainstream view in Washington.

Among American analysts and policy-makers, many argued that engagement had failed to deliver on its perceived and often-touted promises about the sort of international partner China would become. Some stressed disappointment that economic integration and growing prosperity had not led to liberalizing political reforms in China. Instead, after the 2008 Olympics and especially after Xi Jinping became the country's leader, critics noted the reassertion of authoritarian politics under tightened CCP control. Others focused on limitations to China's liberalization of the rules and practices governing foreign trade and investment despite promises undertaken when it joined the WTO in 2001. A minority continued to defend engagement. They acknowledged China's shortcomings and America's frustration with recent trends. But they argued that engagement had, in fact, served the chief and relatively modest purposes for which it was designed, and argued that it remained the only realistic way to provide incentives for China to become a more responsible actor integrated with an international community from which it might yet learn to appreciate the virtues of a more open society.[21] Nevertheless, the critique of engagement prevailed, and it culminated in two key national security documents drafted by the Trump administration and was echoed in a high-profile speech by Vice President Pence. For the first time, U.S. national security strategy explicitly labeled China a "revisionist" power threatening the existing international order that has been favorable to American interests and called for the United States and its allies to adopt strong countermeasures.[22]

In China, these accusations and demands struck a long-sensitive nerve. The CCP regime had emerged from upheavals and revolutions triggered by the bitter experience of encroachments and indignities inflicted by foreign powers that had oppressed and exploited a weak and poor China during the nineteenth and early twentieth centuries. The CCP regime's legitimacy derives not only from improving the people's living conditions—the pre-eminent metric for the post-1978 period. It rests also on fulfilling the long-standing aspiration of Chinese nationalists never again to fall prey to the bullying that characterized the "century of humiliation"—an agenda that has been gaining prominence under Xi, surely in part due to the mounting challenges of sustaining economic performance as a basis of legitimacy.[23]

Facing a worsening external environment and significant domestic economic challenges, how will a China that has become much richer and more influential since 1978 adapt and respond as the era of reform and opening moves into its fifth decade and as Xi prepares for a tenure that (after constitutional revisions abolishing term limits for president were adopted in March 2018) seems likely to extend beyond 2022? In some areas, ambitious economic reform goals have been set and work has begun.[24]

Yet, despite the fanfare accompanying pledges to deepen reform, in practice the Xi regime has mostly moved down a broadly familiar path. Xi has paid rhetorical respect to the Deng era's agenda of "reform and opening." He has extended the Hu-Wen leadership's commitment to an economic-development strategy that emphasizes quality of growth (including sustainable development) rather than focusing only on GDP gains, relying on domestic consumer demand rather than exports or state-driven investment to fuel China's growth engine, and addressing income inequality and re-weaving a social safety net.[25] Extending the broad arc of China's reform-era development agenda, Xi has increased the salience of promoting higher technology and higher value-added sectors, and indigenous innovation. The goal is to make China's companies internationally competitive—even dominant—in newly emerging industries (including telecommunications, biotechnology, artificial intelligence, and robotics), reprising reform-era China's earlier success in becoming the factory to the world.[26]

At the same time, however, the Xi era has raised questions, both old and new, about the nature and trajectory of China's economic reform and development. CCP ideology has begun to downplay the historical role of Deng—the avatar of China's reform era—and emphasize Xi's contributions.[27] The potential for further reform faces constraints rooted in tensions among the key goals the regime set for the era of reform and opening: to make China more prosperous and more internationally influential while also ensuring the CCP remains in control. This multifold strategic agenda has always set limits to domestic reform and international openness. When the CCP leadership believes that economic changes threaten to bring political and social changes that jeopardize one-party rule, or, in the regime's terminology, "unity and stability," it opts for retrenchment.

Developments rooted in greater wealth, market economics, international openness, or technological advancement lead to inflation, unemployment, real-estate bubbles, stock-market crashes, unmanaged information flows, political dissent, social unrest, or vulnerability to foreign pressure, and prompt China's leaders to prioritize countering threats to the party's control over reforming the economy and opening to the outside world. State intervention in markets, growing party presence in firms, slower progress or reversal of domestic economic reforms, and greater control over inbound and outbound international economic activity resurge, often at the cost of delaying what are recognized to be necessary reforms. Perhaps tellingly, the Xi regime's most dramatic initiatives have centered on a wide and deep anti-corruption crackdown; a tightening in the ideological, political, and cultural spheres; a major reorganization of China's military; and the launch of efforts (such as the Asian Infrastructure Investment Bank, the Belt and Road Initiative, and the Regional Comprehensive Economic Partnership) that may give China greater influence in shaping international economic rules, potentially in ways that entail lesser demands on China to assimilate to existing, market-oriented norms and rules.[28]

To be sure, a decisive turn away from the general direction of decades of reform and opening up may not occur. There may well be constraints that limit the regime's political appetite for such moves. Because the regime seeks to maintain its leading position without relying solely on the coercive tools of authoritarian rule that are costly and perhaps, in the long run, ineffective, China's leadership recurrently faces great pressure to relent on retrenchment and resume reform efforts that will improve economic performance and enhance legitimacy.

Nonetheless, the Xi Jinping era also has generated a distinctive set of uncertainties about the future of the reform era's long march of gradual but progressive marketization of the economy and convergence with largely liberal international economic norms. Some see a formidable alternative "Chinese model" or Chinese-style state capitalist-model—one that can provide a template for developing countries and a rival to the neoliberal paradigm and the postwar international economic order.[29] Others—including most of the authors in this volume—are more skeptical. From this perspective, the original reform-era development model may be running its course, and China's leaders now face formidable, but not necessarily insurmountable, tasks that may demand that they innovate in ways that entail taking hitherto unacceptable political risks.[30]

The first part of this volume focuses on domestic economic reform. In an overview chapter, Barry Naughton characterizes the first three decades of the reform era as a period of "enlivening" the domestic economy. In his account, it encompassed several waves of rapid growth-supporting change. The first waves came in the rural sector during the 1980s and early 1990s, with decollectivization of agriculture and the grant of land-use rights to farming households; followed by liberalization of the nonagricultural rural economy and the rise of township and village enterprises producing labor-intensive manufactured goods; followed, in turn, by opening the urban economy to market reforms and the emergence of small-scale private entrepreneurial businesses. The next wave enlivened the state sector, which had been the core of the planned economy, but which faced massive layoffs and insolvency by the early 1990s. Here, key reforms included restructuring remaining state-owned enterprises (SOEs) as corporations capable of surviving and even thriving in a market economy. Primarily in the 2000s, the final waves of enlivening arrived: massive migration of young, underemployed people from the countryside to urban areas with more productive economies; privatization of urban housing, which triggered a massive housing boom; and China's entry into the WTO, which brought a surge of export-led growth.

By the early years of the twenty-first century, Naughton argues, "enlivening" gave way to "steerage." Major market-oriented reform initiatives ceased, notwithstanding ambitious but thus far unimplemented promises for a new wave of reforms at the November 2013 Third Plenum of the Central Committee elected at the Eighteenth CCP Congress, and the persistence of old ways in many areas of the Chinese economy that would benefit from further market-oriented changes. As the "miracle growth" phase waned in a wealthier, maturing economy, and Chinese policymakers lost faith in enlivening, Chinese policy turned toward a new phase of government activism to combat slowing growth in a largely marketized economy. New development strategies focus on identifying and funding "drivers of growth"—principally, high-tech industrial sectors that are strategic emerging industries, part of the innovation-driven development strategy, or were covered by the Made in China 2025 plan—and, secondarily, transport and communication infrastructure projects under the Belt and Road Initiative. Naughton concludes that the model of the Chinese economy that is emerging in this post-enlivenment era is a not-yet-well-understood blend of interventionist and, in some respects, risky state policy and reliance on innovative private—but, in some respects, state-dependent—enterprises.

Economic reform began in the countryside. In Jean Oi's account of four decades of rural reform, initial successes and mounting difficulties both stem from strategies of partial reform, permitting market-oriented changes while not transgressing core principles of the socialist system. Oi assesses decollectivization without privatization of land ownership; rural industrialization without a fully private sector; and rural to urban migration while retaining the *hukou* system of household registration.

Decollectivization, which gave peasants rights to manage land and receive benefits from its productive use, and increased prices for agricultural outputs—from state procurement agencies and consumers' newly freed markets—produced big gains in productivity and income. But decollectivization deprived local governments of revenue, which led them to impose heavy fees on rural households that generated unrest. This, in turn, prompted policies to recentralize control over local cadres and revenue collection in the 1990s and to reduce fees and taxes on peasants in the 2000s. In this context, the decision not to privatize land ownership brought unintended consequences: with land still owned by the collective, local authorities expropriated villagers' land-use rights as a new source of revenue. Industrialization brought rapid growth to rural China in the 1990s, but collectively owned township and village enterprises (TVEs), along with private firms that worked closely with local officials, dominated. This pattern initially contributed to growth by ameliorating local officials' opposition to the development of new enterprises. But support from the local state also meant lower barriers to enterprise creation, softer budget constraints, and weaker firms than would have been the case had rural industrialization relied on a true private sector. TVEs became a burden on local government finances and were privatized in a belated and disruptive transition. China's retention of the *hukou* system, which in principle binds people to living where they are registered, initially fostered economic development, limiting what otherwise might have been the flood of urban migration that has vexed other developing countries, and giving rural authorities roles as labor brokers for peasants relocating to cities. But the *hukou* system also led to systematic discrimination against migrants, denying them access to urban public goods and leaving them vulnerable to forced repatriation. As *hukou*-linked rights to rural land became more valuable, former rural residents were unwilling to give up their *hukou*, which impeded reforms, including policies associated with the New Socialist Countryside. For Oi, all these areas reveal links between chronic problems of local government finance and the perils of partial reform.

Although reform in the rural economy was far from simple and varied across time and space, the story of reform in other sectors of the Chinese economy has been more complex and fragmented. The two remaining chapters on domestic reform shift the focus to narrower, but illustrative, issues within the broad areas of urban enterprises and the financial sector.

Yasheng Huang tackles the question of changing patterns of ownership of enterprises in reform-era China. He takes as background the transformation of China's industrial and service economy from state socialism and pervasive state ownership to the multiple and complicated forms of enterprises that legal and policy changes allowed during the first decades of reform, including: state-owned enterprises, limited liability companies, privately owned enterprises (including very large ones), stock exchange–listed corporations, foreign-invested enterprises, and others. Accounts of this dimension of China's reform-era economic trajectory, including Nicholas Lardy's *Markets Over Mao*, often stress the rise of the private sector and market-oriented enterprises relative to the state sector, relying primarily on output measures. Huang argues that such assessments overstate the change or ask the wrong question.

Huang analyzes the impact of policy on different enterprise types, focusing on changes under Hu Jintao and Xi Jinping—the period after the first waves of reform had created China's complex landscape of firm ownership. He argues that output measures do a poor job of separating private (or non-SOE) enterprise gains due to efficiency from gains due to favorable policy, and that fixed-asset investment—which is heavily influenced by state policy—is a better measure of policy impact. Huang aligns varieties of capitalism (and socialism) with China's categories of enterprise ownership: state socialism and SOEs; state capitalism and limited-liability companies (given the role of state financing and control in the types of enterprises often structured as LLCs); crony capitalism and privately owned enterprises (given the reliance of large private firms on political connections and the increasing reach of the party-state into private firms); entrepreneurial capitalism and foreign-invested, stock market–listed, and small-scale private enterprises (which are the types of firms least entangled with the party-state).

While noting limitations in Chinese data, Huang finds that fixed-asset investment data indicate that the Xi leadership has largely continued, but also accelerated, the Hu era's "statization" of the economy and entrenchment of state capitalism. Huang also finds that crony capitalism has persisted (notwithstanding Xi's anti-corruption drive). These patterns have come at the expense of state socialism and, a bit less clearly, entrepreneurial capitalism. Under Xi, state capitalism also has evolved, reducing the state's direct operating role in enterprises (which has been a hallmark of SOEs) while increasing state influence through providing funds and acquiring control over enterprises (in part through expanding roles of party committees, even in private enterprises).

Victor Shih turns to questions of finance, focusing on the trajectory of the corporate bond market as illustrative of the limits to financial sector reform. In Shih's account, the development of bonds as a major component of a liberalized system of finance has been troubled since its inception in the 1980s. Political and policy concerns consistently have driven, and distorted, the development of bonds and bond markets, from a determination to avoid the instability associated with an inflation-driven panicked sell-off in the late 1980s, through reliance on bonds to finance costs associated with SOE reform in the 1990s, through dependence on bonds to fund priority policies during Zhu Rongji's premiership in the 2000s, to the complicated challenges and policy responses of the mid-2010s that are the principal focus of Shih's chapter. Shih discusses how potentially promising signs of the emergence of a corporate bond market in the early 2010s wilted as state policy returned to chronic habits of political intervention and used bonds to serve other policy goals. In this case, the policy uses of bonds were multiple and interactive: to provide liquidity in response to a crashing stock market and rising foreign exchange outflows; to address crushing local government debt (accumulated in pursuit of economically unsound projects and, in some cases, to sustain growth in the aftermath of the 2007–2008 global financial crisis) by converting debt owed to banks into bonds that banks were required to buy; and to recapitalize banks burdened with bad debt (partly as a result of lending to local governments).

In Shih's assessment, the immediate consequences include a dangerous debt bubble (aggravated by nonbank financial institutions using problematic bonds as collateral for loans to buy more of the same) and the stifling of an economically healthy and reform-supporting corporate bond market. More fundamentally, the combination of the ability of the People's Bank of China (PBOC—China's central bank) to deploy massive financial resources and the broader regime habit of using bonds, and financial sector policy more generally, to serve policy ends and address immediate economic and political challenges, account for the weakness of reforms in this important area and the attendant costs and risks to the financial system.

The four chapters that compose the second part of this book examine China's economic opening up to the outside world. This opening was initiated along with domestic reforms in 1978, but it later accelerated substantially to become a major feature of China's economic rise in the twenty-first century.

David Dollar's chapter provides an overview of this experience, as well as an evaluation of a perception that has grown more widespread among foreign analysts—that the world's engagement with China, especially by the United States, has failed to achieve its purposes. At least in terms of China's economic engagement, Dollar disagrees. Reviewing the evidence of the past four decades, Dollar concludes that engagement, though far from completely successful, has made substantial progress as intended along important dimensions—encouraging China to become more of a market economy, to integrate with the global economy, and to embrace international norms on trade and finance. Combining a summary of the historical trends with available data to measure performance, Dollar details changes in China's policies and performance on trade, currency exchange rates and balance of payments issues, inbound foreign direct investment and related questions about forced technology transfer, outward direct investment from China including its culmination in the widely discussed Belt and Road Initiative, and the role China has played in major international economic institutions.

Having identified areas where engagement has proven beneficial for China and for others, as well as areas where China's performance has fallen short of expectations or created new problems for others, Dollar concludes that the record is one that justifies labeling international economic engagement with China as mostly, although not entirely, successful. He also finds that this record justifies at least tempered optimism about the prospects for addressing remaining problems. Building on the successes of China's international economic engagement will require additional reforms in China's policies as well as reforms of the existing international economic order that should not be viewed as inherently unreasonable.

The remaining three chapters examine key aspects of China's economic opening to the outside world. Yukon Huang analyzes China's rise from irrelevance as a trading nation when the reforms were launched in 1978 to its current position as one of the world's leading powers in trade. Like Dollar, Huang looks at domestic and international decisions that facilitated this remarkable achievement, as well as problems and tensions that success has generated—especially in China's economic relations with the

United States and Europe. Drawing on a rich set of data, Huang sorts out the extent to which tensions over trade balances, investment, and technology reflect perceptions, as opposed to objective reality. He puts these tensions in perspective by comparing China with other Asian economies that have emerged as major traders. He shows that part of the story about growing tensions (especially over trade and investment restrictions, technology transfer, and intellectual property rights) is a familiar one and one that suggests the tensions will ease as a rising trading power—in this case, China—reaches higher income levels.

Still, and again like Dollar, Huang emphasizes that the current tensions are likely to persist and perhaps deepen unless both sides face up to the distinctive problems posed by China as a mixed economy, by China's emergence as a security concern for major trading partners, and by new international economic worries about technology and information sectors that have emerged in the twenty-first century. Huang doubts that the World Trade Organization (WTO) will provide an adequate institutional venue for addressing problems that China's economic emergence has generated. Reforms at the WTO may be helpful, but Huang suggests that a better approach to addressing the tensions between China and its trade partners would be for them to negotiate bilateral investment treaties.

Xiaojun Li examines China's experience with inbound foreign direct investment (FDI). As noted in the other three chapters in this section, FDI played a major role in China's remarkably rapid rise to global economic prominence. Inbound investment, beginning in 1979 and expanding greatly thereafter, was an important catalyst contributing to economic growth, enhancing productivity, and jump-starting international trade. Li's chapter examines the data on FDI in China across sectors and regions, and the evolution of China's regulatory environment for FDI. His discussion points to a decline in the share of foreign-invested enterprises (FIEs) in the economy as the number of private and large state-owned Chinese firms has surged along with overall economic growth. But, as Li also points out, even as the share of FIEs has declined, FDI continues to play a crucial role as a key driver of China's international trade and as a source of tax revenues. Moreover, because the current leadership is determined to shift China to a path of sustainable growth that emphasizes the service sector and tapping the productivity benefits of innovative technologies, it is as important as ever that China remain an attractive destination for FDI.

Unfortunately, Li notes, the country's leaders have thus far failed to address adequately foreign investors' deepening dissatisfaction with the business environment they face in China. He underscores the need for Beijing to implement reforms that effectively answer investor concerns about fairness, predictability, and transparency. Nevertheless, like Dollar and Huang, Li sees grounds for tempered optimism that the current difficulties can be overcome. He also sees negotiating bilateral investment treaties as a plausible way to build a regulatory framework that will help deal with foreign investors' concerns about market access and fair treatment while operating in China. Li also suggests that developments in China may make the prospects for progress on these issues brighter than in the past. Specifically, he emphasizes Xi Jinping's increased political strength, which could enable him to overcome previously intractable resistance to needed changes, and the growing number of Chinese firms doing business abroad that want reciprocal protection for their own investments overseas.

Finally, Tom Miller's chapter turns to one of the most dramatic features of China's economic opening to the outside world, one largely unanticipated at the outset of the reform era—its rise as a source of foreign investment around the world. Miller contrasts China's recently burgeoning outward direct investment with the first two decades of the reform era, when the story of China and foreign investment was overwhelmingly about capital flowing into China. In the early years, low production costs made China an attractive place for foreign investors to establish factories manufacturing goods for the global market and components for their transnational supply chains.

Miller highlights two steps that changed China's role in international investment. First, at the very end of the twentieth century, Jiang Zemin proclaimed his "go-out" policy (*zou chuqu*), which called for a prospering China's companies, at first mostly state-owned enterprises but a decade later joined by private firms, to go abroad in search of investment opportunities that would benefit China. The second step was the integration of this push for outbound direct investment with the bold strategic vision announced in 2013 by China's new leader. As part of his call to rejuvenate the country and restore it to a position as one of the world's most advanced, prosperous, and powerful states by the middle of the twenty-first century, Xi promoted an idea first dubbed "one belt, one road" (OBOR) but later termed the Belt and Road Initiative (BRI).

Miller describes the massive scale of this initiative, its expanding geographic scope, its economic and political goals, and some of its early successes and failures. He emphasizes the dual purposes of China's BRI—to facilitate connectivity through infrastructure development that can benefit China's economy and the economies of recipient countries, and to nurture political ties and influence among states along the continental belt and maritime Silk Road that extends from China's southern and western borders, across much of Asia and part of Africa, to Europe. In addition, Miller discusses the anxious reactions that BRI investments have triggered in some recipient countries and among observers who are concerned about the consequences of China's distinctive approach to investment and development assistance.

Although the BRI has been underway only since 2013, Miller sees warning signs in the mounting problems and challenges that have arisen as the optimism at the time of its launch has given way to doubts about the economic viability of many of its projects, the resulting debt burdens incurred by recipients (and the related problem of possible "debt traps," as foreshadowed by Sri Lanka's transfer of a near-default port project to Chinese control), and the political resistance engendered in recipient countries, which worry that investments and outstanding loans will be translated into political leverage that undermines national sovereignty. The blowback that BRI-linked outbound investment is encountering leads Miller to a more pessimistic view about the future consequences of a rising China's economic opening to the outside, and the possibility of managing the resulting frictions, than we see in the chapters that focus on trade, inbound investment, and other aspects of reform-era China's external economic relations.

More than once, China's economy has confronted fateful moments during the reform era—the political crisis that unfolded in spring 1989 and ensuing international opprobrium, the return to vigorous reform and opening following Deng Xiaoping's southern tour in 1992, the reform of state-owned industry and the country's accession to the WTO in 1998–2001, and the response to the 2007–2008 global financial crisis. Forty years into the reform era, China may have reached another fateful moment—one in which the regime could fundamentally rebalance and deepen reform in the domestic economy and recast China's relations with the outside world. The fortieth anniversary of the seminal December 1978 party plenum coincided with long-emerging major challenges for China's existing approach and mounting difficulties in its external economic and related political relations—especially with the United States, where long-robust support for engagement has crumbled amid complaints about China's international and domestic economic policies and practices and a growing sense of strategic rivalry.

The contributors to this volume cannot provide definitive answers about the paths the Chinese regime will choose or foretell the inevitably uncertain evolution of the circumstances in which China's leaders will make those choices. But they do provide insights into the wide range of economic issues and daunting problems facing China. They also provide historical context by drawing lessons from the past four decades that should facilitate evaluation of the prospects for China and its economy as the reform era enters its fifth decade.

Notes

1. See "Full Text: China's New Party Chief Xi Jinping's Speech," BBC News, November 15, 2012; Zhao Yinan, "'Chinese Dream' Is Xi's Vision," *China Daily*, March 18, 2013.

2. Xi Jinping. "Secure a Decisive Victory in Building a Moderately Prosperous Society in All Respects and Strive for the Great Success of Socialism with Chinese Characteristics for a New Era: Delivered at the 19th National Congress of the Communist Party of China," *Xinhuanet*, October 18, 2017; "Speech Delivered by Xi Jinping at the First Session of the 13th NPC," *China Daily*, March 21, 2018.

3. World Bank, Databank, World Development Indicators (China data for 1978, 1979), https://databank.worldbank.org/data/source/world-development-indicators.

4. World Bank, Databank, World Development Indicators (China data for 1978, 1979).

5. For excellent overviews of China's economic reforms, see Susan L. Shirk, *The Political Logic of Economic Reform in China, California Series on Social Choice and Political Economy* (Berkeley, California: University of California Press, 1993); Arthur R. Kroeber, *China's Economy: What Everyone Needs to Know* (New York, New York: Oxford University Press, 2016); and Barry J. Naughton, *The Chinese Economy: Adaptation and Growth* (Cambridge, Massachusetts: MIT Press, 2018).

6. Andrea Willige, "The World's Top Economy: The US vs. China in Five Charts," World Economic Forum, December 5, 2016.

7. World Bank, Databank, World Development Indicators (China data for 1978, 1979).

8. David Barboza, "China Passes Japan as Second-Largest Economy," *New*

York Times, August 15, 2010; Jamil Anderlini and Lucy Hornby, "China Overtakes US as World's Largest Goods Trader," *Financial Times,* January 10, 2013.

9. Social scientists continue to debate the reliability of data collected through surveys conducted in an authoritarian country where respondents may be concerned about openly expressing their views. For a sample of such work, assessments of the measurement problems, as well as reasons for differences in survey results, see Xueyi Chen and Tianjian Shi, "Media Effects on Political Confidence and Trust in the People's Republic of China in the Post-Tiananmen Period," *East Asia: An International Quarterly,* vol. 19, no. 3 (Autumn 2001), 84–118; Zhengxu Wang, "Explaining Regime Strength in China," *China: An International Journal,* vol. 4, no. 2 (September 2006), 217–237; Zhengxu Wang and Yu You, "The Arrival of Critical Citizens: Decline of Political Trust and Shifting Public Priorities in China," *International Review of Sociology,* vol. 26, no. 1 (2016), 105–124; John James Kennedy, "Maintaining Popular Support for the Chinese Communist Party: The Influence of Education and the State-Controlled Media," *Political Studies,* vol. 57, no. 3 (October 2009), 517–536; Karl Friedhoff and Craig Kafura, "Views from the G2: Public Opinion in the US & China," *Chicago Council on Global Affairs,* December 1, 2016; Daniela Stockmann, Ashley Esarey, and Jie Zhang, "Who Is Afraid of the Chinese State? Evidence Calling into Question Political Fear as an Explanation for Overreporting of Political Trust," *Political Psychology,* vol. 39, no. 5 (2018), 1105–1121; Darrel Robinson and Marcus Tannenberg, "Self-Censorship in Authoritarian States: Response Bias in Measures of Popular Support in China," *V-Dem Institute,* April 12, 2018.

10. World Bank, Databank, World Development Indicators (China data for 1978, 1979); "New Normal in Economic Development," *China Daily,* October 5, 2017.

11. Damien Ma, "Can China Avoid the Middle Income Trap?" *Foreign Policy,* March 12, 2016; Randall Peerenboom, "China and the Middle-Income Trap: Toward a Post Washington, Post-Beijing Consensus," *Pacific Review,* vol. 27, no. 5 (2014), 651–673.

12. Mitali Das and Papa N'Diaye, "Chronicle of a Decline Foretold: Has China Reached the Lewis Turning Point?" *IMF Working Paper,* January 2013.

13. See Jean Chun Oi, *Rural China Takes Off: Institutional Foundations of Economic Reform* (Berkeley, California: University of California Press, 1999).

14. "China Tops US in Numbers of Billionaires," BBC News, October 13, 2016; Kathleen Elkins, "There Are More Billionaires in the US Than in China, Germany and India Combined," CNBC, May 15, 2018.

15. Martin King Whyte's research has indicated that the fuel for such protests has not been growing socioeconomic inequality itself but rather the perception that connections rather than hard work enable some to succeed. Martin King Whyte, *Myth of the Social Volcano: Perceptions of Inequality and Distributive Injustice in Contemporary China* (Stanford, California: Stanford University Press, 2010).

16. See Pew Research Center, "Chinese Public Sees More Powerful Role in

World, Names U.S. as Top Threat. Domestic Challenges Persist: Corruption, Consumer Safety, Pollution," October 5, 2016, 7–8.

17. For an attempt to specify the effects of China's economic rise on other countries, see David H. Autor, David Dorn, and Gordon H. Hanson, "The China Shock: Learning from Labor-Market Adjustment to Large Changes in Trade," *Annual Review of Economics*, vol. 8, no. 1 (October 2016), 205–240. On the debate this influential article triggered, see "Economists Argue About the Impact of Chinese Imports on America," *Economist*, March 11, 2017.

18. Autor, Dorn, and Hanson, "The China Shock"; Justin R. Pierce and Peter K. Schott, "The Surprisingly Swift Decline of US Manufacturing Employment," *American Economic Review*, vol. 106, no. 7 (2016), 1632–1662.

19. David Autor, David Dorn, Gordon Hanson, and Kaveh Majlesi, "Importing Political Polarization? The Electoral Consequences of Rising Trade Exposure," NBER Working Paper 22637, December 2017; J. Bradford Jensen, Dennis P. Quinn and Stephen Weymouth, "Winners and Losers in International Trade: The Effects on US Presidential Voting," *International Organization*, vol. 71, no. 3 (2017), 423–457.

20. In the United States, these concerns are addressed in large part through the Committee on Foreign Investment in the United States (CFIUS) process, which was amended to provide for more stringent review, largely in response to concerns about China, in 2018. See Jennifer Harris, "Writing New Rules for the U.S.-China Investment Relationship," Council on Foreign Relations, December 2017; "Putting FIRRMA into Practice: What CFIUS Reform Means for Foreign Investment in the United States," Center for Strategic and International Studies, September 25, 2018.

21. Kurt M. Campbell and Ely Ratner, "The China Reckoning," *Foreign Affairs*, vol. 97, no. 2 (March/April 2018), 60–70; Wang Jisi, J. Stapleton Roy, Aaron Friedberg, Thomas Christensen, Patricia Kim, Joseph S. Nye Jr., Eric Li, Kurt M. Campbell, and Ely Ratner, "Did America Get China Wrong? The Engagement Debate," *Foreign Affairs*, vol. 97, no. 4 (July/August 2018), 183–195; Ryan Hass, "Principles for Managing U.S.-China Competition," *Brookings Foreign Policy Brief*, August 2018; Jeffrey Bader, "U.S.-China Relations: Is It Time to End the Engagement," *Brookings Foreign Policy Brief*, September 2018.

22. "National Security Strategy of the United States of America," December 2017; "Summary of the 2018 National Defense Strategy of the United States of America"; "Remarks by Vice President Pence on the Administration's Policy Toward China," Hudson Institute, October 4, 2018.

23. On performance legitimacy, see Yuchao Zhu, "'Performance Legitimacy' and China's Political Adaptation Strategy," *Journal of Chinese Political Science*, vol. 16, no. 2 (2011), 123–140; also, Baogang Guo, *Political Legitimacy and China's Transition*, vol. 8, 2003; Bruce Gilley, "Legitimacy and Institutional Change: The Case of China," *Comparative Political Studies*, vol. 41, no. 3 (2008), 259–284.

24. Cheng Li, "Hailing Success of China's Third Plenum," *On the Record*, November 14, 2013; Fred Dews, "Cheng Li: 18th Party Congress' Third Plenum

Another Turning Point in China's Economic Development," *Brookings Now*, November 14, 2013; Evan A. Feigenbaum, "A Chinese Puzzle: Why Economic 'Reform' in Xi's China Has More Meanings Than Market Liberalization," *MacroPolo*, February 26, 2018.

25. See David Dollar, "China's Rebalancing: Lessons from East Asian Economic History," *The Brookings Institution: John L. Thornton China Center Working Paper Series,* October 2013; "China's Difficult Rebalancing Act," *IMF Survey,* September 12, 2007.

26. See Jost Wübbeke, Mirjam Meissner, Max J. Zenglein, Jaqueline Ives, and Björn Conrad, "Made in China 2025: The Making of a High-Tech Superpower and Consequences for Industrial Countries," *Merics: Papers on China No. 2,* December 2016; Scott Kennedy, "Made in China 2025," *CSIS,* June 1, 2015.

27. Chun Han Wong, "China's Museums Rewrite History to Boost Xi," *Wall Street Journal,* August 20, 2018. See also Samuel Wade, "Remaking History as Reform Anniversary Approaches," *China Digital Times,* August 24, 2018.

28. See Jacques deLisle, "China's Rise, the U.S., and the WTO: Perspectives from International Relations Theory," *University of Illinois Law Review* (2018), 57–71.

29. Joshua Kurlantzick, "Why the 'China Model' Isn't Going Away," *The Atlantic,* March 21, 2013; but see Bonnie Girard, "Is There Really a 'China Model'?" *The Diplomat,* July 13, 2018; Suisheng Zhao, "Whither the China Model: Revisiting the Debate," *Journal of Contemporary China,* vol. 26, no. 103 (January 2017), 1–17; see also Ian Bremmer, "State Capitalism Comes of Age: The End of the Free Market?" *Foreign Affairs,* vol. 88, no. 3 (May/June 2009), 40–55.

30. Minxin Pei, *China's Trapped Transition: The Limits of Developmental Autocracy* (Cambridge, Massachusetts: Harvard University Press, 2006); Minxin Pei, *China's Crony Capitalism: The Dynamics of Regime Decay* (Cambridge, Massachusetts: Harvard University Press, 2016); see also George Friedman, "Recognizing the End of the Chinese Economic Miracle," Stratfor, July 23, 2013.

PART I

Enlivening the Domestic Economy

ONE

China's Domestic Economy

From "Enlivening" to "Steerage"

BARRY NAUGHTON

Much of what happened in China after 1978 is captured in the conventional phrase "enlivening the domestic economy." The descriptive term is evocative and accurate, and it has the additional merit that the English term faithfully reproduces the imprecision of the Chinese original, and in particular the ambiguity about the subject. Who was responsible for enlivening the economy? In any case, the Chinese economy came alive, and coming alive, the Chinese economy and China itself were transformed.

At the very beginning of the process, the veteran leader and economist Chen Yun famously likened the economy to a bird in a birdcage, which he argued should be given as much room as possible while also being constrained inside the "cage" of planners' intentions. By giving certain sectors—notably, agriculture—more space within the cage, Chen Yun certainly succeeded in enlivening that part of the economy. Yet it is also clear that the Chinese economy burst out of the constraints envisaged by a relative conservative like Chen Yun and transformed itself as soon as the constraints placed on it were loosened. The Chinese economy enlivened was also the Chinese economy unbound.[1]

The metaphor of enlivening, however, gradually became a less effective description of the Chinese economy as it moved into the twenty-first cen-

tury. It is not that the economy became less lively—far from it. Rather, as
the features that powered very high-speed growth faded, China's policy-
makers became less attracted to policies of enlivening and decontrol, and
more intent on locating and developing new drivers of economic growth.
Envisioning potential growth primarily in hi-tech "emerging industries,"
and eager to create a competitive advantage where it did not yet exist, Chinese policy-makers became increasingly intent on guiding the economy
toward a hi-tech future. For policy-makers, this new effort at "steerage"
is to be built on the foundation of the market economy that China has
become. Their new ambition is an affirmation of enlivening, but not a continuation of it, since policy-makers today have very specific ideas about the
direction in which the economy should go. As a result, China today is, for
better or worse, on an economic trajectory that is quite different from the
earlier decades of reform.

Enlivening and the Growth Miracle

Understanding enlivening requires that we make a link with broader
processes of economic growth. Looking back, it is clear that Chinese
reform and the enlivening of China's economy coincided almost perfectly
with a so-called "growth miracle." A growth miracle is the historically
unique situation where an economy is able to transform itself completely
within a thirty- or forty-year period. There have been eight or nine of
these miracles—defined as an economy's GDP growing at 7.5 percent over
twenty-five years or more—of which all but one have been in East Asia.[2]
The basic experience of the growth miracle is, therefore, not unique. But
for any economy, it can only happen once, and only at a particular developmental conjuncture. This is because growth miracles are possible only
when an economy combines specific demographic and structural characteristics: in particular, a growth miracle can only begin when a traditional
society has completed the first stage of its initial demographic transition.
When the demographic transition has occurred, death rates have fallen
as society becomes healthier, while birth rates have just begun to fall as
better-off families begin to limit fertility. This creates a "baby boom" that
enters the labor force about twenty years later. If modern economic growth
has begun by the time the baby boom hits the marketplace, growth can
accelerate. If, in addition, agriculture is healthy enough to begin releasing
labor on a massive scale, this growth acceleration can be sustained long

enough to propel the economy into a rapid-growth phase for twenty-five years or more.

The growth miracle, then, is not an inevitable phase of development. A country can fail to accelerate when the opportunity is there, or it can get knocked off the miracle-growth trajectory by poor economic policy-making or by adverse external conditions. The growth miracles we have observed have all been cases of an economy taking advantage of a once-in-a-lifetime opportunity to pass through the ordinary phases of development at warp speed. This was true of Japan from 1950 to 1973; true of Korea, Taiwan, Hong Kong, and Singapore; and true of China. Figure 1-1 shows that China was passing through a period of especially rapid labor-force growth in the 1980s, with employment growing at 3 percent annually. Organic labor-force growth was accentuated by the return to the city of millions of sent-down youth and the return to work of millions of politically marginalized people. China had to find an economic strategy that would provide jobs for these people. This helps explain the tremendous importance of enlivening in China. The enlivening of the Chinese economy took

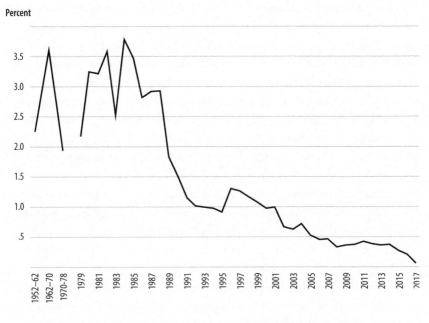

Percent

FIGURE 1-1 Growth of employment (Source: *China Statistical Yearbook, 2018*, p. 110)

place under specific circumstances that permitted the economy to take advantage of unusual opportunity, unleashing the potential of the growth-miracle phase. At the same time, policy-makers were under enormous pressure to provide enough new jobs to absorb this maturing baby-boom, and they also imposed draconian birth-control policies on this group of young people.

China, therefore, went through a growth miracle that was similar in nature to earlier growth miracles, but was the biggest, fastest, longest, and overall most dramatic transformation of an economy in history. At every stage of this explosive transformation, enlivening played a critical catalytic role. Indeed, one way to narrate the history of China's transformation after 1978 concisely is to tell it as a story of seven waves of enlivening.

Outside the Core: The First Three Waves of Enlivening

The first great enlivening took place in the farm economy from 1979 through 1983. In the first step, constraints on farmers were relaxed beginning on what is, by convention, the very first day of the reform era. When the communiqué of the Third Plenum of the Eleventh Central Committee was published in December 1978, it called for giving agriculture a chance to "catch its breath." This vague promise was quickly made good as policy-makers eased off on agricultural procurement quotas and provided better prices to farmers for their output. The liberalization of farm policy was a major policy shift, but it was not until the grant of land to the farmers, spreading nationwide between 1980 and 1982, that the farm economy was really enlivened. With various systems of contracting land to farm households, farmers were given the freedom to decide what to farm, when to farm, and when not to farm. The results are, of course, known to everyone: the farmers who had struggled to feed China for the previous twenty years, left to themselves, quickly produced surpluses that have been more than enough to provide abundance and diversity to China's mass middle-class society.[3] The relaxation of the food constraint, in turn, gave policy-makers much greater room for maneuver, economically and politically, and set the stage for future waves of reform.

In parallel with the transformation of the agricultural economy, but logically dependent upon it for success, was the liberalization of the rural nonagricultural economy. This was the second great wave of enlivening. Left to their own devices, farmers found they could squeeze out a portion of household labor for nonagricultural tasks. Once farmers and villages were allowed to set up businesses, and send out salesmen and purchasing agents to support those businesses, a new explosion of labor-intensive manufactures emerged from the Chinese countryside. These new producers dramatically transformed the availability of simple but diverse products that broke the bleak monotony of consumer-goods supply under the planned economy. In addition, these new "township and village enterprises" (TVEs) provided competition for the state-owned enterprises (SOEs) that had been exploiting their monopoly position in industrial-product markets since the 1950s.

As policy-makers absorbed the lessons of the rural transformation, they began to allow a parallel relaxation in the urban economy. Cities were enlivened first by an explosion of small-scale private businesses that transformed services, retail, restaurants, and then small-scale industry. It took the personal approbation of Deng Xiaoping to allow a seller of dried melon seeds from Anhui (*Shazi Guazi*) to expand a private business beyond household scale. Spanning a decade from about 1983 through 1993, China's cityscapes came alive. Indeed, the "internal opening" of Beijing to small-scale retail business after 1993 was one of the quickest signals that China had resumed liberalization after the post-Tiananmen reform rollback. To be sure, there was at this time no protection for the property rights of private corporations, but when the dams were torn down, there was an enormous reservoir of pent-up labor and entrepreneurship ready to step in and make China's small-scale sector an important contributor to growth and prosperity.

Cracking the Core: Enlivening the State Sector

After the initial three waves of enlivening had taken place, Chinese policy-makers developed the will to engage the "hard core" of the socialist economy, large-scale state industry. These big SOEs were floundering during the 1990s, due to the enhanced competition from TVEs and private firms. Their situation was increasingly critical, as the net profit (after deducting losses) of all industrial SOEs declined, essentially to zero, in 1997. Yet the flip side of the impending bankruptcy of the SOEs was the fact that alternate businesses and ownership forms had reached sufficient scale to absorb the workers, land, and disused structures shed by bankrupt or collapsing SOEs. Moreover, an intensive effort to build fiscal, taxation, banking, and regulatory institutions appropriate to a market economy—sketched out in the 1993 Third Plenum (of the Fourteenth Central Committee)—achieved substantial success during the mid-1990s, sufficient to guide a profound institutional restructuring. As a result, it was possible to enliven the large-scale industrial sector by subjecting the state-owned enterprises to the nearly full brunt of competitive pressures for the first time in their history.

Self-evidently, the restructuring of state-owned industry was not the simple happy story of enlivening such as that which took place in the rural and private sectors. During a drastic and painful period from about 1996 to 2002, the state enterprise workforce shrank by more than 40 percent, and the majority of smaller industrial SOEs went out of business. Many laid-off workers were unemployed for years before either being gradually absorbed back into the labor force at lower wages and status, or accepting early retirement and withdrawing from the formal labor force.

Despite this mid-term pain, the SOE reforms were in the end a story of enlivening as well. The remaining SOEs were substantially restructured around the turn of the century. A considerable number of them were remade into joint-stock corporations, and most of them created corporate subsidiaries that were listed on the Chinese stock market. These surviving SOEs largely recovered their footing, returned to profitability, and made a positive contribution to China's growth during the first decade of the twenty-first century. As figure 1-2 shows, by 2005–2007, state industry had returned to profitability, displaying trends very close to nonstate industry. During the first half of the time period shown in figure 1-2, the profitability gap with nonstate firms was essentially closed. Through painful reforms, even the state sector had been enlivened.

Enlivening a Modern Economy

As the earliest enlivening measures were running out of steam, and as the state sector was absorbing the shock to which it had been subjected, the greatest enlivenment of all was finally building strength. Beginning in the 1990s, but accelerating steadily into the 2005–2010 period, the barriers between urban and rural were finally torn down, and 200 million migrants flooded into the urban economy. This fifth wave of enlivening gave an entirely new scale to the Chinese economy. As figure 1-3 shows, the "floating population"—individuals away from their place of permanent household

Percent

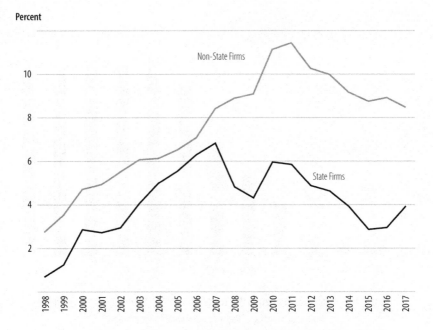

FIGURE 1-2   **Rate of return on industrial assets** (Source: Calculated from *China Statistical Yearbook, 2018*, pp. 428–29, 434–35)

registration for more than six months—increased from almost nothing in 1990 to a peak of 253 million in 2014. These workers, literate, ambitious, equipped with cell phones and the will to build a new, modern China, were the key driver of growth acceleration in the twenty-first century. A comparison of figures 1-1 and 1-3 shows that by the end of the 1990s, the "demographic dividend" was running out of steam and the overall growth of employment was slowing down. However, there were still plenty of underemployed young people in the countryside. The gradual lowering of barriers to movement allowed them to find new jobs and roles in the urban economy. As their potential productivity was brought into play, economic growth remained robust and even accelerated.

Even with rural China on the move, the potential of enlivening was not exhausted. Two more waves loomed, both of which were generally unanticipated consequences of decisions made during the accelerated reform period in the late 1990s. The sixth wave arose because of the decision made in 1998 to privatize urban housing. This decision was itself an offshoot of the great SOE reform and downsizing carried out at this time. In order to

Millions

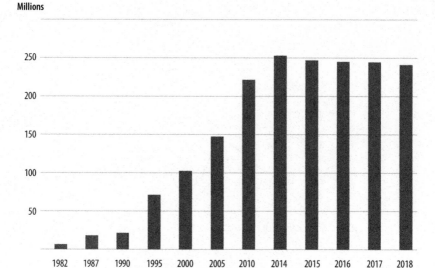

FIGURE 1-3　**Floating population** (Source: *China Statistical Yearbook, 2018*, p. 32; National Bureau of Statistics, "Report on National Economic and Social Development, 2018," February 28, 2019)

allow SOEs to go under without taking workers' living spaces with them, Premier Zhu Rongji agreed to a relatively comprehensive program of low-cost privatization of existing residential property. Most urban housing at that time was owned by the work unit, and each apartment built by the work unit now passed into the hands of the workers and staff who lived there. This simple decision triggered the great Chinese housing boom that accelerated after about 2003. As Chinese households realized they had a valuable and appreciating asset that could be swapped for other, even nicer assets, with even greater appreciation potential, a new wave of upgrading and real estate speculation began. This became another of the great drivers of Chinese growth in the twenty-first century.

Finally, the decision to enter the World Trade Organization (WTO) touched off the seventh, export-oriented, wave of enlivening. As was the case with the housing market, there was a significant lag between the time the nominal decision was made and the time the response to that decision became manifest. China's WTO entry was agreed in 1999, but member-ship did not become final until December 2001, and even then, some of the most important provisions were phased in over the next three years. As the new rules kicked in, and as new producers and merchants entered, as old ones learned new tricks, and as clumsy old businesses were forced out of the way, China's exports began to accelerate. Between 2004 and 2007, China's exports grew more than 30 percent per year, as new players found new markets. The enlivening of China's export economy was the seventh wave, the last in a series of enlivening reforms that released structural potential that had previously been suppressed (see David Dollar's chapter in this volume).

Indeed, then, enlivening is a good description of China's experience, not over forty years, but at least for the thirty years from 1978 through 2008. Seven waves perhaps feels a bit exhausting, but we are characterizing a growth miracle, a process that completely transformed the most populous society on earth.

Enlivening and Market Reform Eventually Ran Out of Steam

After the turn of the century, there was a major shift in the trajectory of economic reform and of enlivening. Even today, we do not have a very good understanding of this turning point. It is clear, however, that major market-oriented reforms pretty much ceased after about 2005.[4] The last major, intentional policy that clearly qualifies as a market-oriented reform was the recapitalization and restructuring of state banks, which was completed in 2006–2007. This complex program wrote off trillions of renminbi worth of nonperforming loans, injected new capital into the banks, and then reorganized the banks (including allowing foreign strategic partners to take minority stakes) and listed them on the stock exchange. This was a huge step forward in terms of returning the banks to solvency and enabling competition between commercial banks, while also diversifying the financial system in order to allow firms of all kinds and ownership structures access to credit. It was the culmination of a process that had started as far back as 1997–1998 as part of Zhu Rongji's reforms. In that sense, it was important "unfinished business" from the Zhu era, in which it was conceptualized and designed.

After the bank restructuring, there was no significant, sustained market-oriented reform—and thus no real new enlivening—until well into the Xi Jinping administration. The Xi-Li government put forward ambitious reforms in the November 2013 Third Plenum, but it is extremely difficult to point to a single reform that has been fully and thoroughly implemented, much less one that is responsible for significant economic changes. In part, this is because of the shift in overall development strategy discussed below, and the changed relationship between the government and the Communist Party, on the one hand, and the market economy, on the other. To be sure, individual elements of reform have the potential to change the economy, if they are followed through on. For example, liberalization of the stock market and expansion of access to bond markets could be significant, if allowed to proceed further. The deregulation of business regulation and cutting of red tape pushed by Premier Li Keqiang might qualify as a market-enhancing reform. Yet even if we were to accept that these embryonic measures might be the first step in a renewed cycle of market-oriented reform—which would go beyond currently available evidence—we would still have to reckon with a reform hiatus of a decade or more. In fact, a great deal changed in the Chinese economy after the new century that caused the policy of enlivening to become far less central.

First, to a certain extent, the economy simply didn't need to be enlivened any longer, for it was already alive. That is to say, a robust, and generally competitive, market economy had been created in the wake of the 1990s reforms carried out under Zhu Rongji. Indeed, in the previous section, we noted that the effects of reforms in the late 1990s worked with a lag effect throughout the first decade of the twenty-first century. This was true not just of housing and foreign trade, but of the economy in general. Moreover, it was based generally on private ownership, especially in the goods-producing sectors. Thus, the share of industrial output produced by private firms has continued to increase steadily.[5] By this reading, the economy was already on a healthy foundation, and no longer needed an "enlivenator."

Yet this explanation doesn't go far enough to be satisfying. The Chinese economy is still hobbled by multiple barriers to entry, limitations on competition, and areas where regulatory authority is unclear and businesses subject to the nearly unchecked discretion of political bosses. Especially in the high-skilled service sectors, rules prevent entry by domestic and foreign private firms. As David Dollar points out in this volume, China's service sector is generally protected, and foreign businesses are restricted much more than in any OECD economy. Finance is a telling example. Despite China's WTO undertakings, foreign banks were effectively prevented from expanding in China by a series of regulatory entanglements that made competition impossible. Nonbank finance—stocks and bonds—remain severely restricted despite repeated declarations from the government of intent to open up. While both bonds and stocks have grown rapidly, they continue to be issued primarily by state-owned enterprises that use funds in accordance with government development priorities. Although the economy continues to benefit from past reforms, it is impossible to argue that it simply doesn't need further reforms.

A more important explanation is that the balance between the necessity of reform and the potential risks from reform shifted dramatically after the turn of the century. Some Chinese economists believe that in the absence of short-term crisis, the system simply cannot mobilize the effort required to launch major reforms. By this interpretation, the reform efforts of the 1980s and 1990s were both enabled by major crisis. In the 1980s, the economy faced multiple consequences of the decades of underperformance from the late 1950s to the late 1970s, and the serious risk that it would be unable to provide jobs and improved livelihood for the hundreds of millions of new workers and newly created families. In the 1990s, a major crisis of government capability emerged, which derived ultimately from a debilitating erosion in fiscal revenues. As figure 1-4 shows, China's budgetary revenues (official definition) declined steadily from 1978 until 1995–1996. This meant not only that policy-makers were forced into action, but also that they had few options besides enlivening the economy, since they really didn't have the resources to pay for any other development options. One is reminded of an incident early in the reform era, when government officials from Guangdong went to Beijing to plead for the freedom to open Special Economic Zones and generally to adopt market-opening reforms one step ahead of the rest of China. Deng Xiaoping is famously said to have told the Guangdong officials that the center could give them no money to support their ambitious objectives, but that it could give "policy" that might allow them to attract funding and other resources. There could be no better statement of the conditions that forced enlivening than this. Today's required reforms are even more complex than those demanded in the 1990s, and also more risky. Measures to open the capital account, for example, have repeatedly stalled out because they create short-run fluctuations and external constraints that policy-makers are extremely nervous about. Thus, there is an interpretation of the Chinese reform process that holds that unless or until pressing problems arise, the Chinese system is unlikely to launch further reforms.[6]

Conversely, the turnaround in Chinese budget conditions after 1996 opened up a new range of policy options. By standard Chinese account-

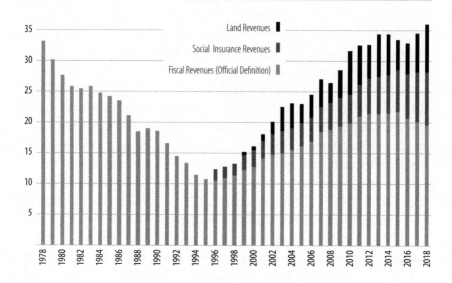

FIGURE 1-4   Fiscal and quasi-fiscal revenues
(Source: B. Naughton (2017); see footnote 7, this chapter)

ing, budget revenues as a share of GDP increased steadily and robustly, doubling from just under 11 percent of GDP in 1996 to 22 percent in 2015. However, the actual performance was even stronger, because the Chinese government opened up a number of new revenue sources that were not included in standard budget accounting. Social insurance revenues in China—unlike virtually every other country—are not included in government revenues (with some minor exceptions). Such revenues increased from virtually nothing to almost 8 percent of GDP in 2018. Even more distinctively Chinese, the revenues local governments reap from their monopoly on land transactions is a major contribution to government resources. Although volatile, such revenues surpassed 7 percent of GDP in 2010 and 2018, and have been above 5 percent of GDP since 2010. Putting these three sources of government revenues together, Chinese fiscal and quasi-fiscal revenues have almost tripled from just more than 12 percent of GDP in 1996 to about 35 to 36 percent in the years 2017–2018.[7] That's as much as developed-country budgets, but with the important difference that China does not yet have heavy social-security outlays to pay for. In developed countries, retirement benefits amount to 10 percent of GDP on average, while China is still well below this figure, so it has much more flexibility. We should be completely clear: the Chinese government has a lot of money.

Not surprisingly, with more money available, Chinese policy-makers have become more ambitious. Under the administration of Premier Wen Jiabao, who had primary jurisdiction over the economy, attention shifted to strengthening rural social security and health care, and to providing the public goods that could be complementary to market-oriented reforms. These measures were important, long overdue, and expensive. Wen succeeded in laying the foundations for a major improvement in health insurance and education systems, while he rarely displayed much urgency on the need for further market-oriented reform. In a broader sense, policy-makers seem to enjoy disposing of larger resources (as the economy grew and the government's tax share of the economy expanded). They began to envision large projects and express the desire to "concentrate resources to accomplish big things." This may have contributed to the policy turning described below.

The discussion up until now has been based primarily on purely economic factors. In fact, some believe that the economic explanations must be augmented by interest-group arguments. They believe that interest groups have become stronger and more entrenched in China since the success of earlier rounds of reforms. For example, as shown in figure 1-2, state-owned enterprises, which were scarcely profitable in the mid-1990s, were brought back to financial health in the early years of the 2000s decade. That meant that control of SOEs became a valuable resource worth defending, and one that could be leveraged for multiple forms of influence. In one spectacular case, the corrupt network around Zhou Yongkang—the first Politburo Standing Committee member ever imprisoned for corruption—was built initially around managers in the petroleum ministry, so clearly the revenues from SOEs in the petroleum sector were sufficient to build a powerful and dangerous interest group. Similar cases could be adduced in sectors from railways to telecom.

We cannot really identify the ultimate interests or driving forces of the important turning point that took place in the early to mid-2000s. We don't know enough about elite level politics in China, and so we can only observe the outcomes: that policy-makers seem to have changed their minds. Whether this was because the constellations of forces and problems they had to deal with had changed, or because their own objectives and sense of purpose had changed, we cannot say. Policy-makers began to claim that their own astute policy-making was the reason for China's explosive growth. That is, they ceased believing in the necessity of enlivening the economy and increasingly decided that, having enlivened the economy, they could begin to guide it in new directions. This isn't really logical, but it is not hard to understand: miracles are miracles and they change everything, including the mindset of policy-makers. Politicians get blamed when things go wrong, and they take credit when things go right, whether or not they are truly responsible. Moreover, they ultimately come to believe their own hype, and become convinced they can lead the economy in new directions. Thus, China's policy-makers turned away from the strategy of enlivening they had pursued to such effect for twenty-five or thirty years and began to search for new growth strategies.

The New Policy Package: Industrial Policy as Development Strategy

Gradually, since 2006, Chinese policy-makers have paid increasing attention to industrial policy. This industrial policy is sometimes called "techno-industrial policy," because it is so overwhelmingly focused on the nurturance of high-technology industries and, to a lesser extent, services. The pause in market-oriented reforms preceded the shift to industrial policy, but not by much. The first key industrial policy projects—the sixteen megaprojects—were launched in 2006, and then, in the wake of the global financial crisis of 2008–2009, a steadily increasing attention was given to "strategic emerging industries," and then artificial intelligence, robotics, and advanced internet.

A Market-Revealing Strategy

To understand this shift, we need to reexamine how we think about enlivening. Traditionally, Chinese actions in enlivening their economy are thought of in terms of tearing down barriers and enabling new types of producers. The entry of private firms, TVEs, and foreign firms into various sectors is often taken as an index of liberalization. However, there is another aspect to enlivening that is intuitively obvious, but almost impossible to measure and so almost never taken as evidence of liberalization. That is, enlivening creates new markets. Each act of enlivening creates its own market, often in ways that were unanticipated by policy-makers. This has been true from the very beginning, when farmers began growing diverse nonstaple crops that quickly found new markets with urban consumers and businesses, and when Wenzhou entrepreneurs uncovered a latent market for colored buttons and bright ribbons (when China was very poor). Much later, WTO membership allowed aggressive private firms to locate new markets in Africa, South America, and Southeast Asia, which had been over the horizon for bigger, state-owned predecessors. From the Wenzhou experience to the entry into WTO, each of China's waves of enlivening opened up a new market.

Because of this market-discovery function, enlivening can be a growth strategy. Each act of enlivenment reveals a new area of market demand. In fact, from 1978 until 2005, enlivening was really the only growth strategy. With structural conditions highly favorable to growth, each wave of enlivening revealed a new area of demand, and labor and capital flowed into that area to meet demand and reap profits. Policy-makers were not able to predict the resulting pattern of demand, and indeed had to be fairly agnostic about the outcomes of policy. Enlivening was a highly viable development strategy, but it took a leap of faith on the part of policy-makers, requiring them to give up their claims of omniscience and accept wherever market pioneers took the economy.

Traditional economics does not deal directly with this market-creation process, but there are two traditions that provide some insight into the current discussion. First, it is an axiom of a fully market-oriented economy that there is "consumer sovereignty," meaning that the ultimate pattern of demand is determined by what households desire, and the decisions businesses make are, in turn, designed to serve the household demand directly or indirectly, today or tomorrow. Even in a pure consumer-sovereignty economy, though, the government must make choices about the pattern of investment in public goods. Transport infrastructure, for example, involves not just meeting today's demand, but also projecting future patterns of development, so it is impossible to draw a black-and-white line between the sovereign consumer and government steerage. However, among these shades of gray, we can distinguish between extremes: on the one hand, a follower government that builds infrastructure (for example) solely in order to accommodate its best estimate of current and future household demand; on the other, a government that lays out a future-oriented infrastructure network, anticipating that households and businesses will move to low-cost nodes, reshaping their activity to conform with government actions.

In this sense, China had begun to depart modestly from the pure consumer-sovereignty model in the late 1990s, because it began to believe in building infrastructure out ahead of demand. All those big, empty airports that seemed as if they would never be filled up, and the expressways that did not link up with existing economic centers were controversial when the Chinese government insisted on building them, because to advisers such as the World Bank, they departed excessively from consumer sovereignty and were likely to be low-return investments. In the event, however, rapid growth meant that most—certainly not all—of these early investments justified the optimism. In any case, the departure from consumer sovereignty was at first relatively small, limited to projecting an ambitiously high rate of growth. In other words, even though China built out ahead of demand, it was until very recently essentially projecting demand and running fast so that it would be there when the economy caught up. Thermal power plants were, until recently, another example of this process.

The second relevant tradition is that of ascribing East Asian economic success to "export-oriented policies." Export-oriented growth policies—in Japan, Korea, Taiwan, and China—had two great benefits. First, they permitted an almost indefinite expansion of labor-intensive manufacturing based on the capacious global market; and second, they exposed domestic firms to a generally fair competitive process in cases where the domestic economic environment was still highly distorted. In its version of export-orientation, China promoted exports pretty much across the board, with its currency valuation and WTO membership affecting virtually all export industries. Comparatively speaking, externally oriented policies in Korea and elsewhere were usually not pure laissez-faire open policies, and instead involved a degree of government intervention (for example, in awarding low-interest rate loans to the most successful exporters). By comparison, China allowed exporters to find markets pretty much on their own. Export-oriented growth in China was thus a process in which the large global market was known in general terms in advance, but policy-makers had few tools to shape highly competitive global markets, and no way to know in advance which domestic firms would be successful or in which sectors. Hence, even in export industries—which were major growth-drivers until 2006—there was still a strong element of market discovery. Thus, while the judgment cannot be "pure," Chinese growth strategy until

2005–2006 was almost entirely based on discovering new markets through enlivening.

Combating Growth Slowdown

After about 2010, Chinese growth began to slow: the miracle-growth period was ending. As discussed earlier, even before this time, Chinese policy-makers were losing faith in enlivenment, as their commitment to market-oriented reform waned and as they began to resume industrial policies that had been abandoned for a decade or more. The global financial crisis of 2009 strongly encouraged this shift. China responded to the clear and present danger of global crisis by unleashing a massive stimulus program. By pumping credit into the economy and encouraging investment by local government and state enterprises, the regime contributed significantly to blunting and overcoming the tidal wave of financial disruption that threatened to drown the world economy. In the wake of that experience, policy-makers gained confidence in their own abilities and adopted a more activist response to the secular slowdown in the economy that became manifest after 2010. Policy-makers began to turn to industrial policy as their primary development strategy.

To be sure, one of the reasons the enlivening strategy had worked so well was that it corresponded with the miracle-growth period. There was explosive growth potential that merely needed to be unleashed. In the post-2010 new normal, it was no longer the case. We can see this clearly through the lens of demographics. One of the underpinnings of miracle growth was the "demographic dividend," meaning that the proportion of the population in the labor force was increasing, and the labor force was growing rapidly. As figure 1-1 showed, that phase is now over, with employment growth having finally declined to zero by the end of 2017. Moreover, as figure 1-3 showed, the "floating population" peaked in 2014, inching down annually since. While there are still plenty of migrants in China's cities, the large net addition to growth created by steadily increasing migration up until 2010 has now evaporated. Clearly, changes in underlying structural conditions are major drivers of the shift in China's policy orientation. Chinese policy-makers began searching for alternative growth drivers as soon as the miracle-growth period approached its end.

However, while the shift in structural conditions helps explain the policy shift, it is not an adequate or complete explanation. As argued earlier, there are plenty of areas of the Chinese economy that are still restricted and distorted, and there is no logical reason why enlivening cannot work in a moderately growing economy. Household consumption was only 39 percent of Chinese GDP in 2016, indicating there is still substantial scope for growing the economy by simply allowing households to claim a higher share of GDP, and moving toward consumer sovereignty and a consumer-driven growth path. China's transition to a post-industrial service economy has also scarcely begun. Enlivening still has potential to illuminate new markets and new technology solutions, and there is nothing inevitable about a shift away from enlivening as growth slows.

However, under the particular China circumstances, slowing growth was one of the proximate causes that led Chinese policy-makers to push for new development strategies. Chinese policy-makers have refused to accept the magnitude of slowdown implied by structural changes and have instead searched for new drivers of growth. Xi Jinping established a target of doubling GDP by 2020 (on a 2010 base) that essentially demands keeping annual GDP growth above 6.5 percent. In this effort, policy-makers do not distinguish between a demand-driven approach and a supply-driven approach. High investment creates demand for heavy industrial products, while hopefully providing more sophisticated capital that improves supply. High-tech industry provides the appearance of being a supply-side policy, based on strengthening productive capabilities. But it must also be a demand-side policy, because an industry can grow only if there is demand for its output. Without a doubt, the quest to keep growth rapid lies behind the adoption of techno-industrial policies as new growth-drivers.

If these policies are a response to slowing growth, they also represent an effort to take advantage of a window of opportunity before China becomes a true elderly society. The end of the demographic dividend does not automatically mean that demographics becomes a drag on growth. To be sure, the extra boost is gone, and the economy must cope with a plateauing of the labor force (in absolute size) and a future rapid decline (after about 2027). However, this is very different from actually having an aged population. Only about 12 percent of China's population is aged sixty-five and older as of 2015, substantially below real aged societies like Japan or Germany, which are in the range of 25–30 percent. Even Korea, Taiwan, and Hong Kong have much larger shares of elderly population than mainland China. So, although China is no longer reaping the demographic dividend, it is today in a kind of demographic "Indian summer." Perhaps we should say that China is today on the high "shoulder" after having descended slightly from the peak of demographic bliss. There is no big pension burden on the government budget today, though there will be in the future. There are still productivity gains to be reaped from the maturing of workers as they grow from their twenties into their forties, and so on. Chinese policy-makers have, implicitly, decided to make use of this demographic Indian summer to drive the Chinese economy to high-tech status. They are trying to outrun the forces that will tend to slow the economy and will eventually cause it to age. They are doing this through aggressive investment in human capital, through high physical investment rates, and, above all, through the pursuit of ambitious techno-industrial policies.

The New Big Push

China's commitment to techno-industrial policies began slowly after 2006, and only started to take coherent shape with the Strategic Emerging Industries (SEIs) during 2010. These are a set of twenty targeted industries (in seven categories), for which substantial subsidies and preferential policies were provided. Returning to figure 1-2, it is clear that profitability of state-owned firms began to diverge from that of nonstate firms after 2007. This coincides with the beginning of the push by policy-makers to give state firms new mandates and developmental responsibilities. This process reached a new milestone with the publication of a formal SEI plan in mid-2012, with targets that were then incorporated into the Twelfth and Thirteenth Five-year Plans (for 2011–2015 and 2016–2020, respectively). Expenditure on the SEIs quickly began a rapid growth. The most striking example is the semiconductor industry, which had $65 billion in dedicated investment funds by the end of 2016.[8] Commitments on a similar scale are evident in electric ("new energy") vehicles. An early developer among the SEIs was solar panels, which surged in 2010–2011 before running into problems with excess capacity and import barriers among developed country markets, including the United States.

In 2015–2016, these policies were expanded in scope and knitted into an increasingly comprehensive development program called the "Innovation-driven Development Strategy" (IDDS), which was reformulated in 2016. This change converted what had been an indicative, rather vague, set of development guidelines into an operational plan for sectoral industrial change, and elevated industrial policy to national strategy.[9] The version of the SEI plan promulgated for the 2016–2020 period has broad targets for industrial sectors and disaggregates implementation tasks to numerous government agencies. It breaks out five large sectors from the original SEI plan and gives output targets for each of them for the year 2020.[10] The SEI plan for 2016–2020 also calls for close coordination with a whole series of other plans. These other plans include the Made in China 2025 plan (initially promulgated May 8, 2015); the Military Civilian Industry Fusion Plan; the Internet Plus Plan; and a special plan for artificial intelligence.[11] Thus, between 2015 and 2016, a full panoply of interlocking plans was promulgated.

The new programs promulgated along with the SEIs were in some ways more sophisticated than the original SEI program, because instead of merely targeting a few specific sectors, these programs envision using new technologies to transform traditional industrial sectors. Thus, Made in China 2025 is designed to assist the application of robotics, sensors, and AI-enabled smart manufacturing to all of China's industry. Each generation of techno-industrial policy has been more sophisticated than the preceding one, and also larger. As new initiatives are introduced, policies have been steadily proliferating. There are no sunset provisions, so the old ones don't disappear. Instead, when problems emerge with excess capacity, ad hoc adjustments are made to scale back subsidies (as has happened recently with solar power and electric vehicles).

While technology is the main focus of China's new "big push," it is by no means the only part of the policy. Increasing state ambition is apparent in the Belt and Road Initiative, which envisions China as the hub of a radiating system of transport and communication spokes. China will organize financing for these infrastructure investments and, in most cases, Chinese construction firms will do the actual work. Telecom and the internet in BRI countries are also intended to stream into the Chinese model. Nor is the external BRI the only target of a new wave of infrastructure investment. Within China, ambitious plans to rebuild major metropolitan areas are afoot. The new city of Xiong'an is planned about a hundred kilometers south of Beijing, to serve as either a new growth pole or as the overflow basin for Beijing's unwanted activities, depending upon your point of view. Indeed, it sometimes seems as if a utopian tinge has crept into Chinese thinking about development strategy. As enlivening is left behind, increasingly ambitious and even utopian schemes seem to be taking its place. In other parts of the world, pessimism about experts and government-managed change seems to be growing just as China is shifting in this direction and accelerating its efforts.

It seems clear, then, that the stalling out of market-oriented reform, combined with the steady acceleration of techno-industrial aspirations, have produced a new development strategy in China. As reforms gradually faded, policy-makers became more and more committed to the idea that government would create new areas of demand, new "drivers of growth," and would increasingly define where the economy was going. The agnosticism about outcomes that accompanied previous Chinese strategies of enlivening has been replaced with a dramatic commitment to fostering high-tech sectors and shaping a new growth trajectory.

Conclusion and Discussion

If the era of miracle growth and enlivening the economy is over, it falls on us to define and describe the new era. It turns out that this is not so easy. As discussed earlier in the section "A Market-Revealing Strategy," we do not have a straightforward metric to quantify the shift toward government steerage. For this shift is distinctive: it is not being carried out through direct government administrative control, but rather through the marketplace, using existing ownership forms.

Markets in the Service of Industrial Policy

China's industrial policies have been launched in an environment that is fairly highly marketized. Moreover, the Chinese government is happy to swing behind private firms if they are proven winners. This is already quite evident in the government's support for the BAT trio: Baidu, Alibaba, and Tencent. These are all private companies, set up by visionary entrepreneurs who were well ahead of any government planners in grasping the potential of the internet. Yet today the Chinese government holds all three close in a tight and affectionate, if involuntary, embrace. The Chinese Communist Party seems completely comfortable with its ability to wield benefits and penalties, carrots and sticks, designed to keep these corporations in line with government interests. To be sure, every now and then the party feels the need to take the trio of BAT entrepreneurs down a notch, as Xi Jinping is said to have done in closed-door criticism at the Financial Work Conference in July 2017. At the same time, the regime depends on the expertise of these internet giants to help it manage the flow of information on the web, develop web-based financial tools, and so forth. The two sides are utterly interdependent, but everybody understands who has the upper hand.

Money from the government to support emerging industries flows freely to private and start-up firms. As pointed out earlier, China has plenty of money available to support this effort for the next decade. To be sure, the government asks state-owned enterprises to do more as well, and gives them advantages in terms of funding and access to opportunities. But nobody expects that to lead to SOE domination of emerging sectors, because that would require a revolution in the thinking and operation of most SOEs. China is far more intent on replicating the Silicon Valley model (with appropriate government controls) than it is in foisting SOE dominance on a thriving tech sector.

This marketization process—and preference for a Silicon Valley–type model—extends beyond the firms doing the innovation and to the financial entities that finance this work. China has developed in the past three or four years a vast array of government-run "industrial guidance funds." At the end of 2017, these funds had a defined fund-raising scope of $1.3 trillion U.S. dollars.[12] This massive sector is managed by governmental agencies and the funds come primarily from the government, SOEs, and state-run banks. However, private entities are also welcome to join these funds as limited partners, providing money in the hope of getting a fat return. Government money, on the other hand, is to be patient and accepting of lower returns, even zero returns (so long as the initial investment doesn't disappear). The Chinese government, in other words, is taking stakes in venture-capital outfits and other investment entities. These are more market-oriented than before, and have reasonably coherent corporate governance structures. This is an experiment, to be sure, and it may not succeed, but it certainly represents an important departure from the way things were done in China a decade or two ago. In short, the Chinese government is paying its own way. It is not imposing distortions on the market economy to get the outcome it wants. Instead, it's paying the differential, using government-owned banks and government contributions to investment funds to shift the investment calculus in the direction that it wants.

Describing the "New Normal"

Chinese policy-makers are quite open in describing their new economic model. They are proud of their far-seeing industrial policies and the efforts and investments they have made in creating new capabilities and supporting a knowledge-based economy. However, we outsiders have been slow to try to understand the implications of this effort. Certainly there are risks:

what China is doing will inevitably involve massive expenses, enormous waste, and a significant chance of failure. There will be successes and failures, and much will depend on how policy-makers handle these divergent outcomes. Will they let failed firms go bankrupt? Will the burden of debt and bad loans on the economy increase? Or will the successful program create new sources of productivity that will allow the economy to grow out of today's problems? It is far too early to tell.

Our understanding of these new policies is limited, in part because they are so new. In part, this is because our standard ways of classifying economies don't really catch what's happening in China today. The proportion of private business and SOEs in the economy doesn't reflect the change in strategy. The size of the government budget and state banks tells us something, but not much. Big government budgets in northern European countries, for example, are almost entirely harnessed to redistributing consumption across generations, fulfilling legal responsibilities to different groups, and therefore have a profoundly conservative impact on developmental patterns. China is certainly different, but how exactly do we show this? In principle, we would want to estimate the expenditure that is made to produce a developmental trajectory that is different from that under consumer sovereignty. As discussed earlier, this would have to describe policies that go beyond a "neutral" policy of government investment in public goods. However, today we do not have the means to compute such a number, but if we did, I believe it would show that the Chinese government in 2005 was very close to a neutral position, whereas by 2017, it was directing much bigger investment flows, potentially equal to several percent of GDP, into areas not clearly suggested by existing demand patterns. This is a momentous change for a government in such a short time.

Conclusion

The past is a poor guide to China's future. Both in terms of underlying structural features and in terms of dominant development strategy, China at the end of the 2010s is very different from the enlivening and transforming China in the first three decades after 1978. The structural changes from the growth-miracle period are straightforward, easy to understand, and similar in form to the changes that Japan, Korea, and Taiwan went through at the end of their miracle-growth periods. But China is determined not to follow the Japanese and Korean example, leading as it did to significant growth slowdowns. Instead, China has launched on its own path of increased intervention and steerage. Our standard measures don't catch this remarkable change. The economy is still marketized—in that sense, the strategy of enlivening has been successful and is being built on. However, the government is no longer depending on enlivening the economy but rather is making a massive effort to steer the economy to a faster growth path, pushing it toward a high-technology future.

Most of the epoch since 1978 was defined by system reform and a development strategy based on enlivening the economy. Those days are gone, and China has entered a new era in which development strategy is defined by a type of government steerage based on industrial policy. But even then, the new era is not stable. The commitment of resources to industrial policy is increasing. It is already at levels unthinkable a decade ago, and is still accelerating.

Notes

1. Chen Yun's classic formulation is in "Several Problems of Realizing the Strategic Objectives Set by the Party's 12th Party Congress," December 2, 1982, in *Selected Works of Chen Yun* (in Chinese), Beijing 1995, 318–320.

2. The one significant non-Asian case is Brazil between 1950 and 1975. New growth miracles have the potential to emerge today in Africa and South Asia, so the membership list is certainly not closed. Commission on Growth and Development, *The Growth Report: Strategies for Sustained Growth and Inclusive Development* (Washington, DC: The World Bank, 2008).

3. Justin Yifu Lin, "Rural Reform and Agricultural Growth in China," *American Economic Review*, 82 (1992), 34–51. Barry Naughton, *The Chinese Economy: Adaptation and Growth* (Cambridge, Massachusetts: MIT Press, 2018), 100–102, 279–305.

4. I define "market-oriented reform" as an intentional policy designed to increase market competition, either by permitting entry by new competitors or by providing better rules for fair competition.

5. Nicholas Lardy, *Markets over Mao: The Rise of Private Business in China* (Washington, DC: Institute for International Economics, 2014).

6. For example, this view has been advanced by senior Chinese economist Zhang Zhuoyuan. See the discussion in Wu Jinglian, "Toward a Renewal of Reform," interview conducted January 5, 2012, in Barry Naughton, ed., *Wu Jinglian: Voice of Reform in China* (Cambridge, Massachusetts: MIT Press, 2013), 11–31.

7. Barry Naughton, "Is China Socialist?" *Journal of Economic Perspectives*, vol. 31, no. 1 (Winter 2017), 1–23. Methodology and definitions outlined in that

source are updated from Ministry of Finance, "Report on National Land Sales and Revenues" (annual; in Chinese); and Ministry of Human Resources and Social Security, "Statistical Report on Human Resources and Social Security" (annual; in Chinese).

8. Junko Yoshida, "Much Ado About China's Big IC Surge; Myth and Reality of China's IC Fund," *EETimes Online*, June 22, 2017.

9. Chinese Communist Party and State Council, "Outline of the Innovation-Driven Development Strategy," Xinhua News Agency, May 19, 2016 (in Chinese).

10. State Council, "Thirteenth Five Year Development Plan for the Strategic Emerging Industries," November 29, 2016 (in Chinese).

11. Xia Xutian and Li Baoqiang, "MIIT: We've Completed the Military-Civilian Industry Fusion Plan," *21st Century Economic Herald*, December 9, 2016; Paul Triolo and Jimmy Goodrich, "From Riding a Wave to Full Speed Ahead: As China's Government Mobilizes for AI Leadership, Some Challenges Will Be Tougher Than Others," *New America DigiChina Project Policy Paper*, February 28, 2018.

12. According to commercial data collected by the firm Zero2IPO.

TWO

Reflections on Forty Years of Rural Reform

JEAN C. OI

After forty years of reform, China can boast a number of successes, especially measured in terms of economic growth. But even Xi Jinping made clear at the Nineteenth Party Congress and at the Thirteenth National People's Congress that much more needs to be done. The process of reform is complex, and it is not surprising that a number of remaining problems stem from China having taken the path of least political resistance early in the reform process. That strategy allowed China to push forward reform by avoiding confrontation of ideologically or politically sensitive issues.[1] Forty years on, the question is: How much longer is this strategy viable? Has China reached a point where much more radical change is needed?

The costs and constraints of China's limited model of reform that ties its hands to certain institutions and ideological principles are increasingly evident forty years later. Unlike the situation in Russia or Eastern Europe, where the "big bang" approach threw out most of the earlier power structures, China has maintained its core institutions. Unlike most other transitional systems that explicitly abandoned communist one-party rule, the Chinese Communist Party (CCP) is still in power. Unlike in almost any other country, veteran communist leaders could legitimately claim that they were victims of the Cultural Revolution and, therefore, not to blame for the serious deviations caused by the Gang of Four and mistakes by

Mao during the previous ten years. These reformers, led by Deng Xiaoping, proclaimed themselves ready to take China back to the correct path with reforms. But to legitimatize both the continued rule of the CCP and themselves, reformers like Deng Xiaoping promised that China would adhere to socialism.

The vow to remain socialist took certain policy options off the table—most important, the privatization of the means of production. Political considerations limited economic policy options and shaped the course and process of reform. In the rural reforms, this precluded the privatization of land when communes were abolished, and instead mandated that the ownership of land remain with the collective. Prohibitions against crossing this ideological red line also help explain why the reforms took off from the countryside. Unlike the state-owned enterprise reforms, sufficient change could be effected in agriculture without challenging core principles of the socialist system.

Barry Naughton's observation, in the preceding chapter, that China's reform was to "grow out of the plan" captures well what happened in the early phases of reform, particularly in the countryside.[2] China kept many of the existing institutions while growing market aspects of the economy. The expectation was that the new institutions would overshadow the old, which would either adapt or eventually fade from the scene. The rural reforms were not so much about what was dismantled, but what was left of the old system and how these institutions were adapted and new institutions were added. This model worked because the state created sufficient incentives for the peasants as well as cadres to adopt and run with the reform policies within existing institutions. Contrary to theories that suggested that communist officials would oppose reform,[3] agents of the Chinese state at the grassroots responded positively to incentives for reform and adapted the Maoist bureaucratic system to grow the economy.[4] An unexpected silver lining of the Cultural Revolution is that it destroyed vested interests, like those in the Soviet Union, which would have likely obstructed reforms in China. Reforms crafted to benefit the economic and political well-being of the state agents responsible for implementing and overseeing those reforms successfully overcame obstacles to change found in other transitional regimes, such as Russia.[5]

Looking back at forty years of reform, one can see that China managed to grow out of the plan in many key respects, allowing the economy to boom. But at the same time, there have been limits to that process.

For example, while it eventually allowed the privatization of the means of production in rural industry (that is, the sale of collectively owned village and township enterprises), it refuses to privatize the ownership of land. Moreover, it has stubbornly adhered to the *hukou* system until recently, and even then has kept the system intact in key mega cities like Beijing and Shanghai. The earlier limits on institutional reform have had significant ramifications for China's ability to complete later stages of reform. To borrow Naughton's term used in this volume, the early phases of reform were aimed at enlivening the economy. That could be accomplished with partial reforms, but, as time has passed, it has become more difficult to continue with this strategy.

This chapter examines three reforms that were successful in the early phases of China's reform process: (1) decollectivization without privatization of land; (2) rural industrialization without the private sector; and (3) migration without integration. All three of these policy successes are examples of reforms that were accomplished without challenging core tenets of the socialist system—that is, adhering to socialist red lines and keeping core existing institutions, whether through collective ownership of the means of rural production, land, or retaining control of institutions from the pre-reform era, such as the *hukou* system that has limited the integration of those seeking to move from rural to urban areas. While all three have seemingly led rather effortlessly from one into the other, as the economy has continued to evolve and grow, the reforms have all stayed within the bounds of a socialist system. However, they have yielded a number of contradictions and unintended consequences that now plague the system.

In the countryside, these partially reformed institutions worked well enough to allow China to generate successful economic growth beyond anyone's wildest dreams in an increasingly marketized economy. Even without privatizing the means of production, by keeping ownership of land collective, the rural reforms successfully kick-started China's economic miracle. Limited reform solved the free-rider problem in agriculture to provide sufficient incentives for peasant households to dramatically increase grain production so much that peasants went from having "difficulty buying grain" to "difficulty in selling grain" within a few years of starting reform.[6]

Even more impressive, the rural reforms opened the door to a rapid diversification of China's rural economy; the rise of rural industry provided alternative and much higher paying jobs for those living in the countryside. Household farming and the reopening of markets additionally provided urban areas with a cheap source of labor as millions of able-bodied migrants from rural areas were able to move to the cities, albeit illegally, in search of a better life and higher incomes. Subsequently, these migrants sent remittances back to their home villages, which helped redistribute income between urban and rural areas.

China's achievements during the past forty years have been record-breaking, and a strong case can be made that this strategy of partial reform was necessary to forward reform. There is no argument about that. The point that this chapter seeks to underscore is that forty years on, China may now be at a point where it must take on the more politically difficult and far-reaching systemic changes that it has been avoiding, if it wants to complete and consolidate its reforms.

Decollectivization Without Privatization

Reforms began in the countryside, where property rights could be divided into a bundle of rights.[7] Only part of Demsetz's bundles of rights had to be changed: decollectivization transferred the right of management and the right to the residual from the land to peasant households, but the right of alienation—that is, the right to sell the land—would remain with the collective. This was not privatization; the ownership of the land was still socialist, because it remained in collective hands. Individual families had the right to the surplus from the use of the land and the right to manage the land, but did not have the right to sell the land. To this day, the ownership of farmland has not been privatized, but households are the unit of production and accounting.

Yet, even with only limited institutional change, the decollectivization of agriculture and the return to household farming were significant enough that they affected peasant economic behavior. Each peasant household could enjoy any surplus from the land that they had the right to manage and work. These changes gave each family hope that they, too, could benefit from Deng Xiaoping's dictum that it was acceptable for some to "get rich first." The collective no longer stood between the peasant producer and the harvest.[8]

While it is important, the household-responsibility system (HRS) would not have been sufficient by itself to explain the increased incentives for production. Some have argued that a far more important and necessary development that spurred production was the dramatic increase in state procurement prices.[9] Starting in 1979, the state increased the price it paid to peasants by as much as 50 percent for all grain procurement sales sold over the basic quota amount. Moreover, this price increase also was accompanied by the restored value of money—in contrast to the Mao period, when everything was rationed and one needed not only money but ration tickets. The structure of China's economy was adjusted so that more consumer goods were being produced and peasants had new reasons to want money to buy the increasing number of goods that were now available in state stores and on the free market. The point is that all of this could be done without any radical change in the system. In fact, rationing officially did not end until much later.

State and market operated side by side during the early years of reform. While the reopening of free markets was important, it was not the driving force for increasing production, contrary to what is assumed in the Washington Consensus. Because there was both plan and market in China's transitional economy, during the early reform period, the market was not always the first choice for either the sale or the procurement of goods. In the late 1970s and early 1980s, state procurements, rather than the free market, provided peasants with a secure outlet for their output at guaranteed prices. Guaranteed state procurements at pre-set high prices made it lucrative for peasants to work harder to grow more and sell more to the state. The impact of price incentives is further reflected in the fact that when the government stopped unlimited guaranteed high over-quota procurement prices and peasants were forced to go to the open market, harvests went down and the state again faced problems with grain production. Peasant productivity responds to price signals and economic incentives, whether these are given by the market or by the state. The commercialization of agriculture eventually emerges and is now expanding.[10]

While limited reforms in the countryside were feasible, the process of agricultural reform was fraught with conflict. The process of decollectivization was in many ways akin to a contentious second land reform.[11] Like the original land reform in the early years of the People's Republic of China (PRC), decollectivization was a terribly quarrelsome process that sometimes took months, with many charges of cadre corruption.[12] Sometimes disputes could only be settled by drawing straws to determine who should get what piece of land. At stake was, of course, the quality and character of the primary means of production for peasant families for the foreseeable future. How rich was the land? How far was it from the family house? How far was it from sources of water for irrigation? Though serious, these problems were not intractable issues of ideological principle—the socialist principle of the collective ownership of land was never violated. However, it was precisely because the collective remained the unit of administration and had the right of ownership of land that negative unintended consequences, some more immediate than others, ensued.

Peasant Burdens and Rural Unrest

Ironic as it may be, the politically correct household-responsibility system, which kept land collectively owned but also managed to provide incentives to peasants to work harder, became the root of a number of problems that have plagued those who remained in China's villages. One obvious and immediate consequence is the fragmentation of land plots that hindered scale production and made mechanization difficult if not impossible. Only with the commercialization of agricultural production have these problems been ameliorated, but that has meant that peasants have had to contract out their right to farm the land, sometimes working as rural labor on what was once their own plots of land.[13] Less obvious but politically more salient, the household-responsibility system gave rise to "peasant burdens" that have led to protests and substantial discontent in parts of China's countryside.

When the abolition of communes made the household the unit of production, it took away the rights to agricultural revenue from the collective, the village. Households gained the right to decide the disposition of the surplus after state taxes and sales were made. The collective was left dependent on peasant households for its only source of revenue from the harvest, the allowed surcharge known as the *tiliu*, which was paid by the households to the collective.[14] But these fees were limited to a small percentage of peasant incomes. If a village had no other sources of collective revenue, there were few or no funds to provide public goods; sometimes there was not even enough to meet the most basic expenditures.

Some village coffers became so drained that village cadres were incapable of governance; some villages became known as "paralyzed villages," where peasants refused to listen to the cadres and the cadres lost their authority because they had little hold over peasants and could no longer provide services due to their lack of resources. Villages devoted primarily to agriculture found themselves in a situation where the only way cadres could get enough revenue to fund the local coffers was to increasingly demand more surcharges and fees from their peasant households—the "peasant burdens" problem. This led to peasant discontent and rural instability.

The late 1980s into the 1990s was a time of problems and instability in the countryside as increasing numbers of farmers protested peasant burdens and cadre corruption.[15] As the literature on village protests documents, villagers became increasingly bold in openly articulating their discontent about these problems.[16] In some instances, they made official complaints to higher levels. In other instances, they took to the roads to protest, sometimes violently. The numerous challenges came to be summed up by the phrase "three agricultural problems": the general malaise in agriculture, stagnant rural development along with increasing debt from failed township and village enterprises (TVEs) (see below), and farmers not prospering.[17] Statements by China's top leaders that these problems could threaten the core of the regime suggest that the state recognized the need to become more proactive as fear increased of the consequences of the unresolved problems emerging over the course of reform.[18]

The center issued many "red-letter directives" that ordered local officials to reduce peasant burdens. But these edicts largely fell on deaf ears.[19] In the troubled context of the 1990s, the central state started to consider more direct action, both with regard to making further changes in the fiscal system and in tightening controls over grassroots cadres.

Recentralizing Control

In the 1980s, the state decollectivized agriculture and stepped back, allowing villages and individual households to go their own way; but in the 1990s, when the unsolved problems and unintended consequences of these reforms became more severe, the state stepped back in. However, the state adopted a bifurcated approach toward households and cadres: it continued to allow markets to develop as the state has remained out of the decision-making calculus of farm households; at the same time, it tightened its grip over township and village cadres and moved fiscal and administrative controls up the bureaucracy, limiting the authority of township or village cadres.

The central state increased its fiscal capacity with the 1994 fiscal reforms in a broad shift to recentralize control, both by fiscal and administrative measures.[20] But the 1994 fiscal reforms, which took much of the extra-budgetary funds from the localities, left local authorities at the township and county levels with insufficient revenues. This only served to aggravate the peasant-burden problem and rural discontent by increasing the need at higher levels, as well as the village, to find new sources of revenue for local administration and governance.

If the 1994 tax reform was driven by the desire to gain control over more revenues, the recentralization of control over cadres was driven by fears of increasing peasant discontent and charges of cadre corruption, after previous indirect-control mechanisms failed. We see this in increased administration and oversight of village- and town-level fiscal revenues, expenditures, and public-goods investments. Zhao Shukai and I, based on our fieldwork in the mid-2000s, found that townships controlled village accounts, depriving village cadres of the right to keep their own books.[21] Where the double-proxy management policy (*shuang daiguan*) is in effect, village funds are turned over to the township economic stations, and villages must submit a request before they can access their funds.

Alleviating Peasant Burdens

By the early to mid-2000s, China's leaders seemed to have a newfound awareness of the degree of discontent and problems that had developed over the course of the reforms, and decided to take direct action to calm discontent in the countryside. The Hu-Wen leadership announced policies to build a Harmonious Society. To quell peasant discontent, the state implemented the tax-for-fee reforms (*feigai shui*) in 2000–2001,[22] which abolished all fees and reformed the agricultural tax to finally eliminate key sources of peasant burdens. By 2006, it took the unprecedented further step of abolishing the remaining agricultural tax so that peasants would owe the state neither fees nor taxes. By 2006, for the first time in China's history, peasants were free from all taxes and surcharges.

Unfortunately for the state and the peasants, the measures that eliminated taxes and fees triggered new problems due to other institutional flaws in the system, which ultimately undermined the abolition of peasant burdens. Here one sees the dilemma of China's piecemeal reform process. Well-intentioned policies that served one set of actors result in negative externalities for another; solving one problem could open the door to new ones. The state's well-intentioned policies toward peasant households created severe fiscal problems for the lowest levels of the administrative bureaucracy. That, in turn, laid the basis for land takings and mounting local government debt, which are currently areas of grave concern.

The effort made by the central authorities to reduce peasant burdens through these well-intentioned policies only aggravated the fiscal problems for villages after decollectivization and for townships after the 1994 fiscal reforms, which took much of the extra-budgetary funds out of the localities, pushing some localities over the fiscal edge into debt.[23] Little by little, localities were faced with waves of debt as costs mounted, including those related to the development and then collapse of TVEs, unfunded education improvement mandates, and the failure of credit associations, among others.

Problems were compounded because the state left land right-of-ownership with the collective. Over time, local authorities turned to land-taking to cope with their fiscal shortfalls—they appropriated peasant land for commercial profit. To raise revenues, local authorities turned to the one resource that decollectivization left to the collective: land. This led to further discontent and, as shown in a later section, it has perverted later reform efforts (the new socialist countryside policy). The anger and protests that stemmed from that undid the calming effects of abolishing fees and taxes and thus undermined the center's efforts to create rural stability.

Thus, decollectivization was a relatively easy solution to enliven agricultural production with only limited reforms. The household-responsibility system was a crucial reform that freed peasants from the land. The reopening of free markets meant that money was again sufficient to secure food. This allowed peasants to migrate and engage in nonfarm labor, all of which yielded much higher incomes than agricultural production. However, close examination of the sources of rural growth suggest that the dramatic growth in the economy was not from agriculture but from the indirect consequences of decollectivization. China's growth stemmed from the emergence of new income opportunities for both individual peasants and for the village as a collective. The household-responsibility system and the opening of markets led to diversification of production and paved the way for migration. No longer did everyone have to grow grain, nor was production dictated entirely by the state-set plan. The peasants who had the knowledge and the skill required to grow cash crops such as vegetables and fruit could reap much higher returns than those who stayed only in grain production. In the long run, grain production has not been the route to increased incomes.

The positives of decollectivization are well known. The point of this section is to show how China's politically expedient household-responsibility system also was the root of problems that have emerged in the wake of decollectivization. The reforms left the village as a collective with little or no revenue sources to adjust to the changed economic circumstances created by decollectivization. It was expected to administer the village as it did before, but without new sources of income. Not surprisingly, myriad problems like the rise of peasant burdens subsequently followed, with some coming sooner than others.

Fortunately for China, some cadres responded to the need to develop new sources of collective income by diversifying production, which led to the rise of village-owned rural industry. These positive externalities of decollectivization allowed China's rural reforms to progress into the 1990s.

The Rise and Fall of Rural Industry

The economic history of most countries suggests that industrialization is the route out of rural poverty. Industrialization is usually accompanied by urbanization, where large numbers of those who had previously farmed for a living become workers and move from rural to urban areas. China had long ago undergone industrialization and had major industries in its many large cities. However, a new process of industrialization emerged in the countryside shortly after the reforms began, around the time of decollectivization, which was very different from what had occurred earlier in China and, for that matter, the rest of the world.

The rapid rise of rural industrialization in the 1980s was crucial for China's reforms. It is not an overstatement to say that it allowed China's economy to take off and counterbalanced the problems already emerging in the agricultural sector, which were described above. Rural industrialization offered new income opportunities for both individual peasants and, perhaps most important, for the village as a collective, which had been deprived of the rights to income from the agricultural surplus by the household-responsibility system.

Rural Industrialization Not Led by the Private Sector

China's rural reforms opened the door to diversification and industrialization, but during the 1980s, political as well as economic necessity promoted a specific type of rural industry: collectively owned enterprises. Private firms would eventually dominate, but that did not happen until the 1990s. The collective ownership of these firms was essential during the early phase of China's reforms. Politically, it meant that the rise of these enterprises would only add to rather than detract from cadre power. TVEs were collectively owned by the township or villages. One cannot underestimate the importance of the fact that these firms were under the control of local officials. This meant that local officials had reason to support rather than oppose this development.

Some peasants started their own household enterprises. In terms of sheer numbers, these privately owned firms dominated.[24] However, collectively owned township and village enterprises employed the largest numbers of peasants and produced the largest output.

Collectively owned rural industry existed during the Mao period, mostly in the form of commune-level enterprises.[25] However, the phenomenon that occurred starting in the early to mid-1980s went beyond anything that could be explained by the limited number of commune-level enterprises. Townships and villages that had never previously had industry established factories, produced goods ranging from simple agricultural-based items like tofu and soap to more industrial items like steel piping and chemicals. Both the scale and the rapid rise of these firms were impressive, especially at the village level, which saw the growth of the largest number of collectively owned firms. Between 1978 and the mid-1990s, employment in TVEs grew by 9 percent annually, from 28 million in 1978 to a peak of 135 million in 1996. TVE value added went from 6 percent of gross domestic product (GDP) in 1978 to 26 percent of GDP in 1996. Along with this growth came the creation of new jobs that were essential for getting a large portion of its population out of poverty. Rural industry absorbed a large amount of the surplus labor that was created by the reform to household farming. Off-farm income jobs allowed the greatest opportunities to get ahead economically.[26]

Some recent work has argued that it was privately owned rural industry, not the collective, that accounted for China's economic miracle.[27] Existing scholarship has long acknowledged that private firms always outnumbered the collectively owned ones.[28] In the 1980s, in areas where local officials were supporting the development of the collective sector, the numerous private firms often remained small, because they were not allowed access to the capital needed to develop industry of any scale. However, there were areas where private firms were dominant from the start, such as in Wenzhou and parts of Fujian. Even though local officials in these areas did not directly control them, these privately owned firms worked closely with local officials so that all benefited. It is in such areas that many privately owned firms were given "red hats" to wear—that is, they were allowed to call themselves a collective—so they could enjoy the preferential access to inputs and services given to collectively owned firms. Huang's research on very poor places like Guizhou, where, he argues, the private sector was dominant from the start and never bothered to hide this type of ownership by wearing "red hats," further adds to our knowledge about the variation in practices that exists in China.[29] It also raises the question of why Guizhou felt confident enough not to hide its private sector and openly provide preferential allocation, which, at least in theory, should have only been given to collectively owned firms. For the country as a whole, however, open support for and the rise of privately owned firms only occurred in the 1990s, after the collectively owned ones started having problems.[30]

If China had, at the beginning of the reforms, promoted a strategy that encouraged the rapid development of a private sector everywhere so as to challenge the power of local officials, the outcome would likely have been much more like that predicted by Kornai. Communist officials would have either blocked reform or preyed heavily upon private business. Instead, in China, only later, when the collectively owned firms began to be a financial burden and private ones turned into a viable revenue source, did officials rethink their options and choose to embrace the private sector. Perhaps equally important, this was after almost a decade of market reforms, by which point local officials realized they could still have power with the rise of private business. This progression of ownership forms, starting with the collectively owned, explains why the China case goes against established notions about the response of communist officials to reform. Collectively owned enterprises enhanced rather than threatened cadre power. These collectively owned firms feed into the route to political success and to bureaucratic promotion—raising GDP numbers for the annual cadre evaluations. In some areas earlier than others, local officials found that this strategy could include helping privately owned firms. Officials who wanted to get ahead politically had incentive to pursue rural industry and generate increased revenues regardless of the ownership structure.

As counterintuitive as it may seem, China's Maoist legacy and particular form of central planning allowed for rapid growth in rural industry.[31] The problems of state-led growth are well known, with the cases of China before reform and the Soviet Union as prime examples of the failures of centrally planned economies. While the centrally planned system of the Mao period can be blamed for the disappointing performance of China's economy, the legacy of the Maoist system coupled with changes in the incentives for those overseeing development was a key variable that allowed rural industry to develop rapidly.[32] In many areas, local officials facilitated and/or spearheaded the rapid growth of TVEs using the existing bureaucratic system adapted for reform to become the sinews of local state corporatism. For collectively owned township or village-owned enterprises and even for those who wore red hats, local officials either directly led or facilitated development.

State-Sponsored Privatization of Rural Industry

The ability of villages and townships to draw on support of the upper levels to start rural industry lowered the entry barriers for the rapid rise of TVEs. However, it was precisely because of the ease with which firms could be established that led to the creation of firms that in a more competitive market system would likely not have been established. The weakness of some firms was unmasked as the numbers increased and a market shakedown occurred, especially as market conditions worsened and the center engaged in economic retrenchment to cool down investment. The ensuing collapse of these firms plagued many villages for a decade after. It is during this economically difficult time, more than a decade after the reforms began, that the state started to relax its stringent adherence to collective ownership of the means of production. Unlike with the ownership of land, where the state held steadfast in refusing to privatize, the state decided in the 1990s to allow privatization of rural industry—the failing TVEs. In fact, the state implemented a state-sponsored privatization of formerly collectively owned firms. In addition, the state explicitly switched its support to private-sector development of small and medium enterprises (SMEs). By the 1990s, this change was economically rational and politically feasible.

During the period between the late 1980s and 1990s, TVEs began to suffer from inefficiencies and soft budget constraints. This was a time of softening markets as well as increased competition and decreasing profits.[33] More than a few TVEs saw hard times by the 1990s, eventually leaving villages with rusting factories and heavy debt.[34] We now know that rural industry became one of the most common sources of village debt.[35] This was even true of those that were seemingly very successful in the 1980s. The financial toll from TVE failures was heavy, both for the individual villages and ultimately for the individual peasant families who had to pay the bill. The rural credit cooperatives, which lent the money for the factories, were mired in red ink. Using survey data to arrange villages along an agricultural dependence continuum, one finds that a wide range of villages, including those that had industrialized, faced a situation where debt was going up rapidly while incomes were slowing or decreasing.[36] Although the sources of the debt were different, there are large increases in debt at both ends of the agricultural dependence spectrum. Villages that were highly industrialized and those most dependent on agriculture accrued increasing debt. By the mid-1990s, most had serious economic problems and were either sold or simply sat idle, rusting away.[37]

In the case of rural industry, we do see the state adapting and abandoning a politically expedient policy decision when economic and political conditions changed. The severity of the economic problems with collectively owned TVEs prompted local officials to switch their support to private firms. As noted above, this move came more than ten years after the reforms began and local officials had come to realize that they could still have power, even with the rise of private industry. By that point, taxes from private firms began to outpace those from collectively owned TVEs. Interviews with bankers and local officials noted that over time they preferred to give loans to the private sector, because those were more secure. Collateral was required in loans to private firms, and it was clear who was responsible for paying back the loans. This was in sharp contrast to the situation for the collectively owned firms, where no collateral was required. Local governments simply signed as the guarantor for a loan, which meant that there was no single person clearly named as being legally responsible for repayment. When there was a market downturn and TVEs faced problems, the number of bad loans to collectively owned TVEs mounted with no relief in sight.

It was in response to problems with public ownership and heavy debt that many localities engaged in state-sponsored privatization, selling village and township enterprises. By the mid-1990s, local officials decided to sell an increasing number of collectively owned firms that had become too costly to support, especially when other sources of revenue generation became available (that is, private firms). From that point on, the private sector has dominated SME in the rural areas. We see that the local corporate state has adapted to help private firms to get ahead.[38]

The failure and debt from TVEs is another example of the limits of a politically expedient reform strategy. The successful collective model of industrialization was adopted in the 1980s because it was both politically feasible and economically necessary. The Maoist legacy allowed rural industry to develop very rapidly, probably even more than if the private entrepreneur model had been followed. However, this also meant that unsustainable firms were established, because officials could mobilize the necessary resources, at least in the short run. But the national retrenchment in the late 1980s created havoc with credit freezes and resulted in a market shake-up. While a market shake-up was ultimately necessary, those that were relatively weak and produced lower-quality goods found themselves unable to compete. Exports were increasingly an important part of the market, but only firms that employed more highly skilled workers or upgraded their equipment to produce the higher-quality products could compete. For many villages and townships that had engaged in rural industry, the collapse of these collectively owned firms resulted in collective local debt, which continued to hang over villages and townships for years.[39] To make matters worse, rural industry also left a legacy of polluted farmland and water supplies. In some places, rural industry has spoiled rivers to the point where water is no longer potable or even suitable for irrigation.[40]

Migration Without Integration

Migration to the cities is the most common route taken by rural residents in search of higher incomes. In developing countries, millions of the poor leave their villages to end up in shanty towns of Latin America or the streets of cities like Calcutta. This is also the case in China, where the same dreams have taken hold of the young, both male and female, who often live in suboptimal conditions. Despite hardships, the number of migrants grew dramatically since the reforms began in the late 1970s and continued unabated until the mid-2010s,[41] when China's cheap source of labor from the countryside started to slow.[42] Even early in the reforms, the building boom served as a source of higher wages for peasants who worked in collectively organized construction teams. While China mirrors other developing countries in its flow of workers from rural to urban areas, the pattern of the flow was politically fashioned and remains politically determined.

As in other countries, peasants have sought industrial jobs, often far from their villages, in different parts of the country. We know that peasants in other developing countries rely on networks to find jobs in cities. However, organization is taken to another level in China. In this instance, political authorities have helped peasants with migration, with local officials often acting as labor brokers. Entrepreneurial officials seek out factories, work out contract terms with the firms, sign a contract for a set number of workers, set out the wages and benefits, and so on, and then recruit local peasants for these jobs. When a large number go to one factory or locality, buses are sent to bring peasants home for the holidays. For example, officials in a relatively poor county in Henan found jobs for locals in much more developed provinces like Guangdong. When local officials act as agents, peasants are assured of a job before they leave their home villages. This may explain the relatively low number of homeless and jobless migrants in the cities.

Hukou

While China has its share of migrants, including beggars, the *hukou* system allowed China to avoid many of the problems seen in India and Latin American countries. The *hukou* system controlled the influx of rural migrants in search of jobs. During the Mao period, the rationing of basic necessities—most important, grain—combined with the household registration system (*hukou*) effectively kept those without urban household registration in the countryside.

The *hukou* system was devised during the 1950s, when China was beginning its central planning, at a time when China was primarily an agrarian economy. The *hukou* system divides the populations into those who have the legal right to live as urban residents and enjoy all the privileges and services associated with urban household registration, and those who have rural household registration and only have the legal right to live in the countryside. Those with rural household registration have no right to be in the urban areas or enjoy services there. Those with rural household registration have citizenship rights, but they are available only in their home villages, where they are legally registered.

The case of the *hukou* system is an example of how an institution created during the previous Mao period of central planning has been retained, even though the context of China has changed greatly. The consequences have been mixed, facilitating but then hindering later reforms. We should also note that the effectiveness of the *hukou* system to control migration changed with reform. Once the complementary institutions that made it effective during the pre-reform period were dismantled, the effectiveness of the *hukou* in controlling population movement eroded. The *hukou* system and migration control were undermined as free markets opened and peasants had a way to secure food and housing. More and more peasants found it possible to venture into the cities even though they did not have the necessary urban household registration.[43] This migration served as a cheap source of labor that has fueled China's growth, allowing the economy to take advantage of the demographic dividend for most of the first forty years of reform.

Unsurprisingly, maintaining the *hukou* system in a completely different economic context from when it was created, where such large numbers of those with rural household registration no longer actually live in the countryside, has created a host of problems that China continues to grapple with to this day. The continued existence of this institution meant that authorities in the cities to where the migrants moved had the right to engage in discriminatory practices, such as denying migrants the right to public goods, and instituting periodic sweeps to clear out the makeshift communities in cities like Beijing.[44]

Maintaining the *hukou* distinction has led to negative externalities by providing an excuse to discriminate against those with rural household registration, denying them citizenship rights when they work and live in the cities, yet at the same time exploiting them as a cheap source of labor. Those from the countryside have endured such discrimination and found ways to survive in the last number of decades, as more and more leave the countryside for the cities. As the reforms have evolved and the state has decided to pursue rapid urbanization, the *hukou* system has turned into an obstacle hindering that process.

Institutional Obstacles to Urbanization

The system of *hukou* has thus created a context that determines who has legal rights of citizenship that, in turn, affects the calculus of urban authorities in their treatment of migrants. While migrant workers are welcomed as a source of cheap labor, local governments did not have a responsibility to provide them their public goods and services. Over time, however, even when local authorities want to provide for its migrant population, they face a dilemma in terms of funding to pay for the public goods and services. Budget allocations from the upper levels to provide basic public goods are based on the number of residents who have legal urban household registrations in a city, rather than the total population a city has to serve. Thus, the continued operation of the *hukou* system creates disincentives for receiving and integrating migrants in the urban areas, even when these cities benefit from a cheap source of labor. The allocation of budgets and who pays for local government expenditures helps explain why the receiving cities are not welcoming to migrants even as they rely on them to keep their economy growing.

Perverting the New Socialist Countryside Policy

Not only has *hukou* created justification for the lack of rights for rural migrants when they get to the urban areas, there are also problems for those who migrate within the rural areas and frustrated government efforts to solve these problems.[45] *Hukou* has become embroiled in the politics of what to do with graying villages that have lost the majority of their population to migration, which have left only the elderly and the very young in the countryside. The quandary is what is a cost-effective way of delivering public goods to these rural residents, whose rights are delimited by where they have their *hukou*. The *nongcun shequ* (rural communities) policy is an effort to rethink the organization of the countryside to recreate communities that circumvent *hukou*, merging sparsely populated villages where all residents will be equally treated as if they all have the same *hukou*. The necessity of such reorganization and reconceptualization becomes critical in determining the rights of migrants within the countryside, when they move from the village where their *hukou* is registered to a village where they work land rented from peasants who have migrated from the village to the city. This type of inter-rural migration has been essential to ensure that land left by those who have gone to the cities is farmed. However, this same migration has created problems of how these in-migrants should be treated when they move into the almost empty villages to work the land, becoming long-term residents with their families. Should they be allowed citizenship rights, including the right to vote in village elections? Relatedly, as migration continues and urbanization grows, should the land rights continue to be tied to rural household registration? Should land finally be privatized? Can halfway measures such as titling but keeping property rights collective be effective in the end? These are the difficult issues that remain to be resolved and continue to cause tensions in both the rural and urban areas.

Migrants within the countryside, like those in cities, suffer discrimination and can't exercise their citizenship right because the *hukou* system dictates that rights are tied to their home area, where they are registered. Not only do migrants have no rights to public goods, they have no right to vote in village elections. When the center tried to address this problem by revising the Organic Law to state that migrants can be given the right to vote if the village assembly approves the application, few villages approved such applications. This is not surprising, given that allowing migrants to vote might eventually change the rules of who is eligible for what rights.

Driven in part by this shift in population and the need to find more efficient ways to provide public goods, since the mid-2000s the state embarked on the ambitious plan to reorganize the countryside—part of the "new socialist countryside" policy—to create the new "rural communities" (*nongcun shequ*).[46] While the implementation of this policy remains limited and uneven across the country, some villages have been merged to create these new rural communities.[47] As a result, in some areas, peasants are being resettled from sparsely populated villages into new rural communities. Even in those villages where there are no mergers with other villages or boundary changes, villagers are convinced to leave their traditional courtyard homes to relocate to new residential areas, often to apartment buildings.

But in many cases, local authorities have frustrated and perverted the reform policies that have tried to provide those in the rural areas with better conditions, including the more effective provision of public goods. While localities often appeared to be eager to implement the policy of creating new rural communities, the inducement for local authorities from the village to the county was that it provided a lucrative means of raising money. It allowed localities an excuse to take land from the peasants, which is the basis for land financing, which has been at the core of local government debt.[48]

Again, the root of such problems can be traced back to decollectivization and the HRS, where control over land was left collectively owned. As indicated above, land became one of the few resources that cadres still controlled. As development proceeded, especially as urbanization spread, land has become like "gold." The value of land has increased so much that some with rural household registration no longer want an urban household registration because it would mean having to give up their rights to land. Yet, the lack of ownership rights means that peasants have been prevented from using land as collateral. Overall, the bigger problem is that of collective ownership and the clarification of the rights of peasant households over the land they have been allocated when the state began to reconfigure the countryside in the wake of the huge waves of migration in the 1990s and 2000s.

Within the villages, when the state has been trying to create new rural communities, most peasants have had to give up their courtyard homes and the associated land to move into the new apartments or houses. The land on which their courtyard homes were located, the residential land (*zhaijidi*), is then used for development. These land reserves would then be either sold to earn revenue or used as collateral by the local government financing vehicles (LGFV) (*rongzi pingtai*). Peasants are supposed to be compensated for that land along with the costs of the demolished courtyard homes, but often the compensation is insufficient, or even when it is fair, that amount pales in comparison to what the local government will get for that land when it flips it for commercial use.

The process of creating these new rural communities has been accompanied by significant rural discontent—further frustrating central state efforts to serve those left in the countryside. While peasants may get new and better housing, there are issues of whether such moves are voluntary, especially for the old, who do not want to leave the family's ancestral home. Contentious disputes have arisen when the authorities have had to compensate the peasants for the houses and the land that they lost in the process. Land conflicts have turned into the most common source of discontent in China.[49] But the state also would have difficulty prohibiting such deals, as it would adversely affect the fiscal viability of localities that have no other sources of revenue.

The state recently decided to try to institute clearer property rights for the peasants over their allocated land. Yet, it faces a new dilemma. Recent research has shown that the decision to implement a national titling system designed to issue formal land certificates to peasants is not being universally welcomed. As surprising as it might seem, this policy has been resisted, sometimes vehemently, even though it "standardizes" and makes "legible" the "rural landscape in which land-use rights can be protected and readily transferred to outside investors to scale up agricultural production."[50]

Need for Fiscal Reform

Is there a way out of the conundrum of rural reforms? While the three reforms described above are distinct, there is a link that binds them: the need for revenues. The efforts adopted to remedy or alleviate the many problems of the first phase of development were complicated, especially in the rural areas, by the 1994 fiscal reform. At approximately the same time that the localities were hit by the collapse of the TVEs, the central state decided to take back the category of extra-budgetary revenues it had given to the localities under the 1980 fiscal reform. One can appreciate why the central authorities took this step when by the end of the 1980s, in some localities, extra-budgetary revenues started to overtake within-budget revenues. From the perspective of the center, the fruits of development were being kept disproportionately at the local levels. The center was getting less than a quarter of total revenues.

The central state undertook the 1994 fiscal reforms to regain control over total revenues. Commonly known as the system of tax-assignment reform (*fenshuzhi*), the 1994 fiscal reforms eliminated the category of extra-budgetary funds and recategorized all local revenues into taxes that (1) belong exclusively to the central authorities; (2) belong exclusively to the localities; or (3) taxes that would be shared between the central government and the localities. Through these changes the 1994 reforms succeeded in shrinking local revenues significantly by eliminating the extra-budgetary revenues that were earlier allotted exclusively to local governments. These 1994 reforms are perhaps one of the most consequential institutional changes during the reform period. Some would argue that it is at the root of local government debt.

While localities had suffered debt before the 1994 reforms, the 1994 reforms created a new set of institutional problems that have resulted in much more widespread debt in almost all localities in China. For many localities, this meant insufficient revenues to carry out even routine administration. The more entrepreneurial localities were able to generate new sources of revenues and to keep those revenues, but even those fell into debt because localities were assigned unfunded mandates by the upper levels.

The state's generosity toward peasants in the 2000s, first abolishing the fees and then the agricultural tax, only further reduced revenues for localities, especially the poorer ones, after the 1994 fiscal reforms had already created fiscal challenges. After the tax-for-fee reforms and the elimination of the agricultural tax, the center decided to provide local governments with funds to make up for lost revenues through fiscal transfers. There were both the general fiscal transfers based on earlier taxes lost through the reforms and earmarked fiscal transfers (*zhuanxiang zhuanyi zhifu*), which were meant to provide additional fiscal support for development projects.[51]

The central state created fiscal transfers to provide a revenue fiscal safety net to stem political opposition from the localities. These fiscal transfers are intended to compensate the localities for the revenue shortfalls and allow localities to meet basic expenditures. The center allocates funds to provinces that then disburse them to counties and eventually to townships, which will then use the money to help their villages and to supplement their own revenues. But the problem with fiscal transfers is at least twofold.

First, the general fiscal transfers may be insufficient to make up for the lost revenues taken by the upper levels with the tax changes. Interviews in selected counties suggest that the localities are still very short of past revenues generated—in part, no doubt, because the transfers are only based on the legal amount of fees that localities were able to collect.

At the same time, while there may still be shortfalls, it must also be acknowledged that, since the policy change, the upper levels now fund more local infrastructural development. However, some research suggests that the disbursement of these funds is not uniform.[52] Moreover, while considerable money is flowing into poor areas to provide public goods, there is also evidence that grants are not always used in the most efficient manner.

There is also the long-term question of whether this system of fiscal transfers is sustainable. Beijing is currently flush with revenues, but what will happen if there is a downturn in central-level coffers? How does this affect the incentives of local officials? Some local officials complain that the cuts in fiscal and political resources have "hollowed out" township administration, leaving it as nothing more than "fake government." The various policies implemented by the central state to reduce peasant burdens and improve peasant-state relations have left many townships in a very precarious position.

Second, the special category of earmarked fiscal transfers has become a source of local government debt. A little-known requirement is that localities needed to provide matching funds to receive such transfers. The 2008 stimulus package is often blamed for causing local government debt to balloon, but one reason is that localities had to take out loans in order to get the stimulus money.

Thus, the size and amount of the needed matching funds associated with the stimulus package only aggravated the fiscal shortfall problems that began with the 1994 reforms. The aftermath of the stimulus package unmasked the dangers of how localities obtained funding for needed investments to grow their economies. This was especially true with infrastructural development, which was needed for the provision of public goods and further economic development. If the localities didn't have enough money, they could borrow, which obviously would lead to debt. Localities also could get help from the upper levels. The center provided earmarked fiscal transfers to aid localities in their infrastructural development. While not obvious, this second method of "aid" from the upper levels also ended in more debt for the localities. The problem is that these fiscal transfers often created a catch-22 situation: localities had to have money in order to get the transfers.[53] The result in more than a few areas is the turn to land-finance, where localities are selling land to obtain needed revenues, and the concurrent rise of local government debt. To underscore the point made earlier, again, this short-term solution, which has led to the increasing debt problem, is the direct consequence of the decision to leave the land ownership in the hands of the collective.

After forty years of reform, China faces a number of obstacles that are frustrating and/or perverting its policies intended to address the problems that emerged from the earlier reform process. Many problems lead back to the institutional problems embedded in a flawed fiscal system.[54] The central authorities have explicitly identified the need to reform the fiscal system. Documents from the Eighteenth Party Congress called for fiscal reform, specifically calling out the need to "progressively abolish *earmarks* for competitive areas and *local funding supplements* . . . [emphasis mine]."[55] Moreover, the 2016 State Council Doc. 49 explicitly and directly warns against unfunded mandates and the need for matching funds. While never mentioning local government debt, it states that "For central projects, the center will spend; central departments must NOT ask for local matching funds."[56] The practice of pushing costs down the administrative hierarchy, *shiquan*, is to stop. The question is how far these reforms will go and how effective they will be.[57]

The Advantages and Pitfalls of Partial Reform

In spite of the incompleteness and problems of China's reforms, the transformation of the economy in the last decades of the twentieth century will no doubt serve as an attractive model for poor countries to try to replicate. Dramatic increases in agricultural output were achieved without dramatic investments of resources other than procurement price increases. Rural industrialization occurred with limited resources and technical know-how, and with limited investment by the central state. The early stage of China's reforms was the ultimate low-cost development model, requiring little from central coffers. China's development experience suggests that countries, even those with limited resources, have the potential to increase enthusiasm for production and output by providing sufficient incentives for producers and for those in charge of overseeing development.

This chapter not only has explained why and how China's politically expedient reforms spurred growth and allowed the regime to push ahead, but also has tried to underscore that the successes that were achieved early in the reforms led to unintended problems. Many of these problems were made worse by institutional flaws and aspects of the planned economy that were never changed. The findings of this chapter raise the larger question of when will China finally embark on the difficult task of tackling head-on many of the issues that it has been able to let linger, instead of allowing the systems to somewhat effectively function without full institutional reforms. Most important, when will China change its fiscal system to provide sufficient and regular revenues to fund local administration?

The Nineteenth Party Congress documents clearly reflect the CCP's new confidence and talk of a "China model." But it is questionable whether there is a Chinese model and whether it can be exported. A key part of the success of China's reforms, especially its rural industrialization, is the institutional support that was embedded in a strong Maoist state from which the reforms emerged. Local state corporatism with its institutions of support for credit, technology, and technical know-how are key in understanding how a backward economy could quickly mobilize so many resources to develop industry in previously unindustrialized areas. The existence of a unified and effective state that runs from the center to the localities is thus the key element of the Chinese experience.

However, caution and caveats are needed, because the model on which the early-reform successes were built has led to significant problems. The increases in grain production were relatively short-lived and very much tied to prices. Local-led rural industrialization allowed for a rapid rise of firms, but had very negative consequences for the many villages that ultimately saw the demise of these firms. China's specific political economy of reform dictated a particular path of change and development. Because of politics, the model was not one that could stress economic efficiency. The decision to promote collectively owned enterprises was the only option that was both economically and politically feasible. Ignoring the political constraints would have been disastrous. It was understandable why private firms were promoted only as the political and economic contexts changed.

There is much to be said for China's more gradual route to development, but the question remains whether "growing out of the plan" or "groping for stones to cross the river" only prolongs well-known problems of the old regime. While it may have been the only feasible and thus successful strategy early in the reform process, the question now is: What is China to do forty years on? Which direction is China now going to go with Xi Jinping at the helm? There are signs that Xi intends to keep tweaking the old institutions to see if the road of reform can be further traveled with old and outdated vehicles such as the *hukou* and collective ownership of land.

But research shows that even giving clearer property rights to peasants over their land through the titling process may not be as easy a fix as some have thought. Again, while there remain pros and cons of privatization, one can understand why the regime would prefer to kick the can down the road rather than privatize land outright. But the titling system, which is still only a halfway measure, would permanently fix who will have land rights, cutting out future generations of those with rural household registration.[58] Those in the countryside are now realizing the value of what they once saw as discrimination (that is, rural household registration), and now they don't want to give up that benefit, because of the increasing value of land. What does this mean, then, for China's goals of rapid urbanization? Will China come up with a way to compensate those who have been discriminated against all these years and only now are realizing the benefits? It seems that some have grown accustomed to and would prefer to keep the status quo, but now the state sees the benefits of trying to go further with reform of land rights. Will politics and the fear of instability cause China to take the safer route and once again put off the most difficult challenge of reform?

As resistance to the land titling reforms raises the possibility that China will become increasingly stuck between the early reform solutions it used to make rapid headway and those solutions needed to move forward, it seems unlikely that growth and economic activity will continue at their previous pace.

If the analysis in this chapter is correct, the solution to land takings and the other problems highlighted in this study is to reform the entire fiscal system, including how urban areas are allocated budgets from the center. The key is to provide stable and reliable sources of revenue to cover administrative expenditures. If urban areas were supplied with sufficient budget allocations to provide public goods and services to all urban residents, not just those with urban *hukou*, migrants would be able to send their children to better schools and integrate into the cities to which they have moved. This would not solve all problems, as many other institutions still need to be reformed. Urban residents would likely still be resentful of being edged out by migrants and fearful of greater competition for their children's schools, but it would be a meaningful step to alleviate some of the problems in China's complex reform process. Finally, there are the daunting challenges that face China when it loses its advantage of cheap and abundant labor from the countryside as its demographic dividend ends.

Notes

1. Jean C. Oi, "Bending Without Breaking, the Adaptability of Chinese Political Institutions," in Nicholas Hope, ed., *How Far Across the River? Chinese Policy Reform at the Millennium* (Stanford, California: Stanford University Press, 2003), 450–468.

2. Barry Naughton, *Growing Out of the Plan: Chinese Economic Reform, 1978–1993* (Cambridge, United Kingdom; New York, New York: Cambridge University Press, 1995).

3. See, for example, the classic work by Kornai, which argues that Leninist

officials would obstruct reform if reforms threatened the planned economy. János Kornai, *The Socialist System: The Political Economy of Communism* (Princeton, New Jersey: Princeton University Press, 1992).

4. Jean C. Oi, "Fiscal Reform and the Economic Foundations of Local State Corporatism in China," *World Politics*, vol. 45, no. 1 (1992), 99–126.

5. Andrew G. Walder, "Bending the Arc of Chinese History: The Cultural Revolution's Paradoxical Legacy," *China Quarterly*, vol. 227 (2016), 613–631; Martin K. Dimitrov, "Understanding Communist Collapse and Resilience," in Martin K. Dimitrov, ed., *Why Communism Did Not Collapse* (New York, New York: Cambridge University Press, 2013), 3–39; Thomas P. Bernstein, "Resilience and Collapse in China and the Soviet Union," in Dimitrov, ed., *Why Communism Did Not Collapse*, 40–66.

6. Jean C. Oi, "Peasant Grain Marketing and State Procurement: China's Grain Contracting System," *China Quarterly*, no. 106 (1986), 272–290.

7. Harold Demsetz, "The Structure of Ownership and the Theory of the Firm," *Journal of Law & Economics*, vol. 26, no. 2 (1983), 375–390.

8. Jean C. Oi, *State and Peasant in Contemporary China: The Political Economy of Village Government* (Berkeley, California: University of California Press, 1989).

9. Louis Putterman, "Group Farming and Work Incentives in Collective-Era China," *Modern China*, vol. 14, no. 4 (1988), 419–450; John McMillan, John Whalley, and Lijing Zhu, "The Impact of China's Economic Reforms on Agricultural Productivity Growth," *Journal of Political Economy*, vol. 97, no. 4 (1989), 781–807; Oi, *State and Peasant in Contemporary China*.

10. Qian Forrest Zhang and John A. Donaldson, "The Rise of Agrarian Capitalism with Chinese Characteristics: Agricultural Modernization, Agribusiness and Collective Land Rights," *China Journal*, no. 60 (2008), 25–47; Weigang Gong and Qian Forrest Zhang, "Betting on the Big: State-Brokered Land Transfers, Large-Scale Agricultural Producers, and Rural Policy Implementation," *China Journal*, vol. 77 (2017), 1–26.

11. Jonathan Unger, "The Decollectivization of the Chinese Countryside: A Survey of Twenty-Eight Villages," *Pacific Affairs*, vol. 58, no. 4 (1985), 585–606.

12. Oi, *State and Peasant in Contemporary China*.

13. Zhang and Donaldson, "The Rise of Agrarian Capitalism with Chinese Characteristics"; Jin Zeng (2018), "We Don't Want Land Certificates!—The Politics of Land Titling in China," unpublished paper presented at the AAS 2018, Washington, DC.

14. Oi, *State and Peasant in Contemporary China*.

15. Thomas P. Bernstein and Xiaobo Lü, *Taxation Without Representation in Contemporary Rural China*, Cambridge Modern China Series (Cambridge, United Kingdom, and New York, New York: Cambridge University Press, 2003); Kevin J. O'Brien, "Rightful Resistance," *World Politics*, vol. 49, no. 1 (1996), 31–55; Lianjiang Li and Kevin J. O'Brien, "Villagers and Popular Resistance in Contemporary China," *Modern China*, vol. 22, no. 1 (1996), 28–61; Kevin J. O'Brien and Lianjiang Li, "Suing the Local State: Administrative Litigation in Rural China,"

China Journal, no. 51 (2004), 75–96; Kevin J. O'Brien and Lianjiang Li, *Rightful Resistance in Rural China,* Cambridge Studies in Contentious Politics (New York, New York: Cambridge University Press, 2006).

16. O'Brien, Li, "Rightful Resistance"; Li and O'Brien, "Villagers and Popular Resistance"; Lianjiang Li and Kevin J. O'Brien, "Protest Leadership in Rural China," *China Quarterly,* no. 193 (2008), 1–23; Cai Yongshun, "Local Governments and the Suppression of Popular Resistance in China," *China Quarterly,* no. 193 (2008), 24–42; Bernstein and Lü, *Taxation Without Representation;* O'Brien and Li, "Suing the Local State"; O'Brien and Li, *Rightful Resistance.*

17. See recent work on the problems in countryside, such as Juan Wang, *The Sinews of State Power: The Rise and Demise of the Cohesive Local State in Rural China* (Oxford, United Kingdom: Oxford University Press, 2017).

18. Jean Oi, "Old Problems for New Leaders: Institutional Disjunctions in Rural China," in Y. Zhu, Z. Luo, and R. H. Myers, eds., *The New Chinese Leadership: Challenges and Opportunities After the 16th Party Congress* (Cambridge, United Kingdom, and New York, New York: Cambridge University Press, 2004), 141–155.

19. Bernstein and Lü, *Taxation Without Representation;* Oi, "Old Problems for New Leaders"; Jean Oi and K. Shimizu, "Uncertain Outcomes of Rural Industrialization: A Reassessment," in T.-K. Leng and Y. Zhu, eds., *Dynamics of Local Governance in China During the Reform Era—Challenges Facing Chinese Political Development* (Lanham, Maryland: Lexington Books, 11–32).

20. Jean C. Oi, Kim Singer Babiarz, Linxiu Zhang, Renfu Luo, and Scott Rozelle, "Shifting Fiscal Control to Limit Cadre Power in China's Townships and Villages," *China Quarterly,* no. 211 (2012), 649–675.

21. Jean C. Oi and Zhao Shukai, "Fiscal Crisis in China's Townships: Causes and Consequences," in E. J. Perry and M. Goldman, eds., *Harvard Contemporary China Series 14* (Cambridge, Massachusetts: Harvard University Press, 2007), 75–96.

22. See, for example, John James Kennedy, "From the Tax-for-Fee Reform to the Abolition of Agricultural Taxes: The Impact on Township Governments in North-West China," *China Quarterly,* no. 189 (2007), 43–59; and Linda Chelan Li, "Working for the Peasants? Strategic Interactions and Unintended Consequences in the Chinese Rural Tax Reform," *China Journal,* no. 57 (2007), 89–106.

23. Yia-Ling Liu, "From Predator to Debtor: The Soft Budget Constraint and Semi-Planned Administration in Rural China," *Modern China,* vol. 38, no. 3 (2012), 308–345; Lynette H. Ong, *Prosper or Perish: Credit and Fiscal Systems in Rural China* (Ithaca, New York: Cornell University Press, 2012); Kennedy, "From the Tax-for-Fee Reform to the Abolition of Agricultural Taxes"; Li, "Working for the Peasants?"

24. Yasheng Huang has argued that this point has not been sufficiently appreciated (Huang, Y., "China Boom: Rural China in the 1980s," 2010). However, scholars such as Oi noted that while they were the largest in number, their overall scope, employment, and output were surpassed by the collectively owned firms. Jean C. Oi, *Rural China Takes Off.*

25. Christine P. W. Wong, "Interpreting Rural Industrial Growth in the Post-Mao Period," *Modern China*, vol. 14, no. 1 (January 1988), 3–30.

26. Scott Rozelle and R. N. Boisvert, "Quantifying Chinese Village Leaders' Multiple Objectives," *Journal of Comparative Economics*, vol. 18, no. 1 (1994), 25–45; Barry Naughton, *The Chinese Economy: Transitions and Growth* (Cambridge, Massachusetts: MIT Press, 2007).

27. Yasheng Huang and John Lammey Stewart Memorial Library Fund, *Capitalism with Chinese Characteristics: Entrepreneurship and the State* (Cambridge; New York: Cambridge University Press, 2008); Huang, "China Boom: Rural China in the 1980s."

28. Oi, *Rural China Takes Off*; Jean C. Oi and Andrew G. Walder, eds., *Property Rights and Economic Reform in China* (Stanford, California: Stanford University Press, 1999).

29. Huang, "China Boom: Rural China in the 1980s."

30. See Oi, *Rural China Takes Off*; Oi and Walder, eds., *Property Rights and Economic Reform in China*, especially the chapter by Chen (49–70). Huang argues the opposite, saying that the 1990s saw the decline of the private rural enterprise. The problem may in part be one of definition ("China Boom: Rural China in the 1980s"). Without question, the privatization of previously collectively owned enterprises took place in the 1990s. The fact that rural enterprises as a whole declined during that period is a separate issue.

31. Oi, *Rural China Takes Off*.

32. Oi, *Rural China Takes Off*.

33. James Kai-Sing Kung, "The Evolution of Property Rights in Village Enterprises: The Case of Wuxi County," in Oi and Walder, eds., *Property Rights and Economic Reform in China*, xiv.

34. There are early signs of this in studies such as Sally Sargeson and Jian Zhang, "Reassessing the Role of the Local State: A Case Study of Local Government Interventions in Property Rights Reform in a Hangzhou District," *China Journal*, no. 42 (1999), 77–99. Also see Oi, *Rural China Takes Off*.

35. Lynette Ong, "The Political Economy of Township Government Debt, Township Enterprises and Rural Financial Institutions in China"; Oi and Zhao, "Fiscal Crisis in China's Townships: Causes and Consequences."

36. Author survey. Also see Oi and Shimizu, "Uncertain Outcomes of Rural Industrialization."

37. The negative experience of some villages with rural industrialization brings attention to an interesting possibility. Some villages that never attempted to industrialize actually found themselves in a better economic condition than the ones that attempted to industrialize but failed, accruing heavy debt in the process. Contrary to common assumptions, survey evidence reveals that the financially troubled villages in the 1990s include those that never attempted to industrialize and those that attempted to industrialize but failed (author survey; also see Oi and Shimizu, "Uncertain Outcomes of Rural Industrialization"). Moreover, privatization of these firms does not necessarily improve performance. H. B. Li

and Scott Rozelle, "Privatizing Rural China: Insider Privatization, Innovative Contracts and the Performance of Township Enterprises," *China Quarterly*, 176 (2003), 981–1005.

38. For a description of the actual change in the composition of industry in a county, see Jean C. Oi and Steven M. Goldstein, *Zouping Revisited: Adaptive Governance in a Chinese County*, Studies of the Walter H. Shorenstein Asia-Pacific Research Center (Stanford, California: Stanford University Press, 2018).

39. Oi and Zhao, "Fiscal Crisis in China's Townships: Causes and Consequences."

40. For pollution problems from TVEs, see Mara Warwick, "Environmental Information Collection and Enforcement at Small-scale Enterprises in Shanghai: The Role of the Bureaucracy, Legislatures and Citizens," PhD dissertation, Stanford University, California, 2003; Elizabeth Economy, *The River Runs Black: The Environmental Challenge to China's Future* (Ithaca, New York: Cornell University Press, 2004).

41. On the earlier migration see, for example, Scott Rozelle, Li Guo, Minggao Shen, Amelia Hughart, and John Giles, "Leaving China's Farms: Survey Results of New Paths and Remaining Hurdles to Rural Migration," *China Quarterly*, no. 158 (1999), 367–393, and Scott Rozelle, Jikun Huang, and Linxiu Zhang, "Emerging Markets, Evolving Institutions, and the New Opportunities for Growth in China's Rural Economy," *China Economic Review*, vol. 13, no. 4 (December 2002), 345–353. Also, Yuen-Fong Woon, "Labor Migration in the 1990s: Homeward Orientation of Migrants in the Pearl River Delta Region and Its Implications for Interior China," *Modern China*, vol. 25, no. 4 (1999), 475–512.

42. Gabriel Wildau, "China's 'migrant miracle' nears an end as cheap labour dwindles," *Financial Times*, May 4, 2015, and Gabriel Wildau, "China migration: At the turning point," *Financial Times*, May 4, 2015.

43. Dorothy J. Solinger, *Contesting Citizenship in Urban China: Peasant Migrants, the State, and the Logic of the Market*, Studies of the East Asian Institute, Columbia University (Berkeley, California: University of California Press, 1999).

44. This has been best documented for Zhejiang village in Beijing. See Li Zhang, *Strangers in the City: Reconfigurations of Space, Power, and Social Networks within China's Floating Population* (Stanford, California: Stanford University Press, 2001).

45. Solinger, *Contesting Citizenship in Urban China*.

46. Kristen Looney, "China's Campaign to Build a New Socialist Countryside—Village Modernization, Peasant Councils, and the Ganzhou Model of Rural Development," *China Quarterly*, no. 224 (2015), 909–932.

47. Division of villages is also possible and has occurred in some localities.

48. Liu Lifeng, "Land Financing and Its Sustainability in the Context of Urbanization," in Jean Oi, Karen Eggleston, and Wang Yiming, eds., *Challenges in the Process of China's Urbanization* (Brookings Institution, Walter H. Shorenstein Asia-Pacific Research Center), 49–74; Yia-Ling Liu, "From Predator to Debtor: The Soft Budget Constraint and Semi-Planned Administration in Rural China,"

Modern China, vol. 38, no. 3 (2012), 308–345; Yinqiu Lu and Tao Sun, "Local Government Financing Platforms in China: A Fortune or Misfortune?" *IMF Working Paper* QP/13/243, December 16, 2013.

49. See for example, Sargeson (2013) and Whiting (2011). Xin Sun, "Selective Enforcement of Land Regulations: Why Large-Scale Violators Succeed," *China Journal*, no. 74 (2015), 66–90; Meg Rithmire, "Land Politics and Local State Capacities—The Political Economy of Urban Change in China," *China Quarterly*, no. 216 (December 2013), 872–895; Siu Wai Wong, "Land Requisitions and State-Village Power Restructuring in Southern China," *China Quarterly*, no. 224 (December 2015), 888–908; Daniel C. Mattingly, "Elite Capture: How Decentralization and Informal Institutions Weaken Property Rights in Rural China," *World Politics*, vol. 68, no. 3 (2016), 383–412; Loren Brandt, Susan H. Whiting, Linxiu Zhang, and Tonglong Zhang, "Changing Property-Rights Regimes: A Study of Rural Land Tenure in China," *China Quarterly*, vol. 232 (2017), 1026–1049; Sally Sargeson, "Violence as Development: Land Expropriation and China's Urbanization," *Journal of Peasant Studies*, vol. 40, no. 6 (2013), 1063–1085.

50. Zeng, "We Don't Want Land Certificates!"

51. On problems of fiscal transfers, see Mingxing Liu, Juan Wang, Ran Tao, and Rachel Murphy, "The Political Economy of Earmarked Transfers in a State-Designated Poor County in Western China: Central Policies and Local Responses," *China Quarterly*, no. 200 (2009), 973–994.

52. CCAP/UC Davis/University of Toronto Research Team (2007), "Tax-for-Fee Reform, Village Operating Budgets and Public Goods Investment: Report for the World Bank, Beijing Office," and Jean C. Oi, Kim Singer Babiarz, Linxiu Zhang, Renfu Luo, and Scott Rozelle, "Shifting Fiscal Control to Limit Cadre Power in China's Townships and Villages," *China Quarterly*, no. 211 (2012), 649–675.

53. For details of this, see Jean Oi, Adam Liu, and Zhang Yi, "The Dictator's Fiscal Dilemma: Decentralization or Local Debt," manuscript in progress.

54. This section draws heavily on Oi 2018 ("Local Government Debt and the Future of Central-Local Relations").

55. November 15, 2013.

56. 2016 Document 49 from the State Council (国发 [2016] 49号).

57. 2016 年国发 49 号文件. Xun Wu, "China's Growing Local Government Debt Levels," *MIT Center for Finance and Policy (2016)*, also states that the 2016 mandating the shutdown of "non-standardized financing channels, later specifically including the LGFV, but that they would be gradually shut down."

58. Zeng, "We Don't Want Land Certificates!"

THREE

Varieties of Capitalism in China

Private-Sector Development During the Xi Jinping Era

YASHENG HUANG

The year 2018 marked the fortieth anniversary of Chinese reforms. In his speech commemorating this event, Xi Jinping singled out the private sector for praise for its contributions to Chinese economic development.

But the reality on the ground belies his effusive endorsement of the private sector. Arguably, the year 2018 also marked the most difficult year for the Chinese private sector since the early 1990s, when the post-Tiananmen leadership curbed the private sector. According to the chief economist of China Merchant Bank, all eleven thousand businesses that went bankrupt between 2016 and the first half of 2018 were private. Also, the political environment for the private sector turned noticeably negative for much of 2018 (until the sharp economic deceleration seemed to have forced Xi to change his tune in late 2018). One online commentator went so far as to claim that it is time for the private sector to relinquish its historical role in the Chinese economy. That comment led to much consternation and even panic among many Chinese private entrepreneurs.[1]

How much of this is due to Xi Jinping? We know that Xi Jinping has been a transformative—used in a neutral sense—political leader. He has mounted a large-scale anti-corruption campaign that has brought down probably tens of thousands of officials. He has consolidated power to an unprecedented degree that China has not seen since Mao Zedong. In March 2018, he abolished the only explicit institutional constraint on his power—a constitutional provision that limits the presidency to two terms. He has also taken a more confrontational approach in foreign policy, such as building naval bases in the South China Sea and launching a massive infrastructural program known as "One Belt, One Road" that challenges the Washington Consensus either in intention or in effect. To the extent there is a consensus view among scholars, business leaders, and other watchers of China, it is that the era of Xi Jinping constitutes a clear break from the cautious, consensus-building approach of his predecessors.

The question is whether on the economic front the Xi era has also constituted as sharp a break from the economic approaches of his predecessors to a similar extent on the political front. This chapter will focus on one particular aspect of economic policies, the microeconomic program of private sector development (or lack thereof) during the Xi Jinping era. We have anecdotal and journalistic evidence that the Xi leadership seems to have imposed more controls on China's private sector, and some observers in China have argued that China's economic slowdown is, in part, attributed to this less-than-liberal policy stance toward the private sector.

While the anecdotal accounts are indicative, they do not convey a systematic picture of the private sector policies during the Xi Jinping era. It is worth noting that the private sector has not been granted full property-rights protection and political security during any period of the reform era. Policy stances toward the private sector can vary substantially among different generations of Chinese leaders and we need a more systematic way to assess and demonstrate these policy variances. We ask and attempt to answer the following question: To what extent does the Xi Jinping era represent a break in terms of private-sector development? Or does the Xi Jinping era represent more of continuation of a previously established pattern?

Getting a handle on this question requires specifying the metrics that we use to measure private-sector development. This is by no means straightforward. The United States Supreme Court Justice Potter Stewart famously described pornography in the context of what constitutes obscene speech as "I know it when I see it." Arguably, defining China's private sector is even harder. We cannot be sure if it is a private firm even if we see it. For example, one is hard pressed to come up with a definitive answer whether companies such as Huawei, HNA, and Haier are private, despite the fact that these are among the best known and largest companies in China.

The definitional complexity has always been there, but it is possible that it has risen during the Xi era. Xi has enforced more rigorously a requirement—stipulated in the party constitution, but often ignored—that a congregation of three Chinese Communist Party members mandates an establishment of a CCP branch. The CCP has enforced this requirement on privately operated enterprises (POEs, or "私营企业" in Chinese). Both from press reports and my own visits to POEs, the impression is that there has been an escalation of the newly established CCP branches. I will go into some details later, but one impact of the establishment of the CCP branches is a—further—blurring of the line between private ownership rights and private control rights of enterprises.

The other challenge of measuring private sector development has to do with the metrics we use to assess the policy and operating environment of private firms. In the academic literature, there are two principal approaches. One draws from the surveys. For example, the Chinese Academy of Social Sciences has conducted a private-sector survey every two to three years since 1993. The survey method has its own advantages and disadvantages. For the topic at hand, the disadvantage is infinite: there has not been a comprehensive private-sector survey since 2014. This seems to be deliberate. The Chinese government has curtailed or has banned altogether many of the survey efforts under way prior to the Xi era.

The other common method has been using output shares by the private sector as a measure of policy and regulatory development. This measure has the advantage of being available and systematic and it is the right measure of the size and the contributions of the private sector. As a policy measure, it is deeply problematic. The main problem is that it confounds two effects—the microeconomic efficiency performance effect and the macro policy and regulatory effect. If we see an increase of the output share by the private sector, it can be an indicator of rising efficiency of the private sector relative to the state sector or it can be an indicator of policy liberalization. Or a combination of both. We have a substantial attribution problem, using this measure.

I proposed using fixed-asset investment (FAI) data as a more reliable indicator of policy and regulatory development. In this chapter, I will present FAI data series on the Hu-Wen era (2002–2012) and on the Xi era (since 2013). The FAI data series has its own problems, including the implied sectoral biases and some of the threshold changes. However, a productive approach is to lay out these biases explicitly and interpret any findings bearing these biases in mind. With that caveat, the FAI data are still a superior indicator of policy developments compared to the alternative data series.

Based on the levels and the compositions of the FAI data between 2006 and 2017, I reached the following tentative conclusion on the private sector development under Xi Jinping: Xi has, by and large, inherited and continued a statist policy orientation of the Chinese economy established by his predecessors, but he has done so seemingly with a sharper edge and most likely with a more explicit rationale than his predecessors. That rationale can be formulated as follows: he seems to have a policy to substantially reduce the direct operating role of the state while increasing the funding, ownership, and strategic-control roles of the state. There is no evidence that Xi—or his predecessors—has intended to increase *both* ownership *and* control rights of the private sector. I said "both . . . and . . ." deliberately. There may be some permissiveness of either the ownership role or some control role of the private sector, but not both. This conclusion is sensitive to a number of assumptions that I will make plain in the course of discussion.

In the political science literature, there is a long-standing idea known as "varieties of capitalism."[2] To an extent, we can argue that China has its own version of varieties of capitalism. There is the state capitalism—defined as one in which the state and the private sector collaborate with each other and they jointly exercise ownership and control rights over economic assets. There is crony capitalism—the kind of capitalism that relies heavily on access to the power of the state to perform and expand. There is also the entrepreneurial and arm's-length capitalism, the kind of capitalism that comes closest to the capitalism in a Western market economy.

To translate the political science idea of varieties of capitalism into this economic context, we can say that these three forms of capitalism vary in the degree the control rights of firms are collaborative or noncollaborative with the state. Notice the difference with the traditional approach of studying ownership of firms in China. The conventional approach focuses on the revenue rights of firms and often assumes that we can infer meaningful information on control rights from information on revenue rights. The approach adopted in this chapter rejects this assumption. We make our best efforts to locate the residence of control rights and formulate Xi's policy in terms of this "varieties of capitalism" idea.

The evidence seems to support the following interpretation. Xi appears to have supported the expansion of state capitalism more than his predecessors, whereas he has continued with the patterns of development of crony and entrepreneurial capitalism that he inherited from the leadership of Hu Jintao and Wen Jiabao. Overall, Xi has moved China more on a state-capitalistic path. That path has two components. One is that it has a smaller role of SOEs; the other is that it has a smaller role of the most arm's-length capitalism as well. In other words, it is the middle form of capitalism—private revenue rights but coupled with increasingly stringent state control rights—that is emerging to be the dominant corporate form in the Chinese economy. Although the rhetorical critique of the private sector might have increased under Xi, there is no evidence based on FAI data that the "Xi effect" constituted a discrete, sharp break with an earlier era. He did not launch state capitalism, but he seems to have accelerated the pace of this path compared with his predecessors.

In this chapter, I first discuss definitional and measurement issues when studying the Chinese private sector. I then use FAI data to present an overall ownership landscape of China between 2006 and 2017. I discuss any potential "breaks" during the Xi era. The final section presents my conclusions.

Definitional and Measurement Issues

Measuring private sector development is fiendishly hard. One issue is definitional. The Chinese style of market reforms has spawned a variety of hybrid and highly ambiguous ownership forms. The official statistical definition often refers to the nonstate sector, and this definition is based on the registration types of firms. The nonstate entities include collective enterprises, de jure private firms, shareholding enterprises, domestic joint-ownership firms, and foreign-invested enterprises. In some studies, SOEs that have issued shares on stock exchanges are also counted as part of the nonstate sector.

I will use registration-based definition as a guide, in part because enterprise data are organized on the basis of registration types and it is the most convenient method. But it can be inaccurate. For one thing, sometimes firms may not change their registration types even after their underlying ownership has changed. One example is an SOE that has been partially or substantially privatized, but the newly privatized firm may not change its registration type. Or the statistical reporting system may not adequately capture the ownership change in its data collection. In these cases, data on the private sector may have a downward bias.

It is not inconceivable that the bias can go in the other direction. In 2018, by an account in the *Financial Times*, there were ten cases of large-scale private firms being nationalized.[3] Some of these nationalization cases may be temporary, as in the case of Anbang, but in the cases of permanent nationalization, the statistical reporting system may contain a bias in the other direction in overestimating the size of China's private sector.

A more serious threat to the fidelity of the ownership data is the likelihood of increasing separation between ownership and control. The separation does not refer to the type of separation between ownership and control in a market economy where professional managers control the operation of a firm owned by shareholders. In China, the separation occurs when the government asserts increasing controls on a full-blown privately owned firm. These controls may not amount to day-to-day controls of a firm's operation, but they may very well impinge upon, interfere with, or even completely override the strategic decision-making of the rightful owner.

There is some indication that the government's assertion of control rights over private firms has become more aggressive and explicit. A vice-minister of the Ministry of Human Resources and Social Security remarked in September 2008 that private enterprises should be "jointly" run by private entrepreneurs and workers.[4] The comment led to a degree of panic among Chinese private entrepreneurs who associated this stance of the government with Mao Zedong's justification for nationalizing China's private sector in the mid-1950s.

This development lies behind controversies surrounding firms such as Huawei. From what we can know on the basis of public information, Huawei does not have explicit government shares, but the suspicion in the international press and among foreign governments is that Huawei has an extremely close working relationship with the government. The decisions to deny Huawei the license to sell mobile phones in the United States and to restrict its businesses in Europe, Australia, and the United States are based not so much on the revenue rights of Huawei as on the residence of its control rights. The blurring of revenue and control rights has the additional impact on further blurring the border between SOEs and private firms. And in the case of China, because the control rights are often established through extralegal mechanisms (such as the requirement to establish CCP branches), we cannot infer the allocation of control rights by the allocation of ownership rights. This is fundamentally different from a market economy where the diffusion of ownership rights is *prima facie* evidence of a potential separation and concentration of control rights. We cannot make the same inferences about Chinese firms. (Later in this chapter, I will suggest one way to make an educated guess: by the size of the firm.)

It is more likely that this type of bias has increased in recent years, but other than anecdotal accounts, it is extremely difficult to systematically track this development. In the rest of this chapter, I will make an attempt to assess this development, but by its very nature this will be a difficult exercise.

The definition of private firms aside, there is a separate issue, the metrics of which are appropriate to measure the development and operating environment of the Chinese private sector. In the economics literature, the most common measure is the output share of the private sector. For example, using this measure, Nicholas Lardy tried to debunk the notion that there has been an "advance of the state and a retreat of the private sector." He shows that the private sector's output continued to climb and that there was no evidence of the "advancing of the state and the retreat of the private sector."

This output-share measure is problematic. One problem with using output shares as a measure of private sector development is that we cannot clearly distinguish between the effects of policy on the growth of this sector and a variety of other firm-level characteristics that might be also at work. Two dynamics affect the output shares of the private sector. One is the "policy effect": the increase in the private sector share that resulted from liberalization and from a stronger protection of private property rights. But this measure also incorporates what might be called the "efficiency effect." If private firms are more efficient than SOEs—and there is evidence they are—then they generate more value added per unit of input. An increase in the output share of private firms can therefore occur without any improvement in the policy environment as long as there is competition between private firms and SOEs.

Let me give a number of examples to illustrate the complexities involved in how we measure private sector development. In 1985, the ratio of the industrial output value of the private sector to that of the state sector was about 0.03; by 1997, this ratio had risen to 0.7. While the policy environment no doubt improved for the private sector during this period, it would be highly misleading, and it defies common sense, to conclude that the policy treatment of the private sector converged to 70 percent of the policy treatment of the SOEs by 1997. This was a clear overstatement of the progress of reforms between 1985 and 1997.

Another example comes from the former Soviet Union.[5] No one would accuse Leonid Brezhnev of being pro–private sector, but actually, under his leadership, private plots contributed to roughly one half of agricultural household income in the Soviet Union. This happened because private farming was so much more efficient than state farming, so its contributions to income were disproportionate to the inputs allocated to it. Private plots only accounted for 1.4 percent of cultivable land in the Soviet Union.

This example from the Soviet agriculture suggests, at least theoretically, that the ratio of the private to the state sector can rise without any improvement in the policy environment for private-sector firms and with rising inefficiencies of SOEs. Indeed, one can think of a situation in which the private output share rises *because of* policy constraints on the private sector. Credit-constrained private-sector firms have few options to grow other than to increase their efficiency. SOEs, lavished with resources, have no such incentives. Thus, the efficiency differential can be very large precisely because of the policy discrimination.

There is an easy way to expose the flaw with the output-based policy measure. Let us choose a period we know for sure to be adverse for private-sector firms. That way we cannot attribute any increase in private-sector output during that period to policy improvements. This is the 1989–1990 period, when the post-Tiananmen leadership launched a systematic crackdown on the private sector. Private-sector employment fell during this period and many private firms were closed down. Credit was tightened. Yet, despite the adversity in the policy environment, the gross output value of the industrial private sector, as a ratio to the SOEs, increased from 7.6 percent in 1988 to 8.6 percent in 1989 and to 9.9 percent in 1990.[6]

A better measure of the changes in the policy environment should be based on an input allocated to the private sector rather than its share of the output. The most appropriate input-based measure is the fixed-asset investment capital. Fixed-asset investments are equivalent to purchases of plants, property, and equipment in the Western accounting system. There are two reasons why this is a better measure of policy. One is that fixed-asset investments remain substantially controlled by the state and thus changes in the patterns of fixed-asset investments are a more accurate reflection of the policy preferences of the Chinese state. The second reason is that in a poor country, capital is scarce relative to labor. So capital allocation is more indicative than labor allocation of the fundamental orientation of the economic system.

Apart from the empirical inaccuracy of using the output of the private sector as a policy measure, there is also the issue of correctly attributing credit for the growth of the private sector. Treating output increases as a measure of policy implicitly assigns all the credit to the government, including the part of the credit due to entrepreneurial energy and efficiency improvement. If we view the output increase as an efficiency measure, credit would then go to the Chinese entrepreneurs. The fact that the private sector was still able to grow in an enormously difficult business environment is a tribute to the agility and acumen of Chinese entrepreneurs, not to the wisdom of the Chinese government and to the liberal policy climate. A straightforward takeaway from this discussion is that on the basis of output data we cannot identify any policy breaks during the forty years of economic reforms, and as a policy metric, output data are completely useless.

Compared with output data, the coverage of the private sector in the area of investment activities goes back to the earliest years of the reforms. This may be because fixed-asset investment activities went through a government scrutiny process that required a bureaucratic paper trail. The third and probably the most important reason we focus on fixed-asset investments is that they are heavily controlled by the government, as compared to other activities in the Chinese economy. Because this measure directly tracks government policy preferences and practices, it is superior to the output measure. It does not involve the kind of confounding problems of distinguishing between the effect of policy and the effect of firm-level efficiency differentials that cloud the output measures of private-sector development.

There are telling pieces of evidence that fixed-asset investments are subject to heavy government controls. Thomas Rawski,[7] for example, shows that China's seasonal investment cycles, as recently as during the 1999–2001 period, matched almost perfectly those prevailing during the centrally planned era. Since fixed-asset investment is a large component of China's GDP, fluctuations in investment levels have a substantial impact on GDP. Rawski shows that China's quarterly GDP growth patterns differed substantially from those in South Korea, Taiwan, and Hong Kong—an indication that factors such as weather or traditional Chinese holidays are not the principal determinants of the seasonal rhythm of China's GDP.

Rawski quotes a Chinese economist's overall assessment of the Chinese investment process as follows:

> Many basic components of a pure market economy are still in their incipient stage in China, although market-oriented reform started two decades ago. Government-guided investment mechanisms, a state-controlled banking system and dominant state-owned enterprises . . . still run in a framework molded primarily on the previous planned economy.

There are at least two noteworthy issues with using FAI data. One is a sectoral bias. The FAI data only cover those firms that invest in fixed assets. So, the data series may bias upward industrial firms and downward service firms. This can be a problem when measuring private-sector firms, many of which operate in the service sector. There are two counterpoints. One is that service firms also make investments in fixed assets. A shop may need to build a new storefront or to purchase computers or cash machines, all of which go into the FAI data series. Service firms are not as fixed asset–intensive as industrial firms, but our analysis here does not look at just one cross-section of FAIs by different firms, but at FAIs by different firms over time. There is some control of sector-fixed effect in this methodology. It can be a problem if, say, private-sector firms transition from industry into the service sector. Then time series comparisons become problematic.

The second issue with using FAI data is that the Chinese statistical agency has introduced changes in reporting thresholds a number of times. In 1997, the government made a change in the investment reporting/approval procedure. Beginning in 1997, the investment reporting threshold was revised from 50,000 yuan to 500,000 yuan, but this change only applied to SOEs and the urban collective firms. The effect of this change is that the published amount of fixed-asset investments in the state and the urban collective sectors is smaller than the actual amount. In 2011, there was another threshold change. The reporting threshold was raised from 500,000 yuan to 5 million yuan (except for real estate investments and rural individual investments).

The 1997 change lies outside our data range and my calculation using both reporting thresholds shows a very small impact.[8] The 2011 threshold change could be a problem for our analysis if it had a different effect on SOEs than on private-sector firms. If more of the private-sector firms invested less than 5 million yuan than SOEs, then this threshold change would introduce a downward bias. This issue needs to be explored further, but from what we can see in the data, there is no evidence that 2011 constitutes a break in the data series.

The Ownership and Control Landscape of Chinese Firms: An Analysis Based on FAI Data

In the remainder of this chapter, I will apply the aforementioned definitional and measurement approaches to assess private sector development in China between 2006 and 2017 and under Xi Jinping. The FAI data run from 2006 to 2017 and were downloaded from the National Statistical Bureau's website. (The latest available data are for 2017.)

Figure 3-1 presents percentage shares of four types of fixed-asset investment (FAI) entities from 2006 to 2017. These four are: SOEs, limited liability corporations (LLCs), privately operated enterprises (POEs), and other-ownership enterprises (OOEs). As is apparent in the graph, the top two entities are LLCs and POEs. In 2017, these two types of entities accounted for 65 percent of the FAIs. The rest was split between SOEs, at

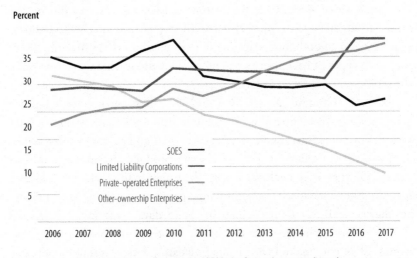

FIGURE 3-1   Four types of FAI platforms (percent shares)
(Source: National Bureau of Statistics of China, "National Data—
Fixed Assets Investment and Real Estate," 2017
(http://data.stats.gov.cn/easyquery.htm?cn=C01&zb=A0501&sj=2017)

22 percent, and OOEs, at 8.8 percent. LLCs (33 percent) and POEs (32 percent) were about comparable in size.

Figure 3-1 establishes a nice baseline of our analysis. The next step is to formulate some hypotheses or narratives about the following issues: (1) the ownership demarcations of LLCs and OOEs and (2) the operating roles of the state in LLCs and POEs. Once armed with ideas about these two issues, we can look at the trend lines of these four types of FAI entities and draw some inferences about private-sector development under Xi Jinping.

The ownership—defined as the identity of persons/entities holding revenue rights—of SOEs and POEs is straightforward. The state owns SOEs and private persons—entrepreneurs or shareholders—own POEs. The reality may be more complicated than this statement implies, but by and large it is a reasonably accurate general statement. (I will return to the issue of POEs and propose that in recent years the cleanliness of the ownership of POEs may have been compromised as well.)

The biggest complications arise vis-à-vis LLCs and OOEs. Their names by themselves are not self-explanatory, and so it is quite challenging to say anything precise about their ownership structure. But it is quite important to get their ownership structure right. As shown in the graph, in 2006, OOEs had the highest share of FAIs and then they tumbled to the lowest share after 2012. By contrast, LLCs rose sharply during the same period, and by 2017 they clinched the top position in the FAI allocation. Getting a good understanding of the dynamics that drove the flip of these two types of FAI entities can tell us a lot about what was going on in the Chinese economy during this period.

LLCs in Chinese are "有限责任公司." They encompass a heterogeneous range of companies. On the one side of the spectrum are pure investment companies, such as venture capital and private equity funds. They make investments in existing projects, products, technology, or businesses. Or they may back start-ups. They may make strategic decisions regarding key managerial appointments, product launch, or fund-raising, but they typically do not participate in day-to-day operations of their portfolio companies. On the other end of the spectrum are development companies. They may make investments in existing businesses, but they may also launch projects on their own. The chief distinction with the investment funds is the operating role of the development LLCs: development LLCs actively participate in the day-to-day operations of their invested businesses.

The next logical question is who are the main owners of these LLCs in China? To that question, the answer is simple: We do not know. We do not have comprehensive data on the ownership structure of LLCs. We can, however, make some educated generalizations. The largest VC in China—among domestic funds—is Shenzhen Capital, a subsidiary of the Shenzhen government. Among the top VC funds in China, probably two are run by the government. (At least this was true as of 2015.) The development LLCs are most likely heavily governmental. Many of them are investment platforms established by local governments, and they are involved in projects that typically have a strong governmental imprint, such as infrastructure. Investment analysts have documented the establishment of hundreds of these local investment platforms, and they were largely responsible for the massive investment boom that took place since 2008.[9] This is confirmed by the data in figure 3-1.

We do not know the composition of LLCs between investment LLCs and development LLCs. Investment LLCs are probably more private-sector driven, both because the control rights are typically delegated to entrepreneurs even in those projects funded by government VCs and because investment LLCs tend to be privately owned in the first place. The relative proportion between the two types of LLCs would be a factor in determining the overall ownership profile of the FAIs made by LLCs, but we do not have such information. One piece of data we do have is that the proportion of the sole state ownership of the LLCs' FAIs has risen over time. In 2014, the wholly state-owned LLCs accounted for 11 percent of the LLCs' FAIs; in 2017 this figure rose to 19 percent. (This rising share by the state-owned LLCs does seem to coincide with the onset of the Xi era, a point I will return to later.) This is a conservative estimate of the state ownership of the LLCs' FAIs, because it does not take into account the FAIs made by those LLCs that may exercise a majority or a sizable minority state-ownership. Based on the limited information we have, one plausible conjecture is that the LLCs represent a hybrid, statist role of the state. Statism here is defined either as a strong funding role of the state (à la Shenzhen Capital) or as a strong funding and an operating role of the state (à la Yaan Development Investment).

The POEs are nominally and operationally private in terms of their revenue rights. This should not be in doubt. However, the reason why this is even a question now is because the state has imposed increasingly onerous operating requirements on POEs. As early as 2006, and possibly even earlier than that, the CCP began to require POEs to establish CCP branches in their enterprises, and it is likely that under Xi Jinping this requirement was enforced more stringently. This question requires further research, but a description of the activities of a CCP in a POE clearly fall within what we normally think of as "managerial functions," such as training, compliance, and, in some cases, employee retentions. Enforcing the establishment of the CCP branches among POEs has probably attenuated the control rights of the private entrepreneurs. It may not have completely decimated the private control rights, but it is hard to imagine the effect to be completely neutral.

Imagine several scenarios. A CCP branch mandates allocating time to studying the documents and instructions of the CCP, and any time allocated to these study sessions is not the time allocated to product development, marketing, customer service, and managing KPIs. Even the most successful Chinese high-tech entrepreneurs are not spared. In June 2018, the Chinese internet circulated a surreal photo in which two of China's most successful high-tech entrepreneurs, Pony Ma of Tencent, and Liu Qiangdong of JD.com, were fully attired in the guerrilla uniforms from the revolutionary era and were seen touring the sacred Yanan, the revolutionary base of the Chinese Communist Party during the civil war and anti-Japanese war. Pony Ma is worth 45 billion dollars.

In another scenario, say, an enterprise is operated by the owner herself and let's suppose that she is not a party member. Establishing a CCP branch in her firm would imply a division of her control rights of the firm with people who are neither the owners of the firm nor her reporting managers. And because the members of the CCP branch report directly to the Department of the Organization of the CCP, not to her, on matters deemed relevant by the CCP, in essence the owner of this firm is forced to split her control rights with the CCP. One can go even further. Because CCP's role is so powerful and its delineation is so vague, it is probably the worst kind of dilution of control rights imaginable. The entrepreneur is unable to specify the division or dilution of control rights *ex ante*, which forces her to accept whatever are the residual control rights *ex post*. It is reasonable, although definitely debatable, to classify POEs as an increasingly statist-oriented category of businesses.

Another dynamic is political connections. Academic research shows that private firms with better political connections tend to outperform those firms without political connections. The main mechanism is their ability to access the Chinese banking system. We find out about these political connections typically when these politically connected POEs run into problems. Companies such as HNA, Fosun Group, and Wanda are all examples of POEs that have been able to expand rapidly—both through greenfield investments and acquisitions—because they could raise hundreds of billion yuan in debt. The rising FAI share of the POEs in figure 3-1 is at least in part due to the debt-fueled expansions on account of political connections. To put it differently, the rising FAI share of the POEs is a numeric expression of rising crony capitalism.

Let me examine the OOEs (other-ownership enterprises). These firms have experienced the steepest decline in terms of their FAI shares, from about 26 percent in 2006 to less than half that level in 2017, 8.8 percent. The OOEs are composed of six types of entities, and their initial share was large, in part, because there are so many types of firms under this single category. They are: (1) foreign-invested enterprises (FIEs), (2) shareholding corporations, (3) individual businesses, (4) shareholding cooperatives, (5) collective firms, and (6) domestic joint ventures. (In the FAI data, there is also another category known as FAIs by other entities. As best I can determine, these are FAIs made by government agencies. I have excluded them from the calculation.) I will single out FIEs, shareholding corporations, collective firms, and individual businesses for discussion. The others are quite small. (The exception is the category of "other entities," which are sizable and rising in their shares. This, as best as I can determine, is the FAIs made by the government agencies in their own "plants and property." This topic requires a separate treatment, which I deal with in my current book project.)

FIEs are the wholly owned or partially owned companies established by foreign firms. Foreign firms include the overseas Chinese firms in Hong Kong, Macau, and Taiwan as well as firms based in other parts of the world. Shareholding corporations are those firms listed on China's main and secondary stock markets. Individual businesses are single proprietorships in which owners both own and operate the business. They may have some employees, but as a rule of thumb, only eight or fewer. Collective firms are firms formally established by the local governments (such as townships), although usually they have some substantial but implicit private ownership rights.

Basically, the statist and the statist-oriented firms in China have grown at the expense of those firms that have clear ownership rights and titles.

The firms that have the clearest ownership titles are those perched at the opposite ends of the ownership spectrum: the SOEs and the OOEs. The fact that both the SOEs and the OOEs have lost FAI shares to LLCs and POEs implies that between 2006 and 2017, China has moved more toward the statist medium of the ownership landscape away from *both* straightforward state ownership *and* straightforward private ownership. I will set aside the welfare and performance implications of this development, but it is important to anchor any analysis on an empirically correct formulation of facts on the ground.

The SOEs have undiluted ownership and control rights. This is probably not a controversial statement. However, it is necessary to justify the proposition that OOEs have undiluted ownership and control rights as well. This statement is based on the following logic. FIEs are probably not subject to the same operating interference as compared with POEs. This is, in part, because the Chinese laws and regulations give some special recognition and leeway to FIEs (although that recognition has been attenuated). Another reason is that FIEs do have some exit options that domestic POEs do not have. Although the CCP branch requirement theoretically also covers FIEs, the exit option of the FIEs is likely to deter an excessive and aggressive enforcement of this requirement.

The listed firms have the most straightforward and clarified ownership structures among Chinese firms. The Chinese state imposes various restrictions and controls on the listed firms, but the fact that these listed firms are at least partially accountable to mostly small investors and that stock prices serve as a feedback mechanism probably go some way to attenuate the incentives to interfere with these firms. Collective firms and individual businesses are basically small and medium enterprises (SMEs). The control costs of these SMEs are probably prohibitively high and their small size probably serves as an immunization against political interference. In brief, these four major components of OOEs operate at the most private end of the ownership spectrum as compared with other firms in the universe of Chinese firms.

The "Xi Jinping Effects"

We can hypothesize two "Xi effects." One is that from 2013 to 2017, Xi led a strong anti-corruption campaign that toppled tens of thousands of corrupt officials. The other effect is a potential movement under his leadership toward a model of state capitalism to a greater (or a lesser) extent than his predecessors. These two "Xi effects" are "co-variants" and it may be hard to tell them apart. In the paragraphs that follow, I will do my best to interpret the FAI data in ways that confirm or contradict these twin effects of Xi Jinping.

The anti-corruption campaign might have slowed down the overall FAIs because real estate and infrastructural projects tend to be the prime venues of corruption. There is support for that. Before 2013, the FAIs were growing at the nominal rate of more than 20 percent a year; after 2013 the growth slowed down to below 20 percent and to a single digit in the last three years. In 2017, the growth rate slowed to a crawl, at 4.9 percent. This is probably the lowest rate since the early 1990s.

It is possible, of course, that the overcapacity also contributed to the slowdown. The rapid FAI growth characterized the entire tenure of Hu Jintao and Wen Jiabao (2002–2012). The rapid FAI growth around 2008 and 2009 was not just related to the Chinese government's response to the financial crisis. It is hard to pin down the slowdown of the overall FAI growth rate to one cause.

A more discerning metric of the Xi Jinping effect should be the composition of the FAIs, not the overall level of FAIs. Here the picture is suggestive of the following conjecture: by and large, Xi Jinping has inherited and continued with the statistization of the Chinese economy started by his predecessors, but he seemed to accelerate the speed and the trajectory of that movement.

Take the FIEs as an example. The biggest drop occurred between 2006 and 2012, when their FAI share went from 9.9 percent to 5.6 percent. The Xi era continued the slide, down to only 3.9 percent in 2017. The turning point seemed to be the Hu-Wen leadership, not the leadership of Xi. In 2000, FIEs accounted for 7.9 percent of the total FAIs, so China was trending more globalized between 2000 and 2006. The likely contributor to the de-globalization turn was the unification of corporate income tax in 2007, the indigenous policy program, and the government's stimulus program that was biased against foreign firms. Those policies were implemented long before Xi ascended to the presidency.

The evidence on a possible "Xi acceleration" is sparse, coarse, and highly imprecise, and showing that such an effect exists requires detailed microeconomic data. But the FAI data on LLCs and SOEs do exhibit a turning point. The FAIs by LLCs surged, mostly crowding out the FAIs by SOEs, but not other types of FAIs. From 2015 to 2016, there was a six-percentage point increase of the LLCs FAI share, and that increase was almost entirely offset by a four-percentage-point drop of the SOE FAI share. This is a pattern we do not see in the previous years. In the previous years, the two data series moved in opposite directions, but at a far lower magnitude. Between 2006 and 2014, a two-way correlation coefficient between FAIs by LLCs and by SOEs is −0.32, but for the period of 2006 to 2017, it is −0.68. The trade-offs between the two types of FAIs became sharper during the Xi era.

We can see this point more clearly in figure 3-2, which presents three sets of simple two-way correlation coefficients: (1) the correlation coefficient between FAI shares by LLCs and by SOEs, (2) the correlation coefficient between FAI shares by LLCs and POEs, and (3) the correlation coefficient between FAI shares by LLCs and OOEs. Since LLCs seem to be the most important FAI dynamic, these two-way correlations can tell us something about the respective effects of LLCs on SOEs, POEs, and OOEs. A negative relationship implies that LLCs are crowding out the other type of FAIs (or vice versa); a positive relationship implies that LLCs are crowding in the other type of FAIs (or vice versa). The coefficients themselves are not indicative of any causal relationships, but it is important to know the direction of the pairwise relationships between LLCs and other types of entities and to indicate the presence of any "Xi effect" if we want to know whether there is a "before" and "after" difference (that is, before and after 2013).

One pattern jumped out from figure 3-2. While the correlation coefficient between LLCs and SOEs was weakly negative, at −0.15, between 2006 and 2012, it is hugely negative between 2013 and 2017, at −0.98. What this says is that there was almost one-to-one relationship in terms of pairwise percentage change between the FAI share gains by the LLCs and the FAI share losses by the SOEs under Xi Jinping. That was not true before 2013. Before 2013, the FAI share gains by the LLCs were achieved more at the expense of OOEs than of SOEs. After 2013, LLCs still gained at the expense of OOEs but more at the expense of SOEs.

It seems highly unlikely that a switch from −0.15 to −0.97 could happen by accident. It is also paradoxical in light of the anti-corruption campaign. One would argue that the effect of the anti-corruption campaign should be strongest on the LLCs, the murky and problematic nexus between the state and the private sector, rather than on the SOEs, firms with rela-

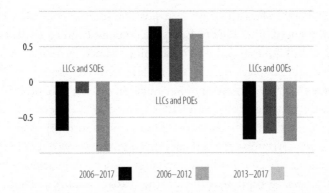

FIGURE 3-2   Two-way correlation coefficients between LLC FAI shares and FAI shares (by SOEs, POEs, and OOEs) (Source: author's calculations)

tively straightforward ownership and control rights. Also, LLCs are the principal drivers of the real estate and infrastructural projects—sectors that are particularly corruption-intensive. *Ex ante*, one would expect to see the anti-corruption campaign to hit the LLCs the hardest. (Of course, this conclusion needs to be revised if the SOEs are shown to be the more corruption-intensive targets. This is an empirical issue.)

The fact that we do not see this anti-corruption effect suggests that the switch from −0.15 to −0.97 is a result of a deliberate microeconomic policy designed specifically to alter the growth drivers of the Chinese economy. Here is one way to formulate Xi's microeconomic policy model based on the observed data: he may have a program in place to dramatically reduce the direct operating role of the state (through reducing SOEs' FAIs) while increasing the funding and the shareholding role of the state (through increasing the LLCs' FAIs). He may not have any intention to increase the funding role, ownership, and control rights of the private sector. The evidence of the latter is that the one part of the private sector most at risk of being subject to the state controls, POEs, gained FAI shares at the expense of the part of the private sector least subject to the state controls, OOEs.

We also do not see the anti-corruption effect where we would expect—the FAIs by POEs. In 2012, POEs accounted for 24 percent of the total FAIs; by 2017, their share rose almost by ten percentage points, to 33 percent. If the theory is right that POEs have been fundamentally driven by crony capitalism, then there is no evidence that Xi has severely curbed crony capitalism. In fact, the massive acquisition sprees launched by HNA, Wanda, Anbang, China CEFC Energy Company Limited (中国华信能源有限公司 in Chinese), led by Ye Jianming, who is currently under investigation) all took place right in the middle of the Xi Jinping era.[10] This is not to say that Xi's anti-corruption campaign did not take place; clearly it did, but the fact that POEs and LLCs seemed to have been immune to its effects suggests that the anti-corruption campaign is primarily aimed at *quid pro quo* corruption—where an official grants something of value, a loan or a regulatory concession, in exchange for a specific benefit—rather than *institutional* corruption, defined as the nexus of politics and businesses to get things done without involving an explicit exchange of benefits.

Another hypothesis is that the anti-corruption campaign has mainly targeted the demand side of corruption—officials—but not the supply side (that is, corrupt businesses that have supplied bribes). Although this needs to be verified, it does seem that the anti-corruption campaign has toppled far more officials than businesspeople. This is an odd way to get to the bottom of corruption. It amounts to a one-sided bet in which bribe suppliers incur no political risks while reaping all the upside of the success of the bribe. To say that this is an effective anti-corruption strategy should require some serious qualifications.

One way to rationalize this demand-focused approach is to argue that the Chinese system has a surplus of official capital and a deficit of managerial and entrepreneurial capital. To insulate growth from the anti-corruption campaign, the government purposely targeted officials while leaving the businesspeople off the hook.

Or corrupt officials are defined as posing a political threat to the leadership, whereas corrupt businesspeople are viewed as politically neutral. Maybe for this and other reasons, POEs have acquired some immunity to political shocks and have been able to expand their FAIs at a rapid rate even under an ostensibly adverse political environment during the Xi era. Another possibility is that Chinese private entrepreneurs are purely transactional with their political patrons and they can switch their political alliances very quickly.

Here is a set of stylized facts about the Xi Jinping era. The anti-corruption campaign may have curbed the topline FAI numbers (that is, the overall growth of FAIs), but it has not curbed the growth of crony capitalism (measured by an important component of FAI: POEs). The state capitalism (LLCs) has been strengthened at the expense of state socialism

(SOEs). Then there is a third component of the China model, and this is entrepreneurial capitalism, and it is worth asking the question about its fate during the Xi era.

This is an arguable point, but one can argue that OOEs are a crude proxy of entrepreneurial capitalism. Here I use "entrepreneurial" not in the conventional sense—that it is a start-up phase of a business—but in a political-economy sense—that it retains some arm's-length distance from the state. Of course, everything is relative. "Entrepreneurial" capitalism is most distant from the state compared with state capitalism and crony capitalism, but it does not mean that entrepreneurial capitalism has no connections to the state. It just has less, either in the form of thinness of its political connections and/or in the form of being less subject to political interventions.

As mentioned before, OOEs comprise six types of entities. Of these six, the individual businesses and FIEs are probably the most distant from the state, and I plotted their FAI shares together with the FAI shares on the part of the OOEs. The two curves are fairly smooth and do not exhibit any breaks that can be clearly identified with known political cycles. The trend is clear. Their shares have fallen dramatically between 2006 and 2017. Entrepreneurial capitalism—as measured here—has not fared well either under Hu-Wen or under Xi. One criticism of this approach is that the falling FAI shares can be accounted for by the structural transformation of the Chinese economy. The Chinese economy has undergone a

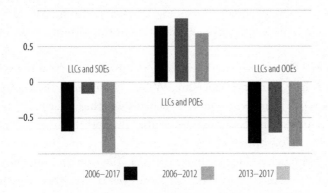

FIGURE 3-3 **FAI shares of OOEs and two alternate definitions of arm's-length capitalism** (Source: author's calculations)

process of capital deepening during this period. Massive infrastructural construction and real-estate buildings are capital-intensive, and thus it is not surprising that the more service-oriented single proprietorships have lost their FAI shares. Also, the more anti-FDI policy environment may explain the falling FAI shares by FIEs.

One way to get at this issue is to do some borderline comparisons. Collective firms are probably more "crony" than individual businesses, but they may operate in similar lines of business. Both of them are domestic. Comparing them implicitly controls for the structural transformation of the Chinese economy and the nationality of their business identities. The pattern is similar. The individual business FAIs have also fallen sharply against FAIs by the collective firms.

Conclusion

With data constraints, this chapter attempts to assess private sector development under Xi Jinping. We rely on the more policy-sensitive FAI data rather than on the performance-sensitive output data. To the extent we can see any patterns in the FAI data from 2006 to 2017, the evidence seems to suggest that Xi has largely continued with the broad contour of the statistization program laid down by his predecessors, but he may have done so with a sharper edge and a more explicit rationale. The pre- and post-2013 compositional change in the FAI data seems to suggest that the Xi leadership has been deliberate about reducing the operating roles of the state while increasing the funding and ownership roles of the state. His far better-known accomplishment—tackling China's mounting corruption—does not seem to be a compelling explanation of the pattern we see in the data.

Let me end this chapter on two broader points. One is about the reform direction of the Xi Jinping leadership. When Xi took over the leadership position in 2012, there were vigorous debates whether he would unleash economic reforms. The communiqué of the Third Plenum of the Eighteenth Central Committee of the Communist Party of China issued in 2012 provided much fodder for those debates. The communiqué outlined an ambitious reform agenda. No less than twenty-six areas of reforms ranging from economics to education and the military were covered in the document.

Now six years into his leadership, we can formulate some solid opinions about Xi's reform agenda, and the judgment converges on the following point: the Xi leadership has explicitly rejected reforming or attenuating the institutional pillars of state capitalism. The Third Plenum communiqué laid out an intellectual vision for reforms, but we also know that Xi has not endorsed the two pathways toward realizing that vision—reforming SOEs and reforming Chinese politics. In fact, he has introduced more changes in the opposite direction.

The suggestion is not that Xi has strengthened the traditional pillar of central planning—the SOEs. In fact, our chapter shows that the SOEs' share of FAI declined during his reign. The evidence, however, centers on the view that Xi has been consolidating and strengthening the model of state capitalism. The FAI shares of the two pillars of state capitalism, the large private corporations and the state-connected firms, rose noticeably under his leadership. The FAI share of the most arm's-length category of firms declined substantially.

Aside from the lack of meaningful economic reforms, what is most worrisome is the state of Chinese politics. The fundamental pillar of state capitalism is the political monopoly of the CCP. It is now abundantly clear that Xi has assigned the highest weight to protecting, perpetuating, and strengthening the monopoly controls of the CCP. The disconnect between the seeming rhetorical rejection of the state capitalism model in the Third Plenum communiqué and the numerous actions and measures taken since 2012 to consolidate the power of the CCP is truly jarring and does not bode well for the future prospects of the Chinese economy.

The other point relates to the broader contour of the Chinese economy. One way to characterize the Chinese economic system is "state capitalism." Ian Bremmer argued in his 2010 book, *The End of the Free Market: Who Wins the War Between States and Corporations?*, that state capitalism was not just an anti-cyclical tool but also a source of China's long-run economic boom. Nicholas Lardy has offered one of the most forceful rejections of the view that Chinese growth resulted from the state capitalism model.[11] In his book *Markets Over Mao*, Lardy demonstrates that Chinese growth has followed a path similar to other successful economies—an overwhelming reliance on the private sector and an expansion of the market economy. He based his relative optimism about Chinese economic prospects on a view that the private sector is now the dominant force in the Chinese economy.

Bremmer is probably empirically closer to the truth, although he is most likely wrong prescriptively. Our data clearly show that the most arm's-length form of capitalism has collapsed in FAI shares. It is important to keep this fact in mind when interpreting Lardy's optimistic view of China's private sector development. China is clearly not a Soviet-type centrally planned economy anymore, but this is not a real issue subject to debate. The real issue here is whether China is a heavily state-controlled economy with many shared characteristics of the commanding-heights economies of the 1970s and the 1980s vintage.[12] In a 1995 study, the World Bank tracked the production and control roles of the state in much of the developing world at that time (outside of the communist countries).[13] What is revealing from the data in that report is that even some of the most statist economies in the world at that time, such as Tanzania, Brazil, India, and Congo, had private-sector output shares in excess of 80 percent of GDP. All had private-sector employment shares in excess of 90 percent of total employment. These figures easily exceed the most optimistic estimates of the size of the private sector in China today.

None of these statist economies from the 1970s and the 1980s turned out to be successful economic performers in the long run. This is an important lesson from history. A large private sector is a necessary but not a sufficient condition for sustained growth. China today has a quantity of capitalism, but so did Brazil and India of the 1980s. State capitalism and crony capitalism all increase the quantity of capitalism, but they do not improve its quality. History is clear on the quantity of capitalism: it is not enough to get a country to a high income, and if history is any guide, the growth prospects under the current policies cannot be taken for granted.

Notes

1. I have written about this topic elsewhere. See Yasheng Huang, "Jack Ma Is Retiring. Is China's Economy Losing Steam?," *The New York Times*, September 28, 2018 (www.nytimes.com/2018/09/28/opinion/jack-ma-alibaba-china-economy.html).

2. Yasheng Huang, *Capitalism with Chinese Characteristics: Entrepreneurship and the State* (Cambridge, United Kingdom; New York, New York: Cambridge University Press, 2008).

3. Peter A. Hall and David Soskice, eds., *Varieties of Capitalism. The Institutional Foundations of Comparative Advantage* (Oxford, United Kingdom: Oxford University Press, 2001).

4. Gabriel Wildau and Yizhen Jia, "China State Groups Gobble Up Struggling Private Companies," *Financial Times*, September 26, 2018 (https://www.ft.com/content/c3eab59a-c09c-11e8-95b1-d36dfef1b89a).

5. Ministry of Human Resources and Social Security of the People's Republic of China, "Vice Minister Xiaoping Qiu Attends National 'Deepening POE's Democratic Management Conference' and Delivers a Speech," September 13, 2018 (http://www.mohrss.gov.cn/SYrlzyhshbzb/zwgk/bld/qxp/ldjh/201809/t2018 0913_301046.html).

6. I cited a number of studies on the Soviet economy to illustrate this point in Huang, *Capitalism with Chinese Characteristics*.

7. Thomas G. Rawski, 2001a, "China Reform Watch: Turning Point," *China Perspectives*, 28–35; Thomas G. Rawski, 2001b, "What Is Happening to China's GDP Statistics," *China Economic Review*, vol. 12, no. 4, 347–354.

8. The impact of the 1997 change is quite minor. For 1996, the government published both the revised and unrevised data. In the unrevised data, the SOEs invested 1205.6 billion yuan in fixed assets and the collective firms invested 366 billion yuan. In the revised data, the SOEs invested 1200.6 billion yuan and the collective sector invested 365.2 billion yuan. This is about 0.4 percent and 0.2 percent in difference, respectively.

9. This area of research is vast. See, for example, Andrew Collier, "Local Debt in China: How Will China Resolve the Impending Crisis?" Orient Capital Research, December 18, 2014.

10. For some of the excellent reporting on HNA and Huaxin, see David Barboza and Michael Forsythe, "Behind the Rise of China's HNA: The Chairman's Brother," *The New York Times*, March 27, 2018 (www.nytimes.com/2018/03/27/business/hna-group-deals-china.html); David Barboza, Marc Santora, and Alexandra Stevenson, "China Seeks Influence in Europe, One Business Deal at a Time," *The New York Times*, August 12, 2018 (www.nytimes.com/2018/08/12/business/china-influence-europe-czech-republic.html?login=email&auth=login-email).

11. Nicholas R. Lardy, *Markets over Mao: The Rise of Private Business in China* (Washington, DC: Peterson Institute for International Economics, 2014).

12. Daniel Yergin and Joseph Stanislaw, *The Commanding Heights: The Battle for the World Economy*, revised and updated edition (New York, New York: Simon & Schuster, 2002).

13. International Bank for Reconstruction and Development, *Bureaucrats in Business: The Economics and Politics of Government Ownership*, *A World Bank Policy Research Report* (Oxford, United Kingdom, and New York, New York: Oxford University Press, 1995).

FOUR

Financial Repression Still

Policy Concerns and Stagnation in China's Corporate Bond Market

VICTOR C. SHIH

At a 2005 Bank for International Settlements (BIS) conference on Asia's corporate bond market, the governor of the People's Bank of China (PBOC), Zhou Xiaochuan, bluntly stated that "China's underdeveloped corporate bond market has distorted the financing structure in the economy, which poses a threat to financial stability. . . ."[1] Following reform pioneers for the financial market, the relatively new central-bank governor clearly saw the deepening of China's corporate bond market as a desirable development over his tenure. Yet, at the end of his tenure in early 2018, corporate bonds continued to be an anemic corner of China's enormous financial system and only accounted for a small share of China's bond market. Despite repeated policy statements calling for the liberalization of the bond market and the development of a deep and market-driven corporate bond market over Zhou's tenure,[2] policy concerns such as stability and low financing costs for state financial institutions drove policy-makers into "quota allocation, administrative approval, and government intervention," practices which Zhou knew in 2005 would render "the prospects for the bond market . . . dismal."[3]

Despite decades of attempted financial liberalization in China, this outcome was an expected one, according to the central bank independence literature. A central bank whose top officials are intimately be-holden to political authorities will be pressured to put political priorities above technical objectives, such as inflation and market efficiency.[4] In few other countries is the political control over the central bank stricter than in China, where top central bankers are also Communist Party cadres and where a party organ, the Central Finance and Economic Leading Group, oversees the activities of the central bank.[5] Economists Marvin Good-friend and Eswar Prasad predicted that a politically subjugated PBOC would be compelled to do the following: (i) buy government debt (that is, to finance a government deficit in whole or in part with newly created bank reserves); (ii) lend to banks, nonfinancial firms, or state enterprises; or (iii) buy foreign assets to support a managed or fixed exchange rate.[6]

As it turned out, the PBOC was pressured to do all of the above over Zhou's tenure, and on an enormous scale. Central bank intervention in the above three ways, especially the first two, ultimately led to the shriveling of the corporate bond market for several reasons. First, by constantly in-tervening in the financial market for policy reasons, the PBOC prevented the market from establishing a yield curve, which would have indicated the equilibrium price of money with different maturities. Instead, the yield curve, such as it was, was almost entirely the product of daily interventions by the PBOC, which meant investors found it difficult to price medium-term macro and inflation risks accurately in the bond yields.[7]

Although central banks around the world intervene in the money market, few major central banks conduct daily, *ad hoc* operations to ensure absolute smoothness in the money market. As the 2017 Q4 *PBOC Report on the Implementation of Monetary Policy* states, "the PBOC closely moni-tored the supply and demand of banking system liquidity and changes in market expectations and used medium term lending facilities (MLF), pledged supplement lending (PSL) and other tools to make up medium term liquidity shortages in the banking system while using reverse repos dominated by the 7-day term to carry out open market operation in a flex-ible way. . . ."[8] This statement makes clear that tools other central banks used occasionally were being used on a daily basis by the PBOC. The deep distrust in the market's ability to adjust itself led to daily interventions by the PBOC on both the short end and the long end of the yield curve. In this tightly managed environment, bond investors' trading became a guessing game of what the PBOC would do next.

Furthermore, decades after the formation of the bond market in China, the PBOC remained under enormous pressure to ensure absolute stability in the interbank bond market. Thus, market participants never grew out of the expectation that the central bank would bail out any major distressed debtor, especially in the interbank bond market. This incentivized investors and credit rating agencies to treat all issuers as low risks, thus compressing yields between issuers.[9] This backstop contributed to the anemic growth of China's corporate bond market, because the presumed PBOC backstop lowered the interest rates offered by bonds issued by risky firms, making them unattractive to investors. Finally, as discussed in detail below, large-scale PBOC interventions to force major creditors (that is, the banks), to buy certain types of bonds crowded out corporate issuers, causing a shriveling of the corporate bond market after 2015.

In the following discussion, I first provide an account of the bond market's development in China since the 1990s and an overview of China's corporate bond market as it stood at the end of 2017. In essence, despite enormous effort in the 1990s to develop the corporate bond market, the role of corporate bonds waned over time after an initial take-off period between 2005 and 2011. In recent years, corporate bonds have been rendered marginal in China's overall bond market because of the overriding need to lower the costs of local government debt via the debt-conversion program launched in 2014. Furthermore, banks, which constantly needed recapitalization, began to rely heavily on the bond market. The enormity of these two policy demands marginalized corporate issuers. In order to partially compensate banks, which lost trillions in high-yielding assets in the conversion program, the PBOC also created a profitable carry-trade opportunity for bond investors by injecting an enormous amount of liquidity into the interbank market. However, this, in turn, led to over-leveraging among nonbank financial institutions. The story of China's corporate bond market is a reflection of one of the lines of reasoning introduced in Barry Naughton's contribution in this volume. Policy-makers had at their disposal such an enormous amount of financial resources that they focused on deploying funds toward policy objectives instead of carrying out further reform. Until the financial resources at their disposal are depleted by a major shock, China's policy-makers will continue to favor the status quo of heavy state interventions in the financial markets.

The Chinese Bond Market: An Overview

Since the formation of the People's Republic, the Chinese government has issued bonds as a way to finance deficits. The issuance of treasury bonds was suspended as a part of the post–Great Leap retrenchment, and bond issuance did not resume until the 1980s, when Chinese banks had a much greater deposit base with which to purchase government bonds.[10] Initially, the main buyers were firms and individuals, who had been financial beneficiaries of the initial wave of reform, but when inflation spiked in 1988, they panicked and sold off their holdings of Chinese treasuries.[11] This led to the only true financial panic in the bond market after 1978. In many ways, preventing such a panic from occurring remained a high priority for China's technocrats into the Xi Jinping administration, even if preventive measures led to other pathologies in the market.

After the post-Tiananmen stasis, China's bond market revived due to the government's need to finance deficits and the escalating costs of SOE reform in the 1990s. Since that point, the bond market became the handmaiden of various government policy priorities as one of the main channels for financing. The major reorientation toward bonds was precipitated by Deng's Southern Tour in 1992, when enthusiastic local and even central government organs directly took money from banks when they needed funds, which was highly inflationary. To put a limit on reckless spending, Zhu Rongji, the newly promoted executive vice-premier at the time, stopped government overdraft in favor of government bond issuance, which was much less inflationary because it did not involve the creation of reserve money.[12] In addition to treasury bond issuance, the newly formed China Development Bank and central enterprises also issued bonds to finance policy objectives such as infrastructure investment, corporate restructuring, and unemployment compensation for SOE workers.[13] The government even issued a special bond to help with reconstruction after the 1998 flood.[14] Later in the 1990s, when banks ran low on capital after a decade of torrential lending to SOEs, the government had to issue more than 270 billion renminbi in special bonds to recapitalize the banks.[15] Due to these policy priorities, annual bond issuance grew from around 50 billion renminbi in 1992 to close to 600 billion by 2000, a twelvefold increase in less than a decade.[16]

To accommodate the rapidly rising bond market, a new structure for trading bonds also emerged in the 1990s, evolving around both trading between major financial institutions in the interbank bond market and trading among retail investors in the Shanghai Stock Exchange. Although the auction and trading mechanisms of these markets improved over the years, even at the outset, a large share of the sales was conducted via "mandatory subscription" (that is, government purchasing quotas issued to banks).[17] Into the early 2000s, bond issuance was still seen by then premier Zhu Rongji as a way to finance even more policy priorities. When the Go West drive was launched in the early 2000s, Premier Zhu ordered the State Planning Commission and the Ministry of Finance to devise a financing plan, much of it evolving around the issuance of policy bonds.[18]

Although state objectives dominated the growth of China's bond market, reform-minded technocrats, mainly in the PBOC, have hoped that a deep and market-driven bond market would someday develop in China, adjusting many distortions in China's financial market. In the mid-1990s, reformers in the PBOC, headed by maverick official Xie Ping, had hoped that the development of the two bond markets would become a core component of interest rate liberalization in China.[19] In essence, market participants in a highly liquid bond market, instead of the government, would determine which firm would pay which interest rate for a given duration.[20] To be sure, that would force some inefficient SOEs into bankruptcy, but that also would accomplish the objective of SOE reform.[21] Reformers in China were influenced by academic economists in the West, who argued that the development of a corporate bond market was desirable because firms could rely on a much wider array of investors to provide financing besides the banks, which on average reduced the costs of financing.[22] Moreover, the development of a bond market created competition for banks, making banks more efficient allocators of money.[23] Finally, since bond investors demanded a high degree of transparency from the issuers, a well-functioning corporate bond market provided information about the short-term and long-term solvency of companies, which made the entire market more resilient in the face of sudden liquidity shocks.[24] These were all desirable objectives from the perspective of reformers in the PBOC.[25]

For Zhou Xiaochuan and China's financial regulators in the early 2000s, the development of the corporate bond market also advanced other needed reform in the financial sector, including bankruptcy laws, better accounting standards, and the diminution of administrative intervention, especially by the National Development and Reform Commission (NDRC).[26] Even in the early 2000s, firms that wanted to issue a bond needed approvals by governments at multiple levels, and the funds raised often could not be spent without government approval.[27] On top of that, bond yields were tightly pegged to the administratively determined interest rates set by the PBOC.[28] Zhou wanted to reform these features of the Chinese financial system.

Yet, although accounting standards improved and interest rates liberalized to some extent over the years,[29] the vision of a deep and liquid corporate bond market still did not materialize at the beginning of 2018, the end of Zhou's tenure. Rampant moral hazard, quota allocation, and administrative interventions still plagued the bond market, preventing its organic growth. Instead of creating a deeply liquid bond market that corrected itself, the Chinese government has fostered a market where participants still mainly reacted to policy signals, as the account below shows.

Figure 4-1 reveals that although corporate bond issuance became dominant in the bond market from 2005 to 2010, its role in the bond market began to wane in 2011. After the middle of 2015, average monthly gross issuance of corporate bonds fell to only 10 percent of gross monthly issuance. But if not corporations, who was issuing bonds? Starting around 2014, the Chinese government, especially local governments, began to issue a torrent of bonds. Into 2015, because banks needed another round of recapitalization to enable continual balance sheet expansion, banks and nonbank financial institutions also began to issue a large amount of bonds, thus eclipsing issuance by nonfinancial corporations (figure 4-1). As detailed below, this did not reflect an organic shift in the preferences of investors, but rather was the result of administrative interventions by the Chinese government.

Figure 4-2 reveals clearly the results of having government and financial issuance dominate the bond market. By the end of 2017, while corporate bonds outstanding hovered around 10 percent of GDP, the overall bond market has grown to 80 percent of nominal GDP from around 50 percent at the beginning of the 2010s. This was not always the case. Corporate notes outstanding rose very rapidly from 2007 to 2011, but their share of the bond market was then eclipsed by the other categories of issuers. In essence, figure 4-2 shows that central and local governments, as well as the wide array of mostly state-owned financial institutions, had debt outstanding to the tune of 70 percent of GDP by the end of 2017. Just as Zhou Xiaochuan had feared, the corporate bond market, as of the end of 2017, remained "dismal."

In terms of corporate bonds' role in financing the "real economy," its contribution to the average monthly total social finance (TSF)—the PBOC's flow metric of financing to the "real economy"—hovered between 10 and 30 percent in recent years (figure 4-3). Since the middle of 2016, however, corporate bonds' contribution to monthly TSF fell to below 15

FIGURE 4-1   Six-month moving average of corporate bond issuance as a share of monthly gross issuance (Source: CEIC)

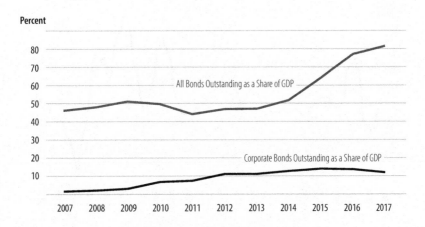

FIGURE 4-2   Corporate and all bonds outstanding as a share of nominal GDP (%) (Source: CEIC)

percent and even briefly entered negative territory. This was a strange collapse in the absence of a financial crisis and suggests a sudden turn in financial policy. Figures 4-1 through figure 4-3 show nothing short of a marginalization of corporate bonds in China's financial landscape, which was a strange outcome in a financial system with assets well over three times GDP. While the slowdown in corporate bond issuance between 2011 and 2015 likely had something to do with general moral hazard in the bond market and yields compression, we focus on the marginalization of corporate bonds after 2015 in the discussion below.

Policy Conundrums: Local Debt Conversion and Liquidity Withdrawal in 2015

Given the pervasiveness of distortion in China's financial market, there are several reasons why the corporate bond market remained stagnant in recent years. However, the coincidence of major policy demands and financial market shocks in 2015 decisively marginalized corporate bonds for the subsequent few years in favor of bonds issued for narrow policy reasons. An unusually challenging year for China's technocrats was 2015. They had to meet onerous policy demands even in the midst of an equity

FIGURE 4-3   Six-month moving average of enterprise bond net issuance as a share of monthly total social finance (%) (Source: CEIC)

sell-off and shocks in the foreign exchange (FX) market. From a liquidity perspective, the foreign exchange (FX) outflows, which drastically slowed the pace of money creation, posed a greater challenge for the PBOC than the stock market sell-off. While a sell-off can be stopped with administrative decrees and PBOC liquidity injections to brokers, outflows decreased the money supply even as the central bank had a mandate to create sufficient liquidity to finance growth and the massive debt conversion program for local government debt.

As seen in figure 4-4, foreign exchange outflows in late 2014 and early 2015 led to some of the slowest growth rates in reserve money since the beginning of the reform. FX inflows had been a steady creator of high-power money in China via PBOC purchase of net inflows with renminbi, which both led to the accumulation of China's FX reserves and money supply creation. This process essentially unraveled starting in the fourth quarter of 2014 as FX outflows rapidly depleted China's reserve money (figure 4-4). By the second half of 2015, reserve money saw consecutive months of negative growth averaging around negative 300 billion renminbi per month (figure 4-4). China would have careened into a financial crisis had that pace of monetary contraction continued unabated. In subsequent years, although the PBOC stabilized its foreign exchange reserve, foreign exchange inflows no longer contributed to the growth in reserve money in any meaningful way.

In addition to a rapidly contracting money supply, the PBOC also faced two enormous new sinkholes for liquidity in 2015. First, the stock market collapse in mid-2015 required the PBOC to inject hundreds of billions of renminbi into the stock market via the China Securities Finance Corporation, Central Huijin Corporation, and the various state-owned brokers.[30] However, the scale of the July 2015 bailout was dwarfed by the liquidity need of the local debt conversion program, which saw a net increase of 3.7 trillion renminbi in municipal bonds in 2015 alone.[31] The PBOC had to ensure sufficient liquidity in the bond market to absorb this enormous wave of local debt issuance even in the midst of serious turmoil.

The implementation of the local debt conversion program had been in the works since the Xi Jinping–Li Keqiang team took power in 2012. As observers had noted as early as 2010, China sustained growth during the 2009 global financial crisis due to an extremely high level of leveraging fueled by borrowing by local government financing vehicles (LGFVs), which were arms of the local governments structured as SOEs.[32] By 2012,

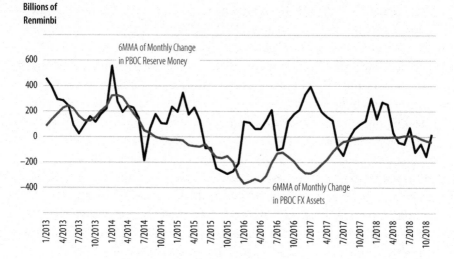

FIGURE 4-4   **Six-month moving average of the monthly change in PBOC reserve money and FX assets (bln RMB)** (Source: CEIC; author's calculations)

outside observers estimated that outstanding LGFV debt stood at 19 trillion renminbi, some 37 percent of China's GDP.[33] As the Chinese government uncovered the horrendous extent of the local debt problems, the Hu-Wen leadership began to explore various remedies. Not wanting a growth slowdown, however, local debt continued to grow unabated through the Hu-Wen years. A half-hearted government audit in 2011 uncovered only 10 trillion renminbi in local debt.[34] When the new administration came to power in late 2012, they immediately ordered a thorough audit, which uncovered more than 18 trillion renminbi in local debt by mid-2013, still a low estimate in all likelihood.

Initially, the new administration put the China Banking Regulatory Commission (CBRC) in charge of the local debt problem in order to prevent LGFVs from increasing their borrowing via trust products and wealth management products (WMPs), which attracted investors with higher interest rates.[35] From the government's perspective, local borrowing through these high-yield channels presented two major problems. First, these channels exacerbated debt levels, because local governments, in most cases, lacked the ability to service high-interest payments, which meant unpaid interest needed to be capitalized into new debt. Second, the ultimate creditors in trust products and WMPs were often households, which would have protested in the event of defaults. Over time, however, the CBRC discovered that it could not resolve the underlying problem of heavy local indebtedness. For one, the political leadership continued to demand that local governments invest more, so as to maintain economic growth. In 2014, for example, Premier Li Keqiang called for a growth target of 7.5 percent.[36] In order to reach the growth target, local governments around China still needed to increase the scale of wasteful investment, which banks needed to finance.

As the local debt problem grew in 2011–2013, experts in the Ministry of Finance began to explore the approach of "open the front door, close the back door." This approach converted local debt parked in high-yielding trust products and WMPs into official municipal bonds.[37] Because the newly issued municipal bonds were guaranteed by the central government, their yields were significantly lower, thus saving local governments hundreds of billions in interest payments. The mechanism for the debt conversion proceeded in the following way. First, local governments issued municipal debt on a large scale, according to a Ministry of Finance (MOF) debt issuance plan. Second, the proceeds of the issuance were used to repay high-interest bank and trust loans, again according to the MOF plan.[38] The borrower could not divert bond proceeds to other uses.

The conversion would not reduce the overall size of local government debt, but would drastically reduce interest payments and cash flow pressure on the local governments. To be sure, because the substitution of high-yielding loans by these bonds reduced banks' profitability, banks were far from pleased by the development. However, the Ministry of Finance's "innovation" was to *force* creditor banks to buy these bonds through "designated allotments" of these securities.[39] The State Council soon ordered creditor banks, many of them smaller local banks, to participate in the debt conversion program, with which banks had no choice but to comply.[40] This was classic financial repression, as banks continued to offer depositors artificially low rates in order to buy low-yielding municipal securities in large quantities. More important, even if banks had wanted to purchase corporate bonds with higher yields, they had to defer those purchases and fulfill their quota purchases of municipal debt that had lower yields.

The political leadership apparently saw this as the perfect solution. In July 2015, in the midst of China's steepest stock market sell-off in recent memory, an excited Li Keqiang announced to a group of economists that "we must increase the scale of (the debt exchange program)."[41] There were no signs that policy-makers thought of deferring the debt conversion program because of the foreign exchange outflows and the stock-market sell-off. Over the course of 2015, the State Council authorized the Ministry of Finance to oversee the issuance of 3.7 trillion renminbi in local municipal debt.[42] In 2016, municipal debt outstanding grew by an additional 5.8 trillion renminbi. Then minister of finance Lou Jiwei victoriously announced in December 2015 that local governments that had undergone debt exchange saw the average interest rate of their debt fall from 10 percent to 3.5 percent, which drastically reduced the cash-flow pressure on these localities.[43]

As the debt replacement shifted into high gear in 2015, however, it also coincided with the contraction in reserve money due to foreign exchange outflows from China. The PBOC needed to quickly replace the shrinking money supply with a new source of liquidity. Without new liquidity, banks would have been forced into a painful choice between providing financing to new investment, which was still necessary to maintain growth, and purchasing the newly issued municipal notes, which served the function of rolling over existing debt without large-scale defaults. As figure 4-5 shows, once the muni-bond program got going, it demanded financial institutions in China to buy, on average, 700 to 900 billion renminbi in net new notes *per month*. The shrinking reserve money seen during the second half of 2015 simply would have made this impossible. A government with less ability to intervene in the financial market would have chosen to focus on stabilizing the financial market while delaying the local debt conversion program. With strict control over the PBOC, however, the Chinese Communist Party decided to proceed with the debt conversion even while the PBOC exerted enormous effort to stabilize the financial market. Zhou and his colleagues at the PBOC needed to find a way to finance all the various demands from the party.

The Zhou Xiaochuan Put

Throughout the course of Zhou Xiaochuan's career as the governor of the PBOC, he pushed for many a reform. However, his ability as a CCP cadre to carry out fundamental reform was also constrained by the multiple political demands placed on his office by higher-level party officials.[44] The political demands made on his office were likely greater in the summer

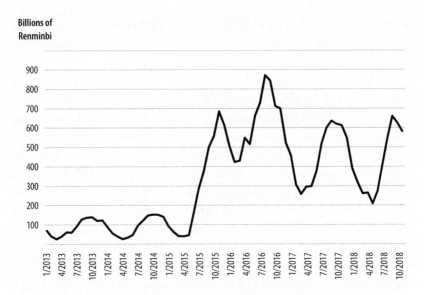

Billions of Renminbi

FIGURE 4-5 Six-month moving average in the monthly net issuance of central and municipal government bonds (bln RMB) (Source: CEIC)

of 2015 than any other time in his tenure, when the stock-market crash and tidal waves of FX outflows coincided with the need to finance the trillion yuan debt-replacement program. Faced with these impossible demands, the central bank did not allow the market to determine where money flowed. Market forces in the middle of 2015 might well have driven additional hundreds of billions of dollars out of China, which would have necessitated a steep devaluation of the renminbi. Instead, the PBOC instituted draconian capital controls and intervened in the interbank market to inject trillions in liquidity with the specific purpose of providing banks with liquidity with which to purchase municipal bonds.

The PBOC accomplished this by lending high-power money to banks via reverse repo operations. In a reverse repo, the lender—in this case, the PBOC or the policy banks—purchases securities from the borrower, but at the same time obtains an agreement from the seller (borrower) that she will repurchase the securities in the near future. In essence, reverse repos were loans from the PBOC secured by bonds as collaterals. The PBOC specifically used this tool to inject liquidity, because it allowed banks to put up newly purchased municipal bonds as collateral to obtain funding, which could be used to purchase even more municipal bonds. Moreover, as figure 4-6 suggests, PBOC injections also allowed banks to lend to one another, especially the deposit-rich large commercial banks such as the Big Four state banks.

As one can see on figure 4-6, the liquidity injections were enormous in scale. PBOC net repo (net borrowing) on the interbank market fell from an average of negative 4 trillion renminbi in November of 2014 to an average of negative 12 trillion renminbi one year later. That represented a net new injection (lending) of 8 trillion renminbi in one year to China's financial institutions, equivalent to 11 percent of China's nominal GDP in 2015. Of course, the flood of liquidity provided by the PBOC also prevented the collapse of high-power money and deposits in the commercial banks, as one can see on figure 4-4. This further empowered large commercial banks to lend an additional 7 trillion renminbi into the interbank market. All told, PBOC reverse repo operations directly or indirectly injected 15 trillion renminbi into the interbank market from late 2014 to late 2015. This massive easing operation reversed the negative growth in reserve money by early 2016, so that reserve money enjoyed average monthly growth of above 100 billion renminbi (figure 4-4). This took place even as the foreign exchange reserves continued to drop in 2016.

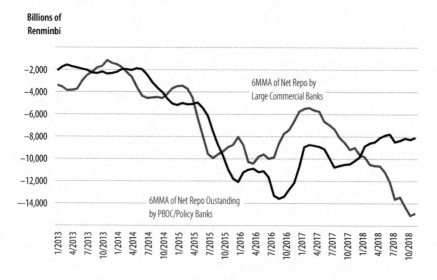

FIGURE 4-6   Six-month moving average of net repo outstanding by the PBOC/policy banks and by large commercial banks (bln RMB) (Source: CEIC)

But which financial institutions took advantage of this flood of liquidity to purchase government bonds? As figure 4-7 reveals, the main borrowers included city commercial banks (CCBs) and nonbank financial institutions (NBFIs) such as brokers, insurance companies, and asset managers. CCB net repo (net borrowing) jumped from 5 trillion renminbi at the beginning of 2015 to 15 trillion renminbi by May. This was not surprising, considering that CCBs were a major lender to local governments, which had forced CCBs into lending trillions to local projects.[45] In the debt-conversion program, CCBs were under great pressure to convert their high-interest loans to local government into low-yield municipal bonds, according to plans drawn up by the Ministry of Finance. With much less ability to absorb new deposits to finance the debt purchase, the PBOC needed to provide CCBs with a helping hand totaling more than 10 trillion renminbi. CCB net repo further rose to close to 20 trillion renminbi by the middle of 2016 (figure 4-7). Meanwhile, NBFIs, which did not even have deposits, saw their net repos jump from 1.5 trillion renminbi to close to 6 trillion renminbi by late 2015.

While NBFIs borrowed from the PBOC as part of the stock rescue program in 2015, they also did so out of profit considerations. Figure 4-8

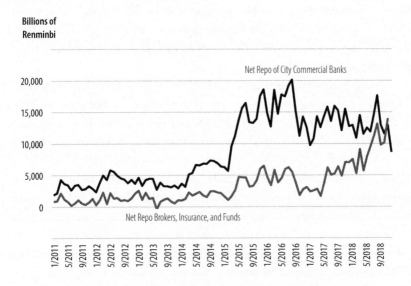

FIGURE 4-7 **Net repo outstanding of city commercial banks and nonbank financial institutions (bln RMB)** (Source: CEIC)

shows the seven-day repo rates, which were heavily influenced by reverse repo rates and quantity set by the PBOC on a daily basis, and ten-year Chinese treasury yields, which reflected longer-term market expectation on interest rates. One can see clearly that starting in early 2015, the PBOC made sure that daily operations drove seven-day repo rates well below ten-year treasury yields, which roughly reflected the yields of the newly issued municipal debt. The lowering of seven-day repo rates allowed all financial institutions, but especially NBFIs, to profit from the carry trade because NBFIs traded actively. In this carry trade, banks or NBFIs borrowed cheaply on the repo market from major commercial banks and used the proceeds to purchase higher-yielding treasuries or municipal bonds. Because the newly purchased securities were essentially risk-free, the carry trade provided a spread between short-term borrowing costs and long-term yields without incurring any default risks. As long as the annualized borrowing costs were below the yields of the purchased bonds, investors earned a spread.

For the city commercial banks, the spread likely represented a minor compensation from the PBOC to these banks, which were compelled to participate in the debt conversion program. Banks were lending at the 7–10 percent range to lower-level LGFVs. Suddenly, they had to accept the 3–4 percent returns of the municipal debt. The spread at least partially compensated CCBs for the collapse in returns on assets. This profit margin, however, was purely the result of PBOC actions and had little to do with market equilibria.

Nonbank financial institutions (NBFIs), which never lent very much to local governments, however, were incentivized by the carry trade to borrow more on the interbank market to buy newly issued debt. In essence, lightly regulated NBFIs could put up a tranche of bonds as collateral to borrow funds from the PBOC or banks, the proceeds of which can be used to purchase another tranche, which, in turn, was used to borrow more money, and so on. The ability of NBFIs to multiply their balance sheets without provisioning created a very healthy appetite for bonds. As figure 4-8 shows, the spread was rather healthy at more than 1 percent (100 bps) for much of 2015, thus providing a very attractive investment option for NBFIs, which engaged in levered bets on bonds. Not surprisingly, net borrowing (repo) of NBFIs jumped from 1.5 trillion at the end of 2014 to as high as 6 trillion renminbi at the end of 2015 (figure 4-7). These transactions, however, represented highly risky bets, because while banks had deposits, NBFIs borrowed almost all of their funds from the interbank market at very short duration to finance their bond purchases. If short-term rates were to spike up, their cash flows would invert, forcing them to liquidate at steep losses.

To be sure, government issuers were not the only beneficiaries of the carry trade engineered by the PBOC. Figure 4-3 shows that corporate issuers also enjoyed healthy demand for their bonds in 2015 and 2016. Yet, as figure 4-1 shows, corporate note issuance was still dwarfed by government and financial institution issuance after 2015. Again, this was the result of the government ordering banks to buy up local government issuance, financed by PBOC reverse repos. Left on their own, banks likely would have preferred to purchase higher-yielding corporate notes.

After the Deluge: The Consequences of Heavy Policy Interventions in the Money Market

Instead of fostering a deep and liberalized corporate bond market, policy demands leading up to 2015 compelled the PBOC to inject a massive amount of liquidity into the interbank bond market in 2015. Creditor banks then used the new liquidity to purchase newly issued municipal bonds in accordance with Ministry of Finance plans. As figures 4-1 and

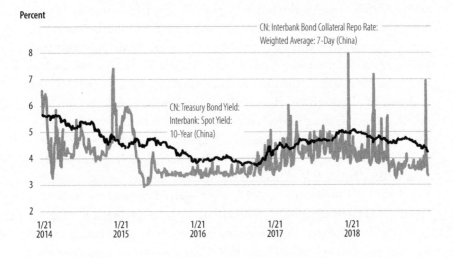

FIGURE 4-8   Seven-day repo rates and ten-year treasury yields (%) (Source: CEIC)

4-3 reveal, a by-product of the local debt conversion program was the marginalization of corporate debt. This, of course, meant that a transparent market, which objectively rated the creditworthiness of and efficiently allocated capital to China's corporate sector would not be forthcoming in the near future.

Another consequence was that the combination of the carry trade, engineered by the PBOC, and the usual assumption of risk-free bonds encouraged NBFIs to engage in highly risky levered bets in China's bond market. Figure 4-9 shows that NBFIs' use of borrowed money (via repos) to purchase bonds rose from 20 percent in late 2014 to close to 40 percent in mid-2015. On top of that, in an environment of cheap short-term capital, NBFIs began to lend money to each other using unofficial repos, called *daichi* (holding on behalf), which might have topped 1 trillion renminbi by late 2016.[46] Unofficial repo had the advantage that the borrower could use one tranche of bonds to lever up infinitely, as long as she found new counterparties willing to lend. If repo rates continued to be low and bond yields trended downward, investors in a heavily levered bet stood to gain enormous profits.

Knowing that these dangerous positions were building up, the PBOC began to slow the pace of liquidity injection in late 2016, which led to spikes in the seven-day repo rates (figure 4-8). The sudden escalation of short-term interest signaled to the market the end of the bond bull market; ten-year treasury yields also began to go up (figure 4-8). Investors that had borrowed heavily to buy ten-year notes suddenly found themselves paying much higher interest while still receiving the same interest payments from bonds purchased prior to the second half of 2016. Their cash flows, which had been positive from the carry trade, turned negative. Some funds that had borrowed heavily on the unofficial repo market defaulted on their creditors, necessitating CBRC and PBOC interventions to stave off a crisis.[47] Overall bond issuance, including municipal bonds, screeched to a halt in the first quarter of 2017 as a result of deep deleveraging by NBFIs in late 2016 (figure 4-9). Although this episode was not nearly as severe as the challenge China faced in 2015, it yet again illustrated the unhealthy cycle of bailout by the PBOC, followed by rapid leveraging and the emergence of a new bubble, which necessitates another round of bailout. Starting in the second half of 2017, the PBOC once again encouraged levering up in the bond market by driving seven-day repo rates lower (figure 4-8). As figure 4-7 shows, NBFIs increased their borrowing to buy bonds from around 5 trillion renminbi to close to 15 trillion renminbi over the course of 2018. Figure 4-9 shows that roughly 40 percent of NBFIs' bond holding was financed by borrowed money by late 2018.

State Power: A Potential Deterrent to Reform

The slow development in China's corporate bond market is reflective of a more general phenomenon alluded to in Barry Naughton's chapter. That is, by dominating all financial institutions in China and by consolidating SOEs in the 1990s, the central government acquired enormous leverage over the economy. In combination with the sizable current account surplus, which infused the banking system with ample liquidity, Chinese policy-makers from the mid-1990s onward simply had little incentives to reform. To be sure, they faced numerous policy challenges, ranging from the global financial crisis in 2008 to outflows in 2015 to the ballooning local debt. Time and again, however, policy-makers resorted to administrative means to overcome these difficulties rather than liberalize the market. China responded to the 2008 global crisis with a massive infrastructure investment program financed mainly by state-owned banks at the behest of the government. The 2015 shocks were overcome by capital control and state injection of funds into the stock market. Policy-makers responded to the local debt problem by administratively ordering banks to purchase municipal bonds.

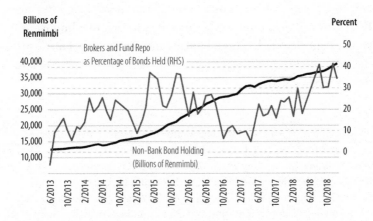

FIGURE 4-9 **Degree of leveraging by NBFIs** (Source: CEIC; author's calculations)

Yet, in all of these cases, administrative means merely deferred the problem, and in most cases, the underlying distortions continued to fester. Despite the short-term effectiveness of the local debt conversion program, for example, the underlying problem was not solved. According to Tsinghua University economist Bai Chong'en and coauthors, local government debt, whether recognized by the government or not, had grown to 45 trillion renminbi by the end of 2015, or 67 percent of China's nominal GDP.[48] In combination with China's official debt of 10 trillion renminbi, China's governmental debt-to-GDP ratio reached 82 percent by the end of 2015, well above the international warning line of 60 percent. Furthermore, the debt exchange program had meant to "close the back door" of LGFV borrowing. However, disclosures from the bond market showed that LGFVs continued to issue their own debt as corporate debt to the tune of tens of billions of renminbi per month, sometimes exceeding even 100 billion per month.[49]

Also, repeated rescues by the PBOC and other agencies meant that market participants have come to expect it, becoming almost totally unprepared for sizable shocks to the financial system. When the economy slows or companies begin to default on debt, banks and bond investors have little willingness to hedge against a large wave of defaults, believing that policy-makers will compel the central bank to rescue the system. The central bank, for its part, time and again faced enormous political pressure to print money and lend to financial institutions, resulting in China having the fastest growth rate in debt in the world.[50] Given the high level of debt in China (estimates range from 250 to more than 300 percent of GDP), there will be a limit to the current approach of administrative interventions coupled with central bank easing. As the debt bubble grows in China, true reform in China's financial market will be more painful and disruptive when it arrives.

Notes

1. Xiaochuan Zhou, "China's corporate bond market development: lessons learned," in Monetary and Economic Department of the BIS, ed., *Developing corporate bond markets in Asia: Proceedings of a BIS/PBC seminar held in Kunming, China on 17–18 November 2005* (Basel, Switzerland: BIS, 2006).

2. People's Bank of China, "*Zhongguo huobi zhengce zhixing baogao 2017 dierji* (The report on the implementation of Chinese monetary policy in the second quarter of 2017)," in PBOC, ed., *The report on the implementation of Chinese monetary policy* (Beijing, China: PBOC, 2017).

3. Zhou, "China's corporate bond market development."

4. Alex Cukierman, "Central bank independence and monetary control," *Economic Journal*, vol. 104, no. 427 (1994), 1437–1448; Alberto Alesina and Lawrence Summers, "Central bank independence and macroeconomic performance: some comparative evidence," *Journal of Money, Banking, and Credit*, vol. 25, no. 2 (1993), 151–162; Christopher Adolph, *Bankers, Bureaucrats, and Central Bank Politics: The Myth of Neutrality* (New York, New York: Cambridge University Press, 2013), xxiii, 357.

5. Sebastian Heilmann, "Regulatory innovation by Leninist means: Communist Party supervision in China's financial industry," *China Quarterly*, no. 181 (2005); Victor Shih, *Factions and Finance in China: Elite Conflicts and Inflation* (New York, New York: Cambridge University Press, 2008).

6. Marvin Goodfriend and Eswar Prasad, "A Framework for Independent Monetary Policy in China," *CESifo Economic Studies*, vol. 53, no. 1 (2007), 2–41.

7. Carl Walter and Fraser Howie, *Red Capitalism* (New York, New York: John Wiley & Sons, 2011).

8. People's Bank of China, The report on the implementation of Chinese monetary policy in the second quarter of 2017.

9. Yu Xie, "Here's why China is flooded with AAA-rated bonds: confusion and rivalry among regulators," *South China Morning Post*, July 17, 2017.

10. Walter and Howie, *Red Capitalism*, 87.

11. Walter and Howie, *Red Capitalism*, 88.

12. Rongji Zhu, "*Zhengdun caishui jiexu, yansu caijing jilu, qianghua shuishou zhengguan, jiakuai caishui gaige* (Rectify order in the budget, restore strictness in budgetary discipline, strengthen management of taxation, speed up fiscal reform)," in Document Research Center of CCP Central Committee, ed., *Xinshiqi Jingji Tizhi Gaige Zhongyao Wenxian Xuanbian* (*A Selection of Important Documents for Economic Structural Reform in the New Period*) (Beijing, China: Central Document Publisher, 1993).

13. Rongji Zhu, "*Zhengdun caishui jiexu, yansu caijing jilu.*"

14. "*1998 nian guozhai shichang yunxing ji dui guomin jingji de yingxiang* (The operation of the bond market in 1998 and its impact on the national economy)," *Zhongguo Hongguan Jingji Xinxi* (*Chinese Macroeconomic Signals*), vol. 1998 (1998).

15. Yuan Wang, *Zhongguo Huobi Zhengce Qushi* (The Trend in Chinese Monetary Policy) (Beijing, China: China Financial Publisher, 1999), 113.

16. Walter and Howie, *Red Capitalism*, 90.

17. Yuan Chen, "Warding off policy-oriented financial risks and promoting effective growth of the national economy," in Bank for International Settlements, ed., *Policy Papers No. 7—Strengthening the Banking System in China: Issues and Experience* (Basel, Switzerland: Bank for International Settlements, 1999).

18. Victor Shih, "Development, the second time around: the political logic of developing western China," *Journal of East Asian Studies*, vol. 4 (2004), 427–451.

19. Ping Xie, "*Lilu shuangguizhi he lilu shichanghua gaige de xuncheng* (The pro-

cess of dual track interest rate and interest rate liberalization reform)," *Hainan Jinrong (Hainan Finance)*, vol. 1995, no. 8 (1995), 5–9.

20. Xie, "*Lilu shichanghua de xiangguan wenti* (Problems related to interest rate liberalization)," *Zhongguo Waihui Guanli (Foreign Exchange)*, vol. 2001, no. 1 (2001), 6–10.

21. Ping Xie, "*Lilu shichanghua de xiangguan wenti.*"

22. Marvin Goodfriend, "Why a corporate bond market: growth and direct finance," in Monetary and Economic Department of the BIS, ed., *Developing Corporate Bond Markets in Asia.*

23. Suresh Sundaresan, "Developing multiple layers of financial intermediation: the complementary roles of corporate bond markets and banks," in Monetary and Economic Department of the BIS, ed., *Developing Corporate Bond Markets in Asia.*

24. Mark Flannery, "Asymmetric information and risky debt maturity choice," *Journal of Finance*, vol. 41, no. 1 (1986), 19–37.

25. Xie, "*Lilu shuangguizhi he lilu shichanghua gaige de xuncheng* (The process of dual track interest rate and interest rate liberalization reform)"; Xie, "*Lilu shichanghua de xiangguan wenti* (Problems related to interest rate liberalization)"; Xinhui Zhou, "*Lilu shichanghua: Lijiu mixin de huati* (Interest rate marketization: A topic that is seemingly new but has a long history)," *Jinrong Shibao (Financial Times)*, September 23, 2000.

26. Zhou, "China's corporate bond market development: lessons learned."

27. Jianhua Zhang, "*Tebie guozhai zijin shiyong qingkuang diaocha ji jianyi* (An investigation on the situation on the usage of special bond capital and suggestions)," *Jinrong Yanjiu Baogao (Financial Research Report)*, vol. 2000, no. 9 (2000), 1–7.

28. Xie, "*Lilu shichanghua de xiangguan wenti.*"

29. Huaipeng Mu, "The development of China's bond market," in Monetary and Economic Department of the BIS, ed., *Developing Corporate Bond Markets in Asia.*

30. "Timeline of China's attempts to prevent stock market meltdown," Reuters, July 8, 2015.

31. Euromoney Institutional Investor PLC, "CEIC China Premium Data," (Euromoney, 2018).

32. Victor Shih, "Local government debt: big rock candy mountain," *China Economic Quarterly*, vol. 2010, June 2010, 26–32.

33. Zhiwei Zhang, Changchun Hua, and Wendy Chen, "China's heavy LGFV debt burden," in Nomura Securities, ed., *Asia Special Report* (Tokyo, Japan: Nomura Securities, 2013).

34. Kang Jia, "*Jia Kang: dangqian difang zhaiwu zuida de fengxian zaiyu butouming* (Jia Kang: the greatest risk of local government debt is the lack of transparency)," *People's Daily*, November 25, 2013.

35. Peng Yi, Zhijin Yang, and Xiaoling Zhang, "*Yuanli 'yinzi yinhang'? 463 haowen shache gongyixing xiangmu juzhai* (Avoiding 'shadow banking'? Document

463 stopped publicly oriented projects from further borrowing)," *21st Century Business Herald,* January 4, 2013.

36. Keqiang Li, "Report on the work of the government," in National People's Congress, ed. (Beijing: NPC, 2014), March 14, 2014 (http://english.gov.cn/archive/publications/2014/08/23/content_281474982987826.htm).

37. Jia, "*Jia Kang: dangqian difang zhaiwu zuida de fengxian zaiyu butouming.*"

38. "*Caizhengbu youguan fuzeren jiu chutai 'difang zhengfuxing zhaiwu fengxian yingji chuzhi yu'an' dajizhewen* (Question and Answer with the Ministry of Finance Spokesperson Concerning Proposal for Dealing with Emergency Risks Related to Local Government Debt)," Ministry of Finance Documents (Beijing, China: Ministry of Finance, 2016).

39. Yumin Li, "*Difangzhai zhihuanhou chengben jiangzhi 3.5 percent, 2016 nian daoqi 2.8 wanyi* (The swapping of local debt lowered costs to 3.5 percent; 2.8 trillion yuan will mature in 2016)," *21st Century Economic Herald,* December 23, 2016, 2–3.

40. "*Guowuyuan guanyu jiaqiang difang zhengfuxing zhaiwu guanli de yijian* (Opinions on strengthening the management of local government debt)," in State Council, ed. (Beijing: State Council, 2014).

41. Jun Cheng, "*Li Keqiang zhuantong jiada difangzhai zhihuan lidu; xiaoxi cheng disanpi zhengzai yunliang* (Li Keqiang supports increasing the local debt swap; sources say a third batch is in the works)," *Hua'erjie Jianwen* (*News from Wall Street*) (Beijing, China: Sina, 2015).

42. Cheng, "*Li Keqiang zhuantong jiada difangzhai zhihuan lidu.*"

43. Cheng, "*Li Keqiang zhuantong jiada difangzhai zhihuan lidu.*"

44. Heilmann, "Regulatory innovation by Leninist means"; Nicolas Lardy, *China's Unfinished Economic Reform* (Washington, DC: Brookings Institution Press, 1998).

45. Shih, "Local government debt: big rock candy mountain."

46. Hong Shen, "Behind China's Bond Selloff, a Risky Twist on the Repo Trade," *Wall Street Journal,* January 17, 2017 (www.wsj.com/articles/behind-chinas-bond-selloff-a-risky-twist-on-the-repo-trade-1484654059).

47. Shen, "Behind China's Bond Selloff."

48. Chong'en Bai, Chang-tai Hsieh, and Zheng Song, "The long shadow of a fiscal expansion," Brookings Papers on Economic Activity (Washington, DC: Brookings Institution Press, 2016).

49. Euromoney Institutional Investor PLC, "CEIC China Premium Data" (www.ceicdata.com/en/products/china-economic-database).

50. International Monetary Fund, "People's Republic of China: 2017 Article IV Consultation," in IMF, ed., Article IV Consultation (Washington, DC: IMF, 2017).

PART II

Opening to the Outside

FIVE

Four Decades of Reforming China's International Economic Role

DAVID DOLLAR

China and Russia challenge American power, influence, and interests, attempting to erode American security and prosperity. They are determined to make economies less free and less fair, to grow their militaries, and to control information and data to repress their societies and expand their influence. . . . These competitions require the United States to rethink the policies of the past two decades—policies based on the assumption that engagement with rivals and their inclusion in international institutions and global commerce would turn them into benign actors and trustworthy partners. For the most part, this premise turned out to be false.

NATIONAL SECURITY STRATEGY OF
THE UNITED STATES, 2017

It is fashionable in Washington now to argue that the strategy of engagement with China has failed. There are two components to this engagement-has-failed notion. The first is the idea that engagement with China should have led to the country becoming more politically open with freer press and speech and moves toward democracy. The second is the notion that engaging China and including it in the international institutions should have led the country to become more of a market economy, integrate into the world economy, and subscribe to global norms of trade

and finance. This chapter looks at this second notion. It reviews four decades of reforming China's international economic role in order to see
what has been achieved with China's opening and to make a judgment on
whether or not China is following global norms.

The chapter is divided into different issues that naturally have some
overlap. The first section, "Trade," examines China's rise as a trading
nation. The next section, "Trade Balance and Currency Issues," looks at
exchange rate and balance of payments issues. Inward direct investment,
and related issues of forced technology transfer, are taken up in the section
titled "Foreign Direct Investment and Technology Transfer." The next section, "Outward Direct Investment and the Belt and Road Initiative," looks
at the recent phenomenon of capital outflow from China through outward
direct investment (ODI) as well as through lending for infrastructure projects, including along the Belt and Road. The section titled "China in the
International Economic Institutions" focuses on China's growing role in
the international economic institutions: the World Trade Organization,
the International Monetary Fund, and multilateral development banks.

The concluding section tries to make an overall assessment. The notion
that economic engagement has failed seems too extreme and hard to
square with an objective assessment. China's integration into the world
economy has been an important factor in global poverty reduction, first in
China itself, but also throughout the developing world. Advanced economies have benefited as well through higher incomes and consumption. The
"China shock" has caused some painful adjustments within rich countries, some of which have handled this better than others through their
safety nets and retraining programs. The largely positive story, however,
is tempered by some worrisome factors. China today is less open to FDI
than other large emerging markets, and it uses its restrictions to encourage technology transfer, especially to its state-owned enterprises. China's
growing capital outflow, natural at this stage of development, has a number
of troublesome characteristics. State-owned enterprises are trying to buy
their high-tech competitors abroad, though they are protected at home
from similar competition. The Belt and Road Initiative, led by lending
from China's big policy banks, lacks transparency and raises questions of
debt sustainability for the borrowing countries. China's role within the international economic institutions is largely supportive, but China's unique
features present new challenges to the WTO. The launching of the Asian
Infrastructure Investment Bank will most likely result in positive changes

to the system of multilateral banks, but nevertheless raises fears that China is bent on creating an alternative system.

The evidence at this point is consistent with the view that engagement has largely succeeded and that China is increasingly conforming with global norms. As the largest trading nation and soon to be largest investor, naturally it wants a large say in the evolution of institutions and norms. However, the practices that do not conform to current norms are serious problems, so there is an open question as to how things will develop in the future. Deng Xiaoping's famous judgment was that Mao Zedong was 70 percent good and 30 percent bad. I do not necessarily agree with that assessment, but those numbers strike me about right as the probability that China will increasingly conform to global norms (which it will have shaped), versus the probability that China goes rogue. Of course, if the established powers move away from engagement, then China is more likely to go rogue.

Trade

Over four decades, China has gone from a virtually nonexistent trader to the largest trading nation. While it is a remarkable story, it is largely what would have been predicted from trade theory. China before 1978 was essentially a closed economy with neither foreign trade of any scale nor foreign investment. A key part of the reform program known as *gaige kaifang* (reform and opening) was to open up the economy in order to expose producers to competition. China's opening to foreign investment was initially confined to four special zones. In 1984, fourteen more cities were given the same opportunities as the special zones. In 1993, this was expanded to the more than thirty provincial capitals plus five inland cities along the Yangzi River and nine border cities.[1] Thus, within a relatively short period of time, dozens of Chinese cities had opened up to foreign trade and investment.

The implicit contract between central leaders and these local governments was clear. The government "has no money. So we will give you a policy that allows you to charge ahead and cut through your own difficult road," was what Deng Xiaoping told party leaders at a policy meeting on the special zones in 1979.[2] Coastal cities in particular competed among themselves to attract foreign investment, and this competition drove improvements in the investment climate. Cities that could provide reliable power and decent transport infrastructure were able to attract investment. The resulting growth and tax revenue fed further improvements in infrastructure.

The great attraction for most of the initial foreign investors was the huge labor force, with decent basic education, working at low wages. China's integration into the world economy is sometimes referred to as the "China shock." What was the shock? In 1978, the ten largest industrial economies produced the vast majority of world GDP. Most trade occurred among them. They had 300 million workers. China had 450 million workers, counting all of the farmers. China had a negligible capital stock; only about 5 percent of what the industrial countries had. China was also poor in natural resources relative to its population. Thus, China's entry more than doubled the global labor force, while leaving the world capital stock and world natural resource stocks virtually unchanged. The expected effect of this would have been to raise wages in China, lower wages for low-skilled workers in advanced economies, and raise the rate of profit worldwide as well as the return to natural resources such as oil and minerals. In terms of trade, China would have been expected to export labor-intensive products and to import ones intensive in the use of capital, technology, and natural resources. This is generally what happened in the four decades since the beginning of opening and reform.

When China first started opening up, it had potential but few actual products that it could trade on the world market. Its initial exports were primary products such as petroleum and food, which made up half of exports in 1980.[3] The agricultural exports gave a boost to the rural economy, which was already benefiting from the household responsibility system. Trade helped the rural economy in another way. Urban reform was slow to take off. In rural areas, Township and Village Enterprises (TVEs) developed as a kind of quasi-private sector more efficient than the urban state enterprises. Aside from primary products, China's initial exports were mostly labor-intensive manufactures. By the early 1990s, the primary product share of exports had dropped to 26 percent as China's comparative advantage revealed itself. In 1995, one-third of China's exports came from TVEs.[4] From the 1990s onward, China emerged as a major exporter of textiles, clothing, and footwear, as well as toys and simple plastic products. In 1995, more than one-third of China's exports came from the textile sector. This share then gradually declined and was down by more than one-half by 2010. At the same time, electronic exports really took off, reaching about half of all of China's exports by 2010.[5]

China's emergence onto the world scene coincided with the rapid expansion of global value chains (and the attraction of China, no doubt, spurred the break-up of the production process for many goods). The GVC phenomenon enabled China to export products that are often labeled as "high-tech" such as computers, smart phones, and televisions. However, China's role has largely been that of assembler. Figure 5-1 shows the global value chain for China's exports of computers and electronics in 2011. The vertical axis shows compensation per hour, a measure of high- versus low-value-added activities. The horizontal axis maps the production process from initiation to the consumer. Inputs are indicated by country-sector codes. At the beginning of the process are high-value design and financial inputs from advanced economies. Then come some sophisticated parts from Japan, the United States, Korea, and Taiwan. China is toward the end of the production process: assembly at low wages and production of some simple parts. The high-value inputs at the end are mostly services, as products are brought to market in the United States, Europe, and Japan. The size of the value-added contribution is indicated by the bubble. China, in fact, has a large amount of value added in these products; this pattern enables China to employ a large number of low-skilled workers. For China's export of these products to the United States, a bit less than half of the total value added comes from China. The point is that breaking up the production process in this way enabled a large number of different labor-intensive activities to settle in China and enhanced the country's ability to exploit its comparative advantage.

Analyzing China's trade in terms of value added provides some additional insights. A majority of China's exports (measured as gross value) come from foreign-invested enterprises. Much of China's success is associated with Hong Kong entrepreneurs who pioneered the garment and footwear exports, and later with firms from Taiwan, Korea, and Japan assembling in China as part of global value chains. In terms of the value added in China's exports, however, the largest single share comes from domestic private firms. State-enterprise contributions are minor.[6] Thus, the export-oriented model enabled the private sector to expand its share of the economy—both foreign investors and the domestic private sector. These tend to be more productive than SOEs, so this structural shift was a contribution to total factor productivity and growth at the macro level.[7]

Figure 5-2 shows the evolution of China's value-added exports from 1978 to 2014, compared to that of the ten largest industrial economies. China's share of total exports grew from basically zero to 25 percent over the period. Over the same period, China's employment increased to 200

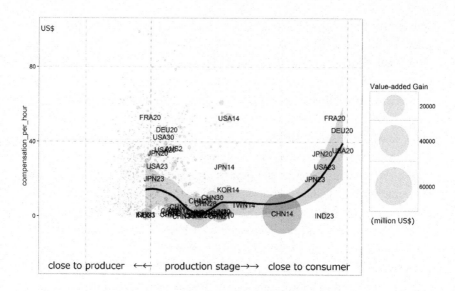

FIGURE 5-1   Value chain for China's exports of electrical and optical equipment, 2011
(Source: Ye Ming, Bo Meng, and Shang-Jin Wei, "Measuring Smile Curves in
Global Value Chains." In Discussion Paper Number 530. Institute
for Developing Economies: Tokyo, 2015)

percent of industrial country employment; its capital stock reached 50 percent of theirs; and its PPP GDP also reached 50 percent of theirs. Its export share was somewhat lower than its share of PPP GDP, but that is not surprising for a large, continental country. The main point is that the amount and composition of its exports was what one would have expected from trade theory.

Trade Balance and Currency Issues

In the early years of economic reform, China ran a trade deficit as is typical for a developing country that needs to import capital and technology. Chinese leaders, however, were determined not to see the country become overly indebted, something they associated with colonialism. The country switched from a modest trade deficit to a modest surplus at an early stage of development. Figure 5-3 shows the current account balance relative to GDP; this is the broadest measure of the trade balance, including directly traded services as well as "factor services"—the main one being

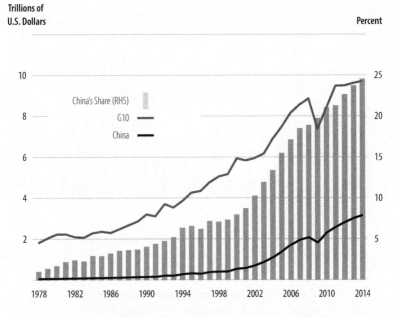

FIGURE 5-2 Value added exports, China and ten largest industrial economies
(Source: Robert C. Feenstra, Robert Inklaar, and Marcel P. Timmer, "The Next
Generation of the Penn World Table," 2013 (http://www.ggdc.net/pwt))

net earnings on capital. China went from an average deficit of about 2 percent during 1985–1989 to an average surplus of about 2 percent during 1990–1992.

The main capital inflows into China were foreign direct investment (FDI). A key part of China's reform was opening to FDI, but up until today it has maintained a positive list system that permits FDI in certain favored sectors and restricts it in others (more on this below). For the balance of payments, FDI provided a modest, steady inflow during the 1990s. Other parts of the capital account were kept severely closed, especially capital outflows. During the 1990s, China accumulated reserves at a steady but unspectacular rate. Its reserves provided an asset to match the FDI liabilities. Throughout the forty years of reform, China was only a net debtor for a very short period, 1986–1989.[8] For the whole reform period, China's current account balance averaged just above 2 percent.

In the early years of reform, China had a multiple currency system in which foreign exchange certificates (FEC) were required for certain

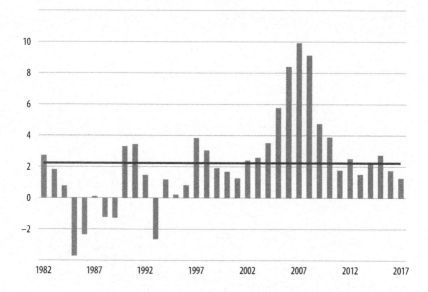

FIGURE 5-3   China's current account balance (% of GDP)
(Source: World Development Indicators, the World Bank)

international transactions. FEC were denominated in yuan but traded at a premium to domestic currency. This was an awkward system, subject to inefficiency and corruption. The currency was unified, and the unified rate devalued in 1994. Then began a long period in which the currency was pegged to the U.S. dollar at the rate of 8.3:1. A pegged exchange rate is a reasonable choice for a poor developing country trying to establish macroeconomic stability and credibility with foreign partners and the domestic audience alike. While China was pegged to the dollar, it had substantial trade with other Asian partners, such as Japan, Taiwan, and South Korea, plus Europe. And these areas all had currencies that fluctuated against the dollar.

In examining whether a currency level is appropriate or not, it makes sense to look at the trade-weighted, or "effective," exchange rate. Figure 5-4 shows the evolution of China's effective exchange rate from 1994 to today. While pegging to the dollar in 1994 provided stability in the yuan in one sense, ironically, it resulted in fairly rapid appreciation of the effective rate between 1994 and 1998. It turns out that this was an appropriate path for China, because the country had commenced its rapid productivity growth in tradables. The problem with a fixed exchange rate in an economy

FIGURE 5-4　China's effective exchange rate
(Index, 2010 = 100)
(Source: Bank for International Settlements)

with rapid productivity growth is that the country becomes competitive in more and more sectors and starts to run a trade surplus. China avoided this initially, as the dollar was appreciating from 1994 to 1998. However, after 2001 the dollar began to depreciate, and China chose to follow it down. It can be seen in figure 5-4 that China's effective exchange rate depreciated 20 percent between 2002 and 2005.

It was shortly after this that China started to run large current account surpluses, nearly 6 percent of GDP in 2005, rising to nearly 10 percent in 2007. There was a certain amount of pride in China at this export prowess in the mid-2000s, but large trade surpluses are not necessarily a good thing for a developing country. And, of course, they have to be matched by someone else's deficit, leading to trade friction and questions about sustainability.

China had the very large trade surpluses for only four years, 2005–2008, and it is a mistake to think that it was the result only of exchange rate undervaluation. But the exchange rate was crucial, because it had so many spillover effects in other areas. To maintain the 8.3:1 peg against the U.S. dollar, in the face of rising trade surpluses, the central bank had to buy excess dollars and keep them as reserves. The reserves grew to $4 trillion. These are low-return assets and having more than a country needs for stability has real costs. The central bank was basically borrowing from Chinese people in domestic currency and lending to the U.S. treasury at low interest rates. It was clear that the currency would eventually have to appreciate, so the central bank was setting itself up for capital losses. It was also reluctant to raise Chinese interest rates to levels that would have been appropriate for a fast-growing developing country, because that would complicate its sterilization task. So, the effort to maintain the peg led to financial repression in China that encouraged investment and a housing boom at the expense of consumption.

The undervalued exchange rate was a great stimulus to the export sector. But it created inflationary pressure on the prices of nontradables and on assets, especially housing. In the heyday of the surplus, 2005–2008, China kept its fiscal policy very tight, and put off needed expenditures in health, education, and infrastructure. That was the real cost of the trade surplus. China was making a lot of stuff for Americans and getting paid with IOUs, while underspending on its own domestic needs.

The costs of undervaluation were becoming apparent by 2005, and China moved off the peg that year. It began a period of gradual appreciation against the dollar. Referring to the effective exchange rate in figure 5-4, it started to appreciate in 2005 and appreciated steadily until 2015. Over that decade it appreciated more than 50 percent. This, apparently, corrected the earlier undervaluation and accounted for ongoing productivity growth. China's trade surplus dropped during the global financial crisis, and then continued to drop further, reaching 1.4 percent of GDP in 2017 and 0.4 percent in 2018. The IMF and most economists consider it fairly valued, as it is keeping any trade imbalance at a very modest level.

The fluctuations in the effective exchange rate in the past few years are interesting. Starting in 2014, the U.S. dollar began appreciating, probably because the U.S. was recovering faster than other advanced economies and the Fed was signaling that it would start to normalize interest rates. Initially, China followed the dollar up, and in figure 5-4 there is a sharp appreciation in 2014. But by the middle of 2015, Chinese leaders began to worry that the appreciation was too much. So they wanted to signal to the market that they were de-linking from the dollar, but they did it together with a 2 percent "mini-devaluation" of the yuan that roiled markets globally. Eventually the authorities did a better job communicating that they planned to manage the currency with respect to a basket. They managed it back down toward trend, and have kept it relatively stable for the past two years.

While China keeps the vast majority of its foreign reserves in U.S. dollars, it has become an increasingly vocal critic of a dollar-dominated global financial system. China's central bank governor, Zhou Xiaochuan, wrote an article in 2009, criticizing the dependence of the world on the dollar and launching a period in which China actively promoted the internationalization of its currency.[9]

Initially, there was steady and rapid increase in measures of internationalization, such as the yuan's share in global payments (figure 5-5). However, the growth came to an end in the middle of 2015, and since then China's share has declined modestly. Up until 2015 there was an expectation that the Chinese currency would continue to gradually appreciate, so that by itself created some incentive for agents to be willing to accept yuan.

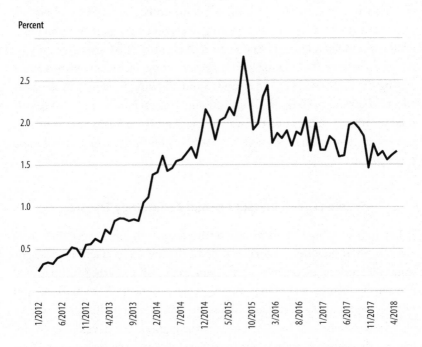

Percent

FIGURE 5-5   Renminbi's (RMB) share as a world payment currency
(Source: SWIFT RMB Tracker)

However, once the expectation of appreciation disappeared, there was not much attraction to holding renminbi.

How do we understand the stalled progress in the emergence of the yuan as a major currency? China's prospects to be the largest economy in the world in about ten years have not changed, and that is one factor influencing the internationalization of currencies. But other factors that are relevant for reserve currency status are coming increasingly into play. Eswar Prasad identifies factors relevant to reserve currency status, in addition to market size: open capital account; flexible exchange rate; macroeconomic policies; and financial market development.[10] At the moment, China has limitations on capital account openness and exchange rate flexibility that severely limit the usefulness of holding renminbi. It is not surprising that the initial enthusiasm over renminbi internationalization has waned to some extent: China is a long way from meeting the conditions to be a major reserve currency country.

While the yuan is far away from being a major international currency, China in 2016 did get it included in the IMF's basket currency, the "special drawing right," along with the big four: dollar, euro, yen, and pound. This was a reasonable, forward-looking decision on the part of Fund management and shareholders. The yuan will eventually be a significant currency. To be included, China had to agree to some technical reforms about setting the daily fixing of the currency and allowing foreign central banks access to various markets in China. Foreign central banks can now usefully hold yuan, and that points the way to the kinds of reforms that would be needed so that ordinary foreign investors in the future can also hold and trade yuan.

Foreign Direct Investment and Technology Transfer

A key part of China's reform was opening up to direct investment from abroad. There is ample evidence that FDI accelerates technological advance in developing countries and enhances overall growth. Multinational firms bring frontier technology, brand names, connections to markets, and management experience. Throughout the 1960s and 1970s there were a lot of restrictions on direct investment throughout the developing world, fearing that these foreign companies would dominate domestic markets and prevent the development of strong domestic firms. However, it turned out in practice that there were beneficial spillovers from MNEs to domestic firms. For example, the supply chain for China's exports of computers and electronics, illustrated in the section "Trade," is largely organized by MNEs from Japan, South Korea, and Taiwan. These firms rely on domestic suppliers; mostly private firms, in the case of China. The MNEs help upgrade the capacity of the domestic suppliers by insisting on quality control, sharing certain technology, and often providing finance. Over time, most developing countries have come to welcome FDI.

In China's case, the regime for foreign investment has gone through four phases, starting with the promulgation of the Equity Joint Venture Law in 1979.[11] This law permitted foreign investment through joint ventures, typically with state enterprises. That restriction plus regulation of foreign exchange resulted in a rather small initial flow of FDI into China, most of it coming from Hong Kong. The second stage, 1986–1991, was characterized by extending the FDI openness to more locations in China and enacting the Law on Wholly Owned Subsidiaries. This set the stage for the third period, from 1992 to 2000. Creating a legal framework for wholly owned subsidiaries, combined with more market-oriented attitudes following Deng Xiaoping's Southern Tour, ushered in a period of rapid inflow of FDI, including from the developed economies. China joining the WTO in 2001 marked the beginning of a fourth phase, in which more sectors were opened and FDI really took off (figure 5-6). FDI is depicted as negative entries because it is a financial liability for the country; China's outward direct investment (ODI) is shown as a positive item on the same graph and will be discussed in the next section.

While China's policy has been to gradually open up the economy to foreign investment, it has always retained a policy of requiring joint ventures in some key sectors. In automobiles, for example, foreign investors have to operate in fifty-fifty joint ventures with domestic firms, most of which are state enterprises. In financial services such as investment banking, the equity cap has been less than 50 percent. The aim of this restrictive policy is to build up the capacity of domestic firms. The OECD calculates an FDI restrictiveness index for its members plus key developing countries. The earliest year for the index is 1997. The first panel of figure 5-7 shows the index for China—total and some key sectors—as well as South Korea as a comparator. Keep in mind that Korea is at a much higher stage of development than China. In 1997, China and Korea were measured to be quite similar. China was slightly above 0.6 for the whole economy, on a scale in which 1 equals completely closed and 0 is completely open. Korea was modestly more open,

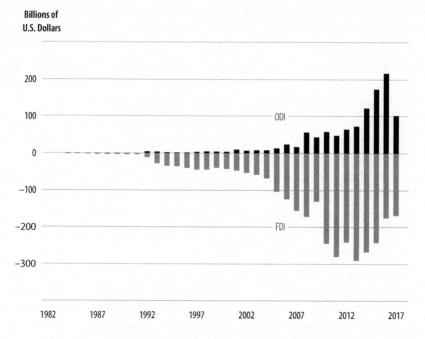

**Billions of
U.S. Dollars**

FIGURE 5-6 China's foreign direct investment (FDI) and outward direct investment (ODI)
(Source: World Development Indicators, the World Bank)

with an index slightly above 0.5. China had some completely closed sectors, such as communications and media, and some highly restricted sectors, such as transport and financial services.

By 2016, Korea had become almost completely open. For the whole economy, the index around 0.1 is similar to the OECD average. Telecom is much more open and financial services are almost completely open. China overall had become significantly more open, reaching about 0.3 on the index. China's opening occurred in steps: there was significant liberalization in preparation for joining the WTO and in the immediate aftermath of accession. Then followed a ten-year period in which there was no further reform. Finally, in the last few years, there has been further significant liberalization as well as promises for additional moves in automobiles and financial services. Thus, the story for China is mixed: it is more open than Korea twenty years ago, and China is about twenty years behind Korea in terms of development, so that is a reasonable comparison. On the other hand, the whole world has become more open to direct investment.

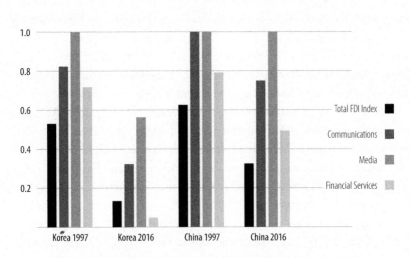

FIGURE 5-7 **FDI regulatory restrictiveness index, Korea and China, 1997 and 2016**
(Index, 1 = completely closed)
(Source: OECD FDI Regulatory Restrictiveness Index)

China's restrictiveness today is about twice the level of the other developing country members of the G20. So, China is outside the norm on FDI openness, but it has moved significantly in the right direction over time, including in the last few years.

FDI restrictiveness is very important, because it is tied to the issue of "forced technology transfer" that has become a hot-button political matter. International auto firms cannot simply produce and sell in China. They have to join a fifty-fifty joint venture and share their technology with the domestic partner. In quite a few manufacturing and service industries, foreign firms are basically training up their competitors for the future. The Chinese government does not like the adjective "forced," because the companies are making a choice to enter the China market on these terms. If they want to profit from their technology in the huge China market, then they have to share the technology and speed up their obsolescence. Many MNEs accept the bargain and figure that they can invent new technologies fast enough that they will always remain ahead of their Chinese competitors. In general, FDI in China has a high return, so the bargain is working out well for the average MNE so far. But it remains to be seen what happens in the future.

The issue of forced technology transfer coerced by China's restrictive investment policies is one of the key tensions between China and its main partners—the United States, European Union, and Japan. But there are also more general issues of intellectual property rights protection in China. Aside from sharing technology through joint ventures, many foreign companies have had their patents and brands compromised, and feel that they have poor redress through the Chinese legal system. As China has developed, foreign investment has gradually moved into higher-tech sectors and services. These are sectors in which there will be more potential disputes than in simple sectors, such as clothing and footwear or electronic assembly. A key question for China then is whether, as it develops, its legal system is keeping up.

This is not an easy question to answer, but empirically we can look at the Rule of Law index from the World Governance Database, which "captures perceptions of the extent to which agents have confidence in and abide by the rules of society, and in particular the quality of contract enforcement, property rights, the police, and the courts, as well as the likelihood of crime and violence." The index, which has a mean of zero and standard deviation of 1.0, is available for a large number of countries starting in 1996.

Figure 5-8 shows the Rule of Law index in 2016 plotted against log per capita GDP in PPP terms, for a large number of countries. China and Korea are identified. The graph also includes the data for those two countries in 1996. China in 1996 had rather poor rule of law (about half a standard deviation below the global mean); however, China was a poor country and had rule of law measured to be good for its income level. That is, it was above the regression line by about half a standard deviation. Between 1996 and 2016, China's income grew enormously, but rule of law barely improved. By 2016 China was well below the regression line, with poor rule of law for its income level. Note that Korea in 1996 was at about the same income level as China in 2016, but had much better rule of law.

So, in looking at investment openness and the related issue of property rights and rule of law, China is lagging behind global norms. Its leaders are talking about opening up more sectors of the economy to direct investment. However, if the rule of law is poor, then it is difficult to really create a level playing field in complicated sectors that require high technology (in the case of manufacturing) or complex regulation (in the case of modern services).

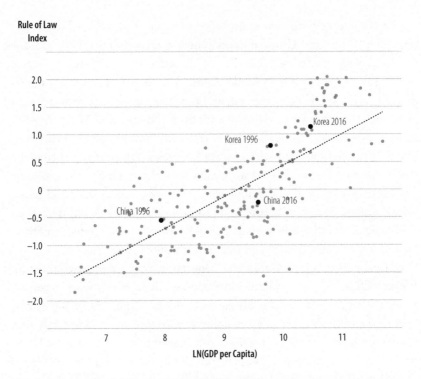

FIGURE 5-8   GDP per capita and rule of law, 2016
(Source: World Development Indicators and Worldwide Governance Indicators, the World Bank)

Outward Direct Investment and the Belt and Road Initiative

In recent years, China has become a major source of capital for the rest of the world. It was noted in Section 3 that China has generally run current account surpluses. These were small in the 1980s and 1990s, and China was not an important supplier of capital to the world. Current account surpluses were large in the mid-2000s, declining in recent years to about 2 percent of GDP. But China's GDP keeps growing, so that 2 percent now is more than $200 billion. Hence, China is in a position to provide different kinds of financing around the world. Its highest-profile effort is the Belt and Road Initiative. This is Xi Jinping's vision of providing infrastructure and connectivity along the ancient Silk Road as well as along a so-called maritime route that goes south from China, past Southeast Asia and South Asia, and on to Europe through the Suez Canal.

China is providing two main types of financing: outward direct investment (ODI) and Chinese development finance (CDF), that is, loans to developing countries primarily for infrastructure, which are largely coming from the two policy banks: China Development Bank and China EXIM Bank. ODI is commercial, and the state and private firms making these investments expect to make a profit. CDB and EXIM are referred to as policy banks in China. They borrow on domestic and international capital markets and lend with a spread, so they expect to be financially self-sufficient. The motivation for China is partly economic: the economy has excess savings and underemployed construction companies and heavy industry. Also, if infrastructure is improved in neighboring countries, then China benefits indirectly as trade expands. There is also strategic motivation as China gains friends and influence through these projects.

China's Ministry of Commerce reports data by recipient country on China's ODI. The total volume increased rapidly in recent years, reaching $200 billion in 2016, before falling back in 2017 (figure 5-6). More than half of the outflow is recorded as going to Hong Kong. It is unlikely that that is the final destination for all of this investment, so it is impossible to know where this finance is going. For CDF, the policy banks do not report detailed lending to individual countries. They do report that their overall portfolio of overseas lending was $675 billion at the end of 2016, more than twice the size of the World Bank. At the time of the Belt and Road Forum, in May 2017, they announced that as of the end of 2016, about one-third of their lending had gone to BRI countries.

A data-set on China's development finance has been compiled by A. Dreher et al. under the title AidData.[12] This data-set contains project-level information on Chinese official development finance to Africa, Asia, Europe, and Latin America from 2000 to 2014. According to AidData, China's development finance was quite modest up until the global financial crisis, after which it increased significantly. It reached a peak of $50 billion in 2009, and since then has moderated to about $40 billion per year. About one-half has gone to BRI countries in the most recent years, which is a bit higher than the aggregate figures reported by the policy banks. The data-set also has a breakdown of projects by sector. By far the two biggest areas are transport (39 percent of total financing) and power generation (32 percent). Less than 3 percent of the lending is in Chinese renminbi. Most of the lending is in dollars at variable interest rates. Most of these loans would be considered nonconcessional, as they reflect the policy banks' borrowing costs plus a spread. However, many developing countries would not be able to borrow from any other source at such attractive rates, so in that sense it is a benefit to those countries. The attraction for borrowing countries is that they get access to a large amount of financing in order to meet their serious infrastructure gaps. The projects are generally carried out by Chinese construction companies, which often bring many of their workers with them.

China's ODI is similar to Western direct investment in that it is attracted to larger markets and to natural resource wealth, as measured by natural resource rents as a share of GDP.[13] It is unlike Western investment, however, in that it is uncorrelated with a measure of property rights and rule of law. After controlling for those other variables, an indicator for the sixty-four BRI countries has a negative, insignificant coefficient.[14] The dependent variable is the stock of ODI at the end of 2015, the most recent year for which there is comprehensive, cross-country data. It probably should be no surprise that BRI has had no impact on China's direct investment, as that should be largely commercial, with much of it going to the United States and other advanced economies.

Turning to CDF, a curious thing about the cross-country allocation is that it is hard to explain it at all. Population is the main variable that has consistent explanatory power. Neither the size of GDP nor natural-resource wealth matters. Unlike China's direct investment, its development finance is not aimed at natural resource–rich countries. Political stability and rule of law are uncorrelated with the allocation. And an indicator variable for Belt and Road countries has an insignificant negative coefficient. Just looking at the raw data, 37 percent of China's financing in the 2012–2014 period went to Africa; 25 percent to maritime Asia; 14 percent to Latin America; and only 14 percent to landlocked Asia.[15] In Africa, in recent years, China has been providing about one-third of the external financing for infrastructure, which is very welcome, given the infrastructure deficit on the continent.

Some additional insight can be gained by focusing on the top twenty recipients of Chinese development finance, 2012–2014 (table 5-1). The list does include some Asian economies that are along the Belt and Road, such as Iran, Pakistan, Kazakhstan, and Indonesia. But it also includes eight African countries: Angola, Côte d'Ivoire, Ethiopia, Kenya, Nigeria, South Africa, Sudan, and Tanzania; and three Latin ones: Venezuela, Ecuador, and Argentina. Among the top twenty recipients, several have rule of law that is above the mean for developing countries—Indonesia, Sri Lanka, Kazakhstan, Ethiopia, Kenya, South Africa, and Tanzania—but others are rated very poorly on rule of law: Venezuela, Ecuador, Angola, Nigeria, Sudan, Iran, and Pakistan. This means that significant amounts of Chinese finance are going to risky environments. The fact that there is no geographic pattern to China's development finance suggests it is more demand-driven by countries that are willing to borrow than supply-driven by a Chinese master plan.

China's growing development finance raises several issues of global governance, one of which is debt sustainability. Developing countries have suffered severe external debt crises from time to time: Latin America in the 1980s, East Asia in the 1990s, and Russia in 1998 are just some of the examples. As a result of these bitter experiences, developing countries have become more aware of the issue of debt sustainability. External debt is different from domestic debt in that it has to be serviced ultimately through exports. Capital flows to developing countries go through cycles: at times, in the search for yield, global investors are willing to lend a lot at relatively low interest rates. It is attractive then to borrow externally in order to fund infrastructure. There is always a risk, however, of capital flow reversal and increases in interest rates. Chinese banks are secretive about their lending terms, but most of these loans are in dollars at flexible, commercial rates. Only about one-quarter of China's development finance, 2012–2014, is concessional enough to meet the standard of "official development assistance."

For the nonconcessional lending, as interest rates rise in New York and London, the cost of servicing loans from China will rise. The ability to service external debt also depends on the value of one's exports. Looking at the list of major borrowers from China, many are exporters of energy or minerals: Venezuela, Ecuador, South Africa, Nigeria, Angola, Iran, and Sudan, for example. Servicing debt may be reasonable at one price for exports, but become burdensome if the price falls significantly. The fall in the prices of energy and minerals in recent years is raising the specter of a new round of debt crises. The current trend of low commodity prices and rising dollar interest rates is putting the squeeze on the finances of developing countries.

Some, but not all, of the countries that have borrowed heavily from China in recent years are at risk of debt distress. The World Development Indicators include recent data on external debt relative to gross national

Country	Average annual borrowing, 2012–2014 ($US billion)	Rule of law, 2015
Pakistan	4.16	−0.79
Laos	2.74	−0.75
Ethiopia	1.85	−0.44
Venezuela	1.82	−1.99
Angola	1.65	−1.07
Belarus	1.48	-0.79
Sri Lanka	1.45	0.07
Kenya	1.29	−0.49
Côte d'Ivoire	1.25	−0.62
Ecuador	1.19	−1.03
Ukraine	1.02	−0.8
Cambodia	0.95	−0.92
Nigeria	0.94	−1.04
Argentina	0.92	−0.8
Indonesia	0.91	−0.41
Tanzania	0.86	−0.43
Kazakhstan	0.85	−0.37
Sudan	0.74	−1.18
South Africa	0.73	0.06
Iran	0.71	−0.95

Note: Average rule of law index for all developing countries is −0.48. (Source: AidData and World Governance Indicators)

TABLE 5.1   Chinese development finance. Top twenty borrowers, 2012–2014

income for most of the countries included in the database on CDF, including all of the top twenty borrowers. For these twenty countries, debt to GNI increased from 35 percent in 2008 to 50 percent in 2015. For the other seventy-seven developing countries there was a modest increase in external debt, from an average of 45 percent of GNI in 2008 to an average of 48 percent in 2015. The average level of debt for the major borrowers from China is not alarming. But the rapid increase is something of a concern. More important, the average disguises a large variation at the country level. In the last couple of years, large increases in debt, taking countries to risky levels, were experienced by Angola, Belarus, Côte d'Ivoire, Ethiopia, Kenya, South Africa, Ukraine, Venezuela, and Tanzania. A number of these countries have very poor governance, and it is not surprising that debt has not been used productively. The rise in external debt to GDP is an indicator to watch, because a strong growth impact would increase GDP and tend to keep the ratio stable, whereas a weak growth effect would show up in debt to GDP rising to unsustainable levels.

Is China violating norms of global finance? At this point, it would be hard to argue that. Of the countries that have borrowed heavily from China, several currently have IMF programs to help with unsustainable fiscal and balance of payments problems: Côte d'Ivoire, Kenya, and Ukraine.[16] Other countries that have borrowed heavily from China, on the other hand, are in good fiscal and financial shape: Kazakhstan and Indonesia would be examples.

On the issue of debt sustainability, a balanced assessment is that most of the developing countries taking advantage of Chinese finance to improve their infrastructure are in sound fiscal condition. A few have taken on excessive amounts of debt, and they have turned to the IMF for the traditional medicine of adjustment policies and emergency finance. Venezuela is the one case in which China's financing may have enabled poor economic policies to persist. But China has reduced its exposure, and it seems likely that Venezuela will go to the IMF in the end.

China in the International Economic Institutions

Along with China's rise as a trading and investing nation has come greater Chinese participation in the international economic institutions, that is, the World Trade Organization, the International Monetary Fund, and the network of Multilateral Development Banks. Is China supporting the international order or subverting it?

In the case of the WTO, China has become a very active member since joining in 2001. Between 2006 and 2015, forty-four cases—representing more than a quarter of the WTO caseload—involved China as a complainant or as a respondent. Only the United States and the European Union had more active cases over the period. Furthermore, in general, when China has lost cases, it has changed the necessary laws and regulations and complied with the ruling. Based on this, one could conclude that

China's integration into trade dispute settlement has been quite successful.

Mark Wu, however, makes a compelling case that the situation is not so rosy. China presents a number of unique challenges for the trading regime, and "since the Great Recession WTO litigation has increasingly bifurcated into an 'Established Powers versus China' dynamic."[17] Between 2009 and 2015, China-related cases accounted for 90 percent of the cases brought by the four large economies against each other. While cases among the United States, European Union, and Japan used to be common, now they increasingly line up together against China.

The problem, according to Wu, is that "China, Inc." is sui generis. "What distinguishes China, Inc.? Contradictions pervade the Chinese economy today. While one might think of the economy as state-dominated, private enterprises drive much of China's dynamic growth. In addition, economic intervention does not always flow through the state. Alongside the state is the Chinese Communist Party ("Party"), a separate political actor that plays an active role in the management of state-owned enterprises ("SOEs"). The economy embraces market-oriented dynamics, yet it is not strictly a free-market capitalist system. . . . These elements make it difficult to determine certain legal issues under WTO rules—such as whether an entity is associated with the state, or how to characterize the overall form of China's economy. These elements also raise the stakes associated with certain activities that fall outside the scope of the WTO's present jurisdiction."[18]

It is difficult, for example, for the WTO to deal with the investment restrictions, forced technology transfer, and IP theft discussed in Section 4. The established powers would like to see the WTO evolve to handle these issues, but China would have to consent. Can the established powers and China negotiate reform of the WTO or separate side agreements? Without this kind of evolution, there is a risk that the WTO will become increasingly irrelevant and that the established powers plus China will feel free to pursue unilateral measures that they deem necessary to address "unfair trade."

China's relationship with the IMF has undergone an interesting transformation. Beijing took over the China seat at the IMF and the World Bank in 1980 and kept a low profile at these institutions for the next decade. At the time of the Asian financial crisis in 1997, China was one of the many vocal Asian critics that believed IMF assistance in the crisis was insufficient and IMF conditionality unnecessarily strict and intrusive. China did not need to borrow and suffer this indignity directly, but it voiced concerns similar to those of the affected countries—Thailand, Indonesia, South Korea. By the mid-2000s, China's relationship with the IMF became even more antagonistic. As China's currency became undervalued in the mid-2000s and its current account surplus ballooned toward 10 percent of GDP, the U.S. Treasury put pressure on the IMF to highlight the issue of global imbalances and currency misalignment. There were several years in the mid-2000s, during which the IMF team was not welcome in Beijing to carry out its annual Article IV review of macroeconomic policies.

Given that background, it is remarkable how the China-IMF relationship has subsequently evolved. Quota reform in the IMF, pushed by the United States, shifted shares toward emerging markets, especially China, primarily at the expense of Europe. China became the number three shareholder in the IMF and, given agreements on quota evolution, it will emerge before long as number two. China now has a lock on one of the senior positions (deputy managing director) in the Fund. The global financial crisis gave rise to a series of very large IMF bailout packages for European economies. Even with the quota increase, the IMF did not have sufficient resources. So, the IMF turned to surplus countries that were willing to contribute to its New Arrangements to Borrow (NAB), which was essentially lending in parallel with IMF core resources. This was appealing to China in that it was a use of reserves alternative to simply buying Treasury bonds.

Given China's growing role in the Fund, it was natural for it to include the yuan in its special drawing right when the SDR underwent its usual periodic review in 2016. As China becomes an increasingly important creditor in the world, it is natural for it to deepen its relationship with the IMF, the international institution that oversees international capital flows and comes in with rescue programs when sovereign borrowers are unable to pay their debts.

An interesting recent development is that China is providing $50 million to fund a China-IMF Capacity Development Center.[19] This virtual center will be under IMF administration, will be anchored in Beijing, and will offer courses both inside and outside China on core Fund topics. Roughly half the participants will be Chinese officials, and half, officials from other developing countries, including countries along the Belt and Road Initiative. One of the important topics that will be emphasized initially is debt-sustainability analysis. The People's Bank of China is the driving force behind this initiative and it represents China in MDBs such as the African Development Bank and the Inter-American Development Bank, which is curious. PBC naturally has more awareness of this issue than other Chinese agencies and wants the knowledge to be spread within China and to strengthen the capacity of other developing countries. In the end, it is the governments of borrowing countries that need to demonstrate discipline and far-sightedness.

Turning to the multilateral development banks, China has had a long and positive relationship with the World Bank, starting with a famous meeting between Deng Xiaoping and Robert McNamara in 1980. Deng told McNamara that China would modernize with or without World Bank assistance, but it would do so more rapidly with the assistance. For many years, China was the largest client of the Bank in terms of loan amount and number of projects. The Bank started with infrastructure projects in power and transport and moved on to more complicated issues such as watershed management, urban water supply and sanitation, reforestation, and urban transport.

The relationship had some bumps along the way, notably when the Bank yielded to international pressure and canceled a poverty project in Western China because it involved resettlement of Tibetans.[20] Chinese officials came to feel that the Bank was getting away from its original mandate to fund infrastructure and growth and getting bogged down in a lot of trendy new issues. It was also getting bogged down in complex rules about environmental and social aspects of infrastructure projects, so much so that many clients stopped coming to the Bank for infrastructure help. In the early years of the Bank, infrastructure accounted for 70 percent of lending; that figure has dropped to about 30 percent in recent years. Developing countries have become frustrated with the complex regulations and long delays involved in Bank infrastructure projects.[21]

Around the time of the GFC, an international commission under the chairmanship of Ernesto Zedillo examined the performance of the World Bank and the other MDBs and made recommendations for modernizing them.[22] This commission had good representation from the developing world (including Zhou Xiaochuan from China) and made a series of practical recommendations: increase the voting shares of developing countries to reflect their growing weight in the world economy; abolish the resident board as an expensive anachronism, given modern technology; increase the lending capacity of the MDBs to meet growing developing-world needs; reestablish the focus on infrastructure and growth; and streamline the implementation of environmental and social safeguards in order to speed up project implementation.

China generally shared these criticisms of the World Bank and its sister institutions such as the Asian Development Bank. In the wake of the Zedillo report, however, there was no meaningful reform. This frustration with lack of reform in the World Bank, combined with a general dissatisfaction with the United States–led global financial system, influenced China to launch a new development bank. Alex He notes: "Indeed, China and other emerging powers have criticized the World Bank and the IMF for their inefficient and over-supervised processes of granting loans. The current gap between the demands for infrastructure investment and available investment from existing international financing organizations in developing countries creates an opportunity for emerging economies to establish a new type of bank with a directed focus in this area."[23] The new bank is also a way for China to put its excess savings to use through a multilateral format, to complement (and perhaps provide some competition with) its bilateral efforts. While the bulk of the current funding for BRI described in the previous section comes from the existing policy banks, in the future the Asian Infrastructure Investment Bank (AIIB) will also play a role.

The charter of the AIIB follows very much in the spirit of the charters of the World Bank and ADB, but it also incorporates virtually all of the Zedillo report recommendations: majority ownership by the developing world, no resident board, authority to lend more from a given capital base, a focus on infrastructure and growth, and environmental and social guidelines that should be implemented "in proportion to the risk" (per AIIB website).

The issue of environmental and social safeguards was a key factor in the brouhaha around the founding of the new bank. The United States and Japan opposed the effort primarily due to concerns over governance, including the issue of environmental and social safeguards. Other major Western nations, such as the United Kingdom, Germany, France, and Australia, all chose to fight these battles from the inside. AIIB has promulgated environmental and social policies that, on paper, are similar to the principles embodied in World Bank safeguards: environmental and social assessments to analyze risks; public disclosure of key information in a timely manner; consultation with affected parties; and decision-making that incorporates these risks. The AIIB approach, however, differs from that of the World Bank by avoiding detailed prescriptions for how to manage the process. The World Bank's regulations—literally hundreds of pages—inevitably make implementation slow and bureaucratic.

AIIB's leadership hopes that the bank can meet international standards but be more time- and cost-effective. This is largely a matter of implementation, and it will take time and experience on the ground to see if the effort is a success. In its first two years of operation, AIIB lent $4.4 billion to twelve different countries, with two-thirds of its projects co-financed with the World Bank or regional development banks. India was the largest borrower. It will take time for AIIB to build up a portfolio of projects that it developed on its own. If AIIB can meet environmental standards more efficiently, that would be a very positive innovation. If AIIB's activities can put pressure on the World Bank and the regional development banks to streamline their procedures and speed up their infrastructure projects, then this would be a positive change to the global system that emanated from China.

Conclusions

Has engaging China economically and integrating it into international economic institutions succeeded? The argument for "yes" would be as follows: China, the most populous country in the world, has emerged as the largest economy in PPP terms; the largest trading nation; and, before long, the largest net creditor. Thus, its strong integration into the world economy is undeniable. Its export prowess up to now has relied mainly on labor-intensive activities, while it imports goods and services intensive in technology, high skills, and natural resources. Given that China is so large, this integration has put downward pressure on wages for semi-skilled labor and upward pressure on returns to capital, including knowledge stocks, skills, and natural resources. Given that so many developing countries depend on the export of natural resources, China's demand has spurred growth throughout the developing world, especially Africa in the past fifteen years. China's emergence has coincided with a strong period of global growth and unprecedented poverty reduction both in China and elsewhere in the developing world.

In rich countries, owners of capital, skills, and natural resources have benefited from the China shock, whereas semi-skilled workers have seen the disappearance of manufacturing jobs and downward pressure on their wages. All of these distributional effects were predictable. Some rich countries, particularly in Northern Europe, have spread the benefits widely through their safety nets and retraining programs. In the United States, on the other hand, public policy has generally reinforced rather than counteracted the market trends toward higher inequality.

In terms of direct investment, China has opened up sufficiently to be the largest developing country recipient of FDI and number two overall, after the United States. MNEs in China are generally highly profitable and reinvest their retained earnings, a sign that they find the investment climate—while not ideal—sufficiently good to keep them investing. MNEs account for a majority of China's exports. But the largest share of value added in the exports come from China's domestic private sector. This is consistent with the fact that most GDP in China now comes from the private sector.

In recent years, China has emerged as a major source of capital in the world, with its direct investment primarily going to the United States and other advanced economies. Aside from direct investment, China lends about $50 billion per year to other developing countries to finance their infrastructure. While this is branded as the "Belt and Road Initiative," it is, in fact, global, with more financing going to Africa than to Asia.

In his keynote address at the 2018 Boao Forum, President Xi Jinping argued that China is a supporter, not a subverter, of the international economic order. China has had a long and productive relationship with the World Bank, has emerged as a key player in and financer of the IMF, and engages actively in dispute settlement within the WTO.

Against these positive outcomes, what would be the argument that engagement has failed? The key to this argument is that there is still a large state-owned enterprise sector in China. It may not have much involvement in trade, but it is a major distortion. Furthermore, the Communist Party has its fingers in all significant private enterprises, raising questions as to whether they truly behave as private firms or not. Overall, property rights and rule of law have not progressed in China as would be expected in a rapidly developing market economy. China maintains an active industrial policy and, in particular, has identified ten frontier industries that it intends to dominate by 2025. It restricts investment in some of these industries in order to attract foreign technology on favorable terms. It plans to subsidize their development through its state-owned banking system. Most of these practices will be difficult to discipline through the WTO.

China's outward investment deviates from global norms in several dimensions. It controls outward direct investment through an approval process that favors state enterprises trying to buy high-tech firms in the West, in the very sectors that China keeps closed. Its development finance for infrastructure is largely welcomed by other developing countries, but it lacks transparency, is carried out on commercial terms, and risks precipitating a new round of Third World debt crises.

What makes an overall assessment difficult is that it requires some speculation about how things will evolve in the future. I am inclined to say that the weight of the evidence (around 70 percent) favors the view that engagement has been and will remain an effective strategy. In thinking about the future, I am skeptical that China's industrial policy will be terribly successful. Most of China's success up to now has come from MNEs and the domestic private sector. Favorable policies for SOEs are mostly going to be a waste. China will probably have some successes, and the whole world benefits from those. But the idea that China will dominate all the high-tech industries does not seem plausible. As China pursues its industrial policy, it will find that certain measures are WTO inconsistent and likely will adjust. I expect that over time China will continue to gradually become more open.

I also expect China to become more transparent in its overseas lending. China recently established an office under the State Council to coordinate its development cooperation. This is a positive step in the direction of how other countries manage development finance. Once there is an agency in charge, it is natural for it to issue regular reports and to coordinate with other international sources of finance. There is always some speculation that China will set up an "alternative set of international institutions." However, this would be very difficult, and it is not at all clear why China would want to do so. The existing institutions work well, and China has growing influence within them. China may very well want some changes that the United States opposes, but if anyone thought that China would simply accept U.S.-dominated institutions, that would have been the height of naiveté.

Notes

1. Richard S. Eckaus, "China," in Padma Desai, ed., *Going Global: Transition from Plan to Market in the World Economy* (Cambridge, Massachusetts: MIT Press, 1997), 415–438.

2. Ezra F. Vogel, *Deng Xiaoping and the Transformation of China* (Cambridge, Massachusetts: Belknap Press of Harvard University Press, 2011), 398.

3. People's Republic of China State Council, "China's Foreign Trade," 2018 (http://english.gov.cn/archive/white_paper/2014/08/23/content_28147498 3043184.htm).

4. Zhihong Zhang, "Rural Industrialization in China: From Backyard Furnaces to Township and Village Enterprises," *East Asia: An International Quarterly,* vol. 17, no. 3 (1999), 61.

5. See chapter 6 by Yukon Huang.

6. D. Dollar, J. Reis, and Z. Wang, eds., *Measuring and Analyzing the Impact of GVCs on Economic Development* (Washington, DC: World Bank, 2017).

7. Nicholas R. Lardy, *Markets over Mao: The Rise of Private Business in China* (Washington, DC: Peterson Institute for International Economics, 2014).

8. Philip R. Lane and Gian Maria Milesi-Ferretti, "The External Wealth of Nations Mark II: Revised and Extended Estimates of Foreign Assets and Liabilities, 1970–2004," *Journal of International Economics,* vol. 73, no. 2 (2007), 223–250.

9. Zhou Xiaochuan, "Reform the International Monetary System," *People's Bank of China official website,* March 23, 2009 (www.pbc.gov.cn/english/130724/2842945/index.html).

10. Eswar Prasad, "Global Ramification of the Renminbi's Ascendance," in Barry Eichengreen and Masahiro Kawai, eds., *Renminbi Internationalization: Achievements, Prospects, and Challenges* (Washington, DC: Brookings Institution Press, 2015), 85–110.

11. Jing Chen and Yuhua Song, "FDI in China: Institutional Evolution and Its Impact on Different Sources," *Proceedings of the 15th Annual Conference of the Association for Chinese Economics Studies Australia,* 2003.

12. A. Dreher, A. Fuchs, B. Parks, A. M. Strange, and M. J. Tierney, *Aid, China, and Growth: Evidence from a New Global Development Finance Dataset, AidData Working Paper #46* (Williamsburg, Virginia: AidData, 2017).

13. David Dollar, "Is China's Development Finance a Challenge to the International Order?" *Asian Economic Policy Review,* vol. 13, no. 2 (2018), 283–298.

14. The Belt and Road countries are identified by the Hong Kong Trade Development Council, 2017, *The Belt and Road Initiative: Country Profiles.*

15. Dollar, "Is China's Development Finance a Challenge?"

16. International Monetary Fund (IMF) (2017). IMF Lending Arrangements as of July 31, 2017.

17. Mark Wu, "The 'China, Inc.' Challenge to Global Trade Governance," *Harvard International Law Journal,* vol. 57, no. 2 (Spring 2016), 264.

18. Wu, "The 'China, Inc.' Challenge," 265.

19. IMF, "*IMF and the People's Bank of China Establish a New Center for Modernizing Economic Policies and Institutions,*" May 14, 2017.

20. Sebastian Mallaby, *The World's Banker: A Story of Failed States, Financial Crises, and the Wealth and Poverty of Nations* (New York, New York: Penguin Press, 2004). Chapter 10 has a good description of this incident.

21. Chris Humphrey, "Challenges and Opportunities for Multilateral Development Banks in 21st Century Infrastructure Finance," *Intergovernmental Group of Twenty-Four,* June 2015.

22. Ernesto Zedillo, "Reempowering the World Bank for the 21st Century: Report of the High-Level Commission on Modernization of World Bank Group Governance," *World Bank Group,* 2009.

23. Alex He, "China in the International Financial System: A Study of the NDB and the AIIB," *CIGI Papers, No. 106,* June 2016, 3–4.

SIX

China's Emergence as a Trading Power and Tensions with the West

YUKON HUANG

China's near double-digit GDP growth over the past four decades is unprecedented in economic history. The global implications became self-evident when China supplanted the United States in 2015 as both the world's largest trading nation and largest economy in purchasing-power terms. China's economic successes, however, are not universally seen as a blessing. Its emergence as a major source of low-cost manufactured goods has benefited consumers worldwide and supported a protracted period of global expansion in the new millennium. But the speed and magnitude of China's emergence spurred a debate about its role in driving global macroimbalances in the prelude to the 2008 international financial crisis and, more recently, as a threat to the technological superiority of the West.

This chapter analyzes the unique geo-economic and institutional factors that led to China becoming a major trading power. The geo-economic story lies in Deng Xiaoping's strategy to concentrate export-oriented industrialization along China's coast, while the institutional transformation involves a multi-decade process to create a more market-driven trade regime. This is followed by an assessment of China's impact on global trade patterns and how this led to trade, investment, and technology tensions with the United States and Europe. These tensions are based partly on misperceptions that have been around for decades, but they also reflect legitimate grievances. As such, these are not likely to be transitory concerns but systemic issues that will affect United States–China economic relations for years to come with ramifications not just for Europe but also for the global trading system.

Three Phases in the Evolution of China's Trade Regime

In terms of outcomes, China's emergence as a powerful trading nation can be broken down into three phases delineated by the share of its trade to GDP (see figure 6-1). The first phase (1980–1990) begins with Deng Xiaoping's opening up the economy and is marked institutionally by the dismantling of China's centrally planned trade system, and spatially by a concerted effort to establish export-oriented industries along China's coastal provinces. Foreign direct investment (FDI) brought in the much-needed foreign exchange, managerial expertise, and marketing links with the West to begin reshaping its economy. At the outset, trade amounted to only 15 percent of GDP, but by 1990, its share had risen to nearly 30 percent, which is more typical of large countries.

The second phase (1990–2000) is marked by massive infrastructure investments, initially along the coast and then in the interior, to connect China with external and internal markets, and by trade liberalization to secure WTO membership. This pushed the share of trade to GDP to 40 percent by the turn of the century.

The third phase (2000–2018) begins with China gaining membership in the WTO in 2001, providing it with ready access to Western markets. Drawing on its enhanced industrial capacity, this allowed China to

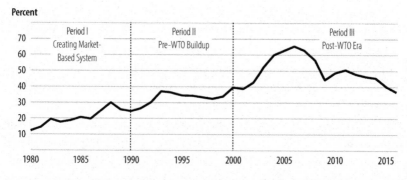

FIGURE 6-1 Evolution of China's trade regime. Total trade as a share of GDP, 1980–2015. (Source: World Bank WDI)

become the center of the East Asian production sharing network. Trade volumes soared, with the ratio of trade to GDP rising sharply from 40 percent to nearly 70 percent of GDP on the eve of the global financial crisis before falling below 40 percent by 2015 with the worldwide slowdown in trade and collapse in commodity prices. This period concludes with the onset of trade and investment tensions with the United States, which many see leading to a possible global trade war.

The two overview chapters provide insights into the reforms that fed into China's rise, which are characterized by Barry Naughton as "enlivening the economy" and David Dollar as moving to the global norms of trade and finance. In contrast, the public often perceives China's success in promoting exports less positively, in alluding to its abundance of cheap labor and alleged undervalued exchange rates and state-supported subsidies. This chapter incorporates into the discussion the importance of policies to promote agglomeration economies and specialization along the coastal provinces and related institutional reforms. China's emergence as an export-oriented manufacturing power was facilitated by a much-welcomed at the time integration into an international financial system created by the United States and Europe. But, ironically, many in the West now see China as having taken unfair advantage of this system.

Deng Xiaoping Reshapes China's Economic Geography

Deng Xiaoping is seen as a visionary who transformed China's economic landscape, but he can also be described as the consummate "unbalanced" reformer, regarding the spatial consequences of his opening-up strategy. He deliberately promoted the coastal region to give China the advantages needed to become globally competitive.

His strategy coincidentally followed the principles underpinning two Nobel Prize–winning growth models that help explain how spatial factors can alter a country's development path and promote trade.[1] One was W. Arthur Lewis's model of economic development with unlimited supplies of labor. Put simply, the Lewis model shows how the transfer of "surplus" labor from rural activities to urban, export-oriented industries can lead to higher productivity, increased investment, and sustained rapid growth. The other was Paul Krugman's principles of the "new economic geography," which showed how the concentration of labor and economic activities in urban areas could generate "agglomeration economies" or the additional productivity gains that come from specialization and economies of scale to promote trade.[2]

Deng's policies transformed China into the world's most efficient assembler cum exporter of a wide range of manufactured goods. He foresaw that the benefits would initially be concentrated along the coast, but over time spread to the interior. Thus, he warned the Chinese people that the priority initially had to be on developing the coast and not the interior, where the bulk of the population lived. But he also predicted that there would eventually be a turning point when the transformation would reverse itself, which, indeed, has been the process unfolding in recent years.

Deng's "open-door policy" provided the incentives for a surge in FDI. This was supported by a strategy of "big inputs, big exports" by importing components and raw materials to stimulate assembly trade. Foreign trade and investment provided the coast not only with capital but also advanced technology and management expertise. With the natural advantages from geographical location supported by preferential policies, major commercial centers in the eastern region took off, while the western region lagged behind as the periphery.

When China initiated its reform process, it was desperately short of foreign exchange but reluctant to borrow from the West. Instead, its industrial capacity was developed mainly through FDI in the Special Economic Zones (SEZs) along its coastal borders and a more liberal regulatory regime, as noted in Xiaojun Li's chapter. Enterprises in those zones enjoyed tax exemptions as well as better infrastructure and often better government services. In 1980, the first SEZs were established in four coastal cities and then in the provinces of Guangdong and Fujian, followed by fourteen coastal cities, the major deltas, and another one hundred and forty coastal cities and counties before going nationwide. Meanwhile, foreign-invested enterprises outside SEZs enjoyed more advantages over domestic enterprises, including concessional tax rates and lower prices for land. Worth noting is that much of China's success in exports is due to foreign-invested firms, whose share in exports rose from 1 percent in 1985 to more than 50 percent today.[3]

Utilized FDI for the two decades leading up to 2000 totaled $308 billion, of which Asia accounted for nearly 80 percent of the accumulated total, compared with 16 percent between the European Union and the United States.[4] Overseas Chinese were able to operate more comfortably than Westerners within a system where the rules were opaque and personal relationships essential to deal-making, and they handled much of the financing and relationship-building. Western multilaterals focused on design and distribution to consumers at home. This pattern has continued, since most of the profits come from marketing rather than from production, which is vulnerable to cost pressures and low profit margins. The emphasis for most of this period was on merchandise exports; only decades later was there a more concerted effort to promote services.

China's expansion of transportation and communication networks, initially along the coast and then gradually inland, sharply reduced the effective distances between major commercial centers internally and externally with global markets. Large amounts, by global standards, were spent over the past several decades on transport infrastructure. Rapid urbanization was a result of this process, as agrarian workers were attracted to jobs in the export-oriented industries. This was one of the more significant "enlivening" measures noted in Barry Naughton's chapter. With urban wages several multiples of what could be earned in agriculture, this spawned a huge migrant labor population of around 250 million, residing mostly in the major commercial cities. Market integration encouraged specialization and economies of scale, contributing to increases in productivity and surging profitability. This led to an exceptional concentration of globalized industries along the coast.[5]

China's Trade Regime: Institutional Evolution

The structural and geographic shifts in production were accompanied by a gradual transformation in China's trade regime. The first two phases (1980–1990) and (1990–2000) cover initially the transformation to a more market-based trade regime and later liberalization to achieve WTO membership. The overall period was marked by policies designed to promote both heavy industries and labor-intensive, export-oriented industries such as textiles. The third phase from 2001 onward focused initially on fulfilling WTO commitments and support for broader trade liberalization. But, in quick succession, China's policy-makers had to deal with ballooning trade surpluses in the mid-2000s that threatened global macro-stability, a financial crisis in 2007–2008 that led to recessions in the West, a prolonged growth slowdown at home, and, in 2018, the threat of a major trade war with the United States.

Transforming the Trade Regime to Join WTO (Phases I and II)

In the first phase, beginning in 1980, foreign trade management shifted from being the exclusive responsibility of a dozen specialized companies to being available to all trading companies. Thousands of corporations became eligible to trade, many of them sanctioned by local, not central, authorities.[6] State plans setting procurement targets were gradually reduced and then eliminated by the late 1980s. The plan was replaced by import licensing, which was relaxed as the foreign exchange constraint was eased. Export promotion measures (export tax rebates, subsidies, foreign exchange retention quotas, and a multiple exchange rates system) were put in place but their roles diminished over time.

In the second phase, with the increasing efficiency of the economy, liberalization measures were launched in the early 1990s to reduce tariff rates and scale back quotas and licenses. However, the level of trade protection was still high—the average applied tariff rate was 43 percent in 1992 compared with 56 percent in 1980, and the coverage ratio of nontariff barriers was 51 percent.[7]

The announcement that China would establish a "socialist market economy" in 1992 provided the basis for more market-oriented economic reforms, including trade reforms to meet the GATT guidelines at that time and later WTO accession conditions. In 1994, the Foreign Trade Law laid out the legal foundation for a more modern Chinese trade policy regime and paved the way for tariff reductions and reforms to the exchange rate system.

The second leg of China's opening up was the gradual reforms in the exchange rate regime. Initially, the Bank of China was the only bank that was allowed to conduct foreign currency business. By 1986, all domestic banks were allowed to do so. Initially, domestic firms had to surrender all their foreign exchange, but over time retention quotas were established, which allowed them to import products with prior approval. The share of foreign exchange retention was gradually increased and then abolished by the end of 1993. A dual exchange rate was used to encourage firms to earn foreign exchange. After unification, the official rate was gradually allowed to increase to 8.27 in 1997 and then pegged to the U.S. dollar (and, as discussed later, allowed to appreciate gradually from 2005 for several years before moving to a managed float pegged to a basket of currencies).

There are three noteworthy features of this initial two-decade period of liberalization. First, as David Dollar's chapter notes, China merely caught up with global norms following its long period of isolation. Second, some of this explosive growth in trade volumes was deceptive, since about half of China's trade was processing-related (assembly of imported parts for export as finished products). And third, while China's integration with the rest of the world was remarkably swift, its evolution left China with a complex and sometimes conflicting set of policies administered by numerous agencies.

Premier Zhu Rongji drove the initiative to join the WTO in Phase II, which Barry Naughton has characterized as the seventh and last of China's enlivening measures. He realized that China's rapid growth provided the basis for popular support for further trade liberalization. Principal among these was removing protective barriers in agriculture. This was possible because rapid expansion in urban employment opportunities mitigated the pressures from rural interests against reducing protection for agriculture.

Negotiations for China's accession to the WTO took more than fifteen years to complete, and membership required agreeing to a more burdensome set of "WTO-plus" obligations than for other countries.[8] Chinese officials had argued that, as a developing country, China should be allowed to enter under more flexible terms.[9] Agreement was reached that required China to make extensive reductions in various trade and investment barriers, while allowing it to maintain some level of protection for a transitional period for some sectors.

Among the many requirements, China was asked to reduce the average tariff for industrial goods from 17 percent to 8.9 percent, limit subsidies for agriculture, provide nondiscriminatory treatment to all WTO members, adhere to basic WTO standards on IPR protection, and open its banking system to foreign institutions.[10] Overall, WTO membership led to major reductions in tariff and nontariff trade barriers (see table 6-1).

The run-up to the WTO accession in December 2001 saw a major reduction in tariffs as well as other barriers, with average tariffs falling from more than 40 percent to less than 15 percent at accession. Eliminating the remaining barriers led to a remarkable change in the degree of openness of the economy.

As indicated in figure 6-2, both exports and imports surged from the late 1990s onward, but a significant trade surplus only began to surface around 2004–2005. Thus, the process is more accurately described as trade rather than export-led in its early phases, which later evolved into huge

Import Coverage of Nontariff Barriers (%)

Barrier	1996	2001
Licenses and quotas	18.5	12.8
Tendering	7.4	2.7
Licensing only	2.2	0.5
State trading	11.0	9.5
Designated trading	7.3	6.2
Any nonstaff barriers	32.5	21.6
No nonstaff barriers	67.5	78.4
Total	100	100

Average Statutory Tariff Rates (%)

Year	Simple	Weighted
1992	42.9	40.6
1993	39.9	38.4
1994	36.3	35.5
1996	23.6	22.6
1997	17.6	18.2
1998	17.5	18.7
1999	17.2	14.2
2000	17.0	14.1
2001	16.6	12.0
After accession	9.8	6.8

TABLE 6-1   WTO tariff and nontariff adjustments
(Source: China and the WTO, World Bank, 2004)

trade surpluses (as indicated in the widening gap in figure 6-2) driven by a combination of expansionary monetary and fiscal policies in the West and a surge in savings rates in China.

Post-WTO Phase III

The third phase, beginning in the early 2000s, involved actions to meet WTO commitments and move closer to a market-oriented trade regime.[11]

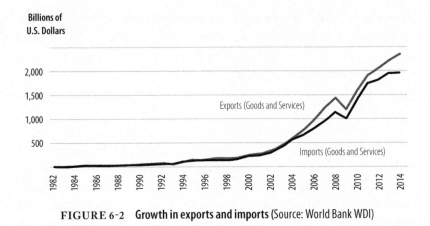

Billions of
U.S. Dollars

FIGURE 6-2 **Growth in exports and imports** (Source: World Bank WDI)

The amendment of the Foreign Trade Law in 2004 allowed all domestic enterprises and individuals to have the right to trade. A large number of trade-related laws and regulations were revised to become consistent with WTO conditions. Judicial reviews were also established to increase transparency and coherence of trade policies.

China's average tariff rates dropped from around 15 percent in 2001 to 10 percent in 2005, with manufactured goods tariffs declining from 14 to 9 percent and agricultural products decreasing from 23 percent to 15 percent. In terms of nontariff barriers, most of the import licenses, import quotas, and specific tender requirements were removed. Trade-related investment measures, including foreign exchange, local content, and export performance requirements in previous FDI laws were made consistent with the WTO agreement. China also made extensive service liberalization commitments beyond the average of developing countries.

WTO accession and the dismantling of barriers to China's exports led to a boom in its exports and a huge rise in its trade surplus. The current account surplus reached a record high of 10 percent of GDP in 2007. As noted in David Dollar's chapter, WTO accession did not prevent trade tensions from surfacing, but it did provide a means for addressing them. China became the major target of WTO dispute cases and, for most of them, it acceded to the WTO's decision and curbed export restrictions, increased export taxes, and reduced rebates on VAT on exports.

The global financial crisis led to a decline in exports and imports, causing Beijing to shift from contractionary to expansionary trade policies.

Actions were taken to promote trade financing and facilitation, loosen export controls, and enhance VAT rebates on exports. Appreciation of the yuan that began in 2005 was halted. At the same time, China continued to liberalize its trade regime, offering national treatment in the areas of government procurement for foreign companies and opening up some services sectors, such as tourism.

Despite these measures, China's pace of trade liberalization reforms has been criticized for having been too slow over the past decade, a notable example of the shift in reform emphasis as highlighted in Barry Naughton's and David Dollar's chapters. Many China observers believe that the leadership was lulled into greater apathy since the economy was booming in the years just before the global financial crisis and preoccupied with dealing with the growth slowdown afterward. In addition, many Chinese felt that they had given way too much in the WTO negotiations; hence there was a lack of consensus within government on reform priorities.

Since the crisis, the average tariff rate has not been significantly reduced. More tariff quotas were, however, abolished with only a limited number of commodities still subject to quota restrictions. Overall, China's average tariff rate was around 9 percent by 2015 with the percentage of tariffs that exceeded 15 percent falling to 14 percent from 40 in 2001.[12] While import prohibitions, restrictions, and licensing have largely been brought into compliance with WTO rules, some items have been subjected to disputes. China continues to be the target of many anti-dumping cases in recent years and is seen by some WTO claimants as using trade remedy investigations as a retaliatory tool.

In sum, over a three-decade period of reform and liberalization, China's trade regime has been brought roughly in line with global norms (see figure 6-3). The country's *de jure* trade policies are comparable to or less protectionist than those of most other developing countries. Average tariff

Dual Exchange Rate Regime	Exchange Rate	Unified and Adjustable Exchange Rate
State-Designated Trading Agencies	Management of Trade	Trade Freely Permitted
High Tariffs, Extensive Restrictions	Tariffs	Moderate to Low Tariffs and Relatively Few Restrictions

FIGURE 6-3   **Schematic evolution of China's trade regime** (Source: author's calculations)

rates are not unusually high, and most restrictions, such as quotas, have been removed.

China's tariff policy has reflected a balance between an industrial policy that shields high-tech industries from foreign competition and a social policy that protects low-income and unskilled workers. Some studies, however, suggest that China's trade policy formation continues to be dominated by ideological preferences and concerns involving national interests, especially security.[13] China's trade policies, as in other countries, have been influenced by lobbying from various interest groups, including local governments and SOEs. Not surprisingly, interests of consumers have been less influential.[14]

Global Impact of China's Trade Expansion

China's direct impact on other countries comes primarily through its emergence as the world's largest trading nation, a premier destination for foreign investment, as discussed in Xiaojun Li's chapter and, more recently, a source of surging outward capital flows, as discussed in Tom Miller's chapter. This chapter focuses on trade-related foreign investment flows that have led to tensions with the United States. These shifts have fundamentally altered China's external economic relations. All this has been part of an outward-looking process, which until recently was seen as having benefited both developing and developed countries. But rising protectionist sentiments have led to pushback against globalization in the West.

Evolving Regional and Global Trade Relations

From being largely a regional player, China is now the primary export destination for some forty countries—compared with ten a decade ago, with key relationships extending to all continents. China has long since replaced the United States as the primary export destination for most Asian economies. This shift was especially significant for ASEAN, given its centrality as a political grouping that both the United States and China have been catering to for decades.

This shift came primarily from the rise of the East Asian production network with China as the hub. China's trade surplus was modest until 2004 and then increased rapidly. Most of this increase was due to its surplus from processing trade while the balance from "ordinary" trade (trade based entirely on domestic materials or components) was minimal or negative.[15] The share of foreign content in China's processing varies significantly across product lines, averaging 50 percent, but is particularly high at around 80 percent for electronics.[16] This percentage has declined in recent years, as China began producing more of the components internally.

China's increasing economic presence has also raised concerns about its political influence. A decade and a half ago, there was widespread concern about whether China represented a threat or an opportunity for its neighbors. Most had assumed that exporting via China rather than directly to the West would result in a lower share of global trade for their respective economies. But from 2000 until 2010, China's surging imports of parts and raw materials from its East Asian partners more than compensated for any declines in their direct exports to the West. Even as China's share of global trade in parts and components soared from around 2 to 11 percent from 1993 until 2006, ASEAN's share increased from 8 to 11 percent. The share of the more developed Asian economies (South Korea, Taiwan, and Japan) remained constant but shifted to higher-value components from less profitable assembly activities.[17]

Overall, the efficiency gains from specialization and economies of scale from using China as the central hub benefited everyone in the Asia region, leading to an increase in its share of global manufacturing exports from 28 to 35 percent. As a measure of the extent of its increased competitiveness, the foreign reserves of the East Asian economies (ASEAN, China, South Korea, Taiwan, and Japan) quadrupled from around $1 trillion in 2000 to $4 trillion by the eve of the global financial crisis in 2008.

However, China's imports from ASEAN have stagnated in recent years while its exports to them have continued to increase. The net effect of shifting from a trade deficit to a trade surplus with ASEAN is that trading with China is no longer such a growth driver for those countries. These shifts have been aggravated by stagnating wages that come from being part of the regional trading network with China. From 2005 to 2014, China's wages rose by 300 percent, pushing them higher than wages in Malaysia, Thailand, and the Philippines.[18] Nevertheless, its labor productivity has been increasing commensurately until recently so that "adjusted" labor costs have been contained. Other Asian countries have had to maintain productivity-adjusted labor costs that are on par with China, with the result that their wage increases in real terms have been modest compared with China's increases of around 8 or 9 percent annually over the past decade.[19]

Post–Financial Crisis Trade Patterns

China's trade relations have been influenced by the dozen or so free-trade agreements that have been agreed upon, notably with ASEAN and recently with South Korea and Australia. A number of new agreements are being negotiated, of which the Regional Comprehensive Economic Partnership (RCEP) involving ASEAN and five other Asian countries is the most prominent. These agreements have been diverse in coverage and content and are seen as having significantly increased trade flows among the participants.[20]

From one perspective, China's trade as a share of GDP has declined to below 40 percent from its high of 70 percent a decade ago (see figure 6-1). This would seem to suggest that its position in the global trade system has been declining relative to other major economies, such as South Korea and Germany, whose ratios have hovered around 80 percent over the past decade, and the United States, whose ratio has risen over the past decade from around 20 to 30 percent.

This impression is deceptive, since China's trade volumes have continued to increase faster than those of any other major economy. But since its GDP has been growing even faster, its share of trade to GDP has been declining. China's increasing share of global trade has come largely at the expense of the shares of the United States, European Union, and Japan (see figure 6-4).

China's export composition is highly diversified. Electronics accounted for the largest share in 2016 at 34 percent, followed by other light manufactures at 25 percent and textiles at 7 percent. China's product mix has been shifting gradually from labor-intensive to more sophisticated products with appreciation of the exchange rate and rising wages. Footwear exports have leveled off, for example, but China is now dominating exports of drones. Imports are also highly diversified. Aside from the components for the production-sharing network such as machinery parts, China imports large quantities of primary products (e.g., crude oil, metals, and soybeans).

According to adjusted U.N. Comtrade data by product,[21] China's share of global exports for six major industrial categories has soared in relation to a selection of other major economies over the two decades, 1995–2015

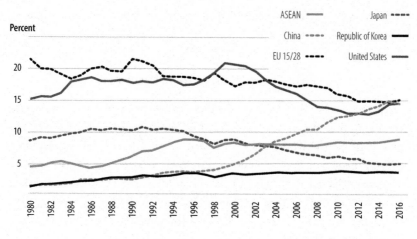

FIGURE 6-4   Shares of global trade, countries and groupings (Source: WTO)

(see figure 6-5). This is most noticeable in the declining share of the United States and Japan and, to a lesser degree, the major EU economies, with Germany as shown, but also France and the United Kingdom. The shares for ASEAN as a group, South Korea, and some other large emerging market economies such as India, Mexico, and Brazil have held their own or even increased their shares. The major category accounting for this relative change is electrical products. China's share for textiles has also remained relatively large as the composition shifted from lower-value to higher-value lines.

Drawing on OECD's database, which only goes up to 2011, China's share of services exports has also been increasing rapidly, but not as dramatically as for goods (see figure 6-6). As a share of GDP, exports of services rose from 2 percent in 1980 to more than 7 percent today. In relation to global trade, China's share rose from less than one percent in 1980 to about four percent in 2014.[22] America's global domination of services, however, remains quite strong, most noticeably in financial services.

Unlike merchandise trade, China has been running a deficit in its services trade since 1992, and this deficit has widened in recent years. A striking aspect of the structure of China's overall trade is that its share of services trade has been averaging less than 15 percent of its total trade, compared with the global average of more than 20 percent. This reflects in part the relatively smaller role that services have played thus far in Chi-

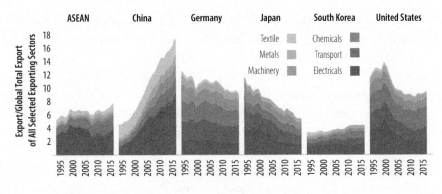

FIGURE 6-5   Share of global manufacturing exports (Source: MIT OEC)

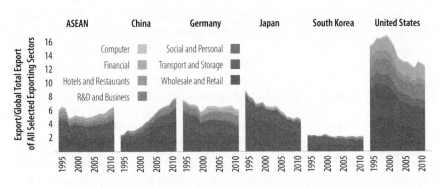

FIGURE 6-6   Share of global service exports (Source: OECD)

na's development relative to industry. This bias has been addressed in the Twelfth and Thirteenth Five-Year Plans.

Evolution of Processing Trade

Some subtle changes have emerged in the role of processing trade in recent years. Reduced demand in consumer goods in the West has led to a decline in China's imported components from its East Asian partners.[23] (See figure 6-7.) This decline in imports has been sharper than the fall-off in China's exports to the West, since China is now producing more of the needed components itself rather than importing them from others. This has occurred despite rapidly rising wages, because production has been moving inland, to lower-cost centers. This suggests that China's production is becoming more vertically integrated and self-sufficient.[24] The decline in processing trade has not just affected ASEAN countries but also China's trade with North Asia. China's trade deficit with Japan, South Korea, and Taiwan declined from more than 5 percent of GDP in 2007 to around 1 percent currently.

OECD studies have shown that China's share of global trade in value-added terms has been increasing rapidly, but not as rapidly as measured in nominal values.[25] This is a result of the significant role that processing trade plays. Electrical equipment accounts for the lion's share of the divergence between value-added and nominal data, since most of the sophisticated components and parts are produced in other countries, notably Japan, South Korea, and Taiwan, and then shipped to China for assembly. As discussed later, relying only on nominal values overstates China's share of global trade as well as its contribution to the trade deficits of the United States and Europe.

Trade Imbalances and United States–China Economic Tensions

China's persistent bilateral trade surpluses are perceived as weakening America's competitiveness and damaging employment prospects. China also has its share of critics in the European Union, with many voices accusing China of mercantilism and unfair trade practices. Charges by the Trump administration reinforce long-standing complaints from both Democrat and Republican congressional leaders about China's exchange-rate manipulation, technology theft, and IPR violations. Moreover, there

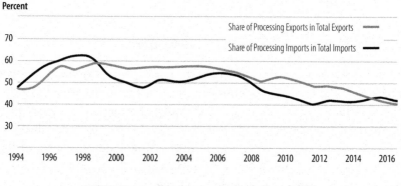

FIGURE 6-7   China's processing trade (Source: CEIC)

has been a noticeable shift in the sentiments of Western firms regarding the difficulties they now have in accessing China's domestic market.[26] This is occurring despite China being ranked consistently as a highly attractive foreign investment destination—second only to the United States. All this has led to calls about "reciprocity"—that foreign firms operating in China should be treated the same way that Chinese and foreign firms are being treated in the United States. As discussed later, all this has fed into punitive actions toward China (as well as other nations), and together with retaliatory measures has generated what many call an emerging trade war.

Geo-Structural Trade Patterns

The geo-structural nature of China's trade relationships plays into these trade frictions with the West. As seen in figure 6-8, after WTO membership, China began to run large trade surpluses with the United States and Europe, although Europe's deficits moderated after its budget reforms and the fall in the value of the euro post-financial crisis. The size of these surpluses underpins the perception noted earlier and discussed later, that China is being blamed for lost jobs, unfair competition, and low wage-growth in the United States and Europe.

China's surpluses with the West have been offset in part with trade deficits with its Asian production-sharing partners, but the magnitude

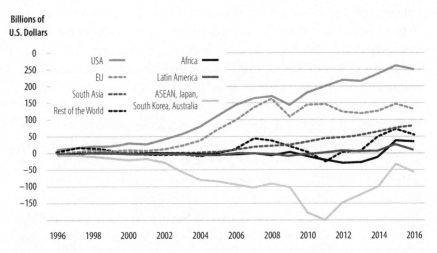

FIGURE 6-8 China's trade balances with selected country groupings (Source: UN Comtrade)

has been shrinking, as China is now producing more of the components needed at home. Depending on fluctuations in commodity prices, trade balances with other regions (notably Africa and Latin America) fluctuated between deficits and surpluses over the past two decades.

Nature of Trade and Investment Tensions

The American public generally sees China's economic rise as a threat.[27] This takes place in a general environment, where free trade is increasingly being criticized for alleged harm to specific producers. These negative sentiments provided the rationale for the Trans-Pacific Partnership (TPP) to exclude China when it was being negotiated, reinforcing the popular view that China's trade practices are unfair. President Trump has now taken this position one step further in dropping the TPP, even though many believed that it was the best option for checking China's influence in Asia. On the other hand, most economists, the business community generally, and a sizable share of the public have a more positive view of trade. They recognize, in particular, the benefits that accrue to consumers and the productivity benefits to firms even if specific industries may be adversely affected.

Some of the criticism relates to the increasing role that the state plays in China's economy, echoing a theme in Barry Naughton's chapter. This is cited as a reason why China should not be granted the market status designation needed to escape the penalties that the WTO allows for dumping. When China joined the WTO, it was deemed a nonmarket economy and thus subjected to harsher criteria in determining whether it was dumping products abroad. China had thought that it would automatically be granted market status at the end of 2016, following the original membership agreement, but both the United States and the European Union have now argued otherwise. This dispute has now been appealed to the WTO.

The dispute about market status, followed by other punitive U.S. trade actions, laid the basis for an emerging trade war in 2017–2018, which affected not just China but Europe and many other countries, including Mexico and Canada. President Trump issued an executive order in March 2017, mandating an "Omnibus Report on Significant Trade Deficits." The United States then followed up with punitive tariffs targeting solar panels, followed by tariffs for national security purposes on steel and aluminum imports, and then, in July 2018, tariffs on $50 billion of imports from

China, followed by another $200 billion based on alleged unfair practices under Section 301 of the 1974 Trade Act. China retaliated with tariffs on about $100 billion of U.S. products. A temporary truce was reached between the United States and China in December 2018, subject to negotiations to be completed within ninety days.

Approximately 9 percent of China's exports to the United States were already subjected to punitive duties, while for the rest of the world it was about 2 percent.[28] As of the winter of 2018, the threat of rounds of retaliatory actions has created uncertainties that have disrupted global markets. As discussed later, the punitive tariffs levied on China were reinforced by a subsequent tightening of investment restrictions that some see as curbing China's ambitions to upgrade its technological base.

Views on Trade Deficits

Many of the protectionist actions being advanced by the Trump administration have been criticized by experts as reflecting a misguided view on the role of trade deficits.[29] Although China's trade and investment policies have been widely perceived as unfair, the general sentiments of both economists and the business community were that punitive tariffs were not the right tool to address the problem.

Trade Deficits—Determinants and Significance

Many experts have pointed out that trade deficits in themselves are neither inherently good nor bad, economically, and no one wins in a trade war. Since a country's overall trade balance is determined by its savings and investment rates, punitive tariffs would do little to reduce America's trade deficits. Moreover, the links between trade deficits, growth, and employment are tenuous at best. The United States has been running trade deficits continuously for forty consecutive years, regardless of whether the economy was doing well or poorly and long before China even became a major economic power.

Although many observers believe China's trade surpluses are driving America's trade deficits, the trade balances of the United States and China are not directly linked. U.S. current account deficits became significant around the late 1990s and peaked around 2005 (see figure 6-9). But China's surpluses did not become globally significant until around 2005. Moreover, when China's surpluses were surging during the years 2005–

2008, America's deficits began to diminish. America's trade problems existed long before China began generating significant trade surpluses, and their respective balances have moved in contradictory directions since then. In 2017, China's current account surplus as a share of its GDP fell to the lowest it has been for a decade, but the U.S. bilateral trade deficit with China hit a record high.

America's bilateral trade deficits were concentrated among the more developed East Asian economies in the late 1990s, notably Japan, South Korea, and Taiwan. But this shifted to China after it became the center of the regional production-sharing network after obtaining WTO membership in 2001. Figure 6-10 indicates that U.S.-manufactured imports from Pacific Rim countries have remained at about 45 percent of total U.S.-manufactured imports from 1990 to 2015, but China gradually captured an increasing share of Asia's exports to the United States as the last stop in the global assembly chain.[30] Thus the U.S. trade deficit is really about a deficit with East Asia more generally, with much of the higher-valued components being produced by countries other than China.

A joint OECD and WTO study estimated that in 2011, roughly a third of the overall value of China's gross exports was composed of imported components. This level increased to more than 50 percent for electrical and optical equipment. The study estimated that if bilateral trade imbal-

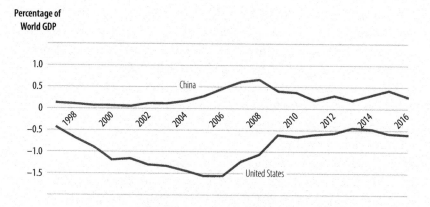

FIGURE 6-9   China and U.S. current account balances (Source: IMF, World Economic Outlook Database, October 2017)

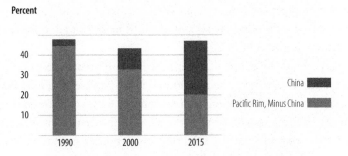

FIGURE 6-10 **U.S. manufactured imports from Asia**
(Source: U.S. ITC Trade Commission DataWeb; CRS)

ances were measured according to the value-added of trade, the U.S. trade deficit in goods and services with China would decline by 35 percent.[31]

Role of Exchange Rates

David Dollar's chapter elaborates on the factors that have shaped evolution of its exchange rate management. Some of the concerns were being driven by the view that China had been deliberately undervaluing its exchange rate to promote exports. After it joined the WTO in 2001, many experts thought that the yuan would be under additional pressure to depreciate, since China had to liberalize its import regime as a condition of membership. But the reality was far different, since China ended up gaining a significant share of the global export market. Institutional reforms and surging productivity increases due to infrastructure investments were probably more important that any exchange-rate manipulation in driving China's export success.

But appreciating the exchange rate can help moderate trade imbalances once they emerge. When China's trade surpluses increased to 5 percent of GDP, it moved away from a fixed peg to the U.S. dollar and began to appreciate the yuan in 2005. The combination of a steady appreciation of its nominal exchange rate and increasing domestic prices contributed to China's real effective exchange rate appreciating by about 50 percent by the end of 2015, compared with a nominal increase of 35 percent since 2005.[32]

While this rapid appreciation eventually helped to moderate China's trade surplus, even more important was the surge in China's investment rates and related increase in imports coupled with slackening import demand from the recession-afflicted West. China's current account surplus fell from a high of around 10 percent of GDP in 2008 to 2 to 3 percent by 2012, and to 1.4 percent in 2017.

Nevertheless, the sense that China still manipulates its currency remains strong. In 2015, China moved to a more flexible system that would have the yuan adjust in line with movements in a basket of trade weighted currencies. Recent movements in the U.S. dollar have continued to influence the value of yuan by affecting cross-border capital movements, making it difficult to totally delink the yuan from fluctuations in the U.S. dollar. The result is that shifts in China's foreign reserve holdings have become a significant factor influencing market expectations about the yuan's value, resulting in a managed float with intermittent periods of appreciation and depreciation relative to the U.S. dollar.

In response to long-standing concerns about the manipulation of a country's currency by not just China but also other nations, criteria were developed in the U.S. 2016 Trade Facilitation and Enforcement Act to judge whether foreign currencies are being manipulated. The most recent assessment, in April 2017, concluded that China was not manipulating its currency and, in fact, had been drawing down its foreign reserves in recent years to prevent the yuan from depreciating.

Role of Savings and Investment Rates

Deciphering whether a trade deficit should be viewed with alarm or is largely a nonissue begins with understanding that a country's trade balance is shaped by its savings and investment rates. Comparing the savings and investment rates of the United States and China with their current account balances offers insights into the links (see figure 6-11).

America's current account deficits come from inadequate domestic savings driven by large budget deficits and a secular decline in personal savings rates beginning around the late 1990s. Securing the additional savings needed for investment by borrowing from abroad is then reflected in America's overall trade deficit. America's 2017–2018 tax reforms are likely to increase rather than moderate the budget deficits, leading many economists to predict that its trade deficit will rise in the future.

China's current account surpluses emerged as savings rates increased much faster than investment rates, beginning around 2004, and the gap has narrowed only in recent years. Closing the gap further would require China to either increase its investment rate or to lower its savings rate.

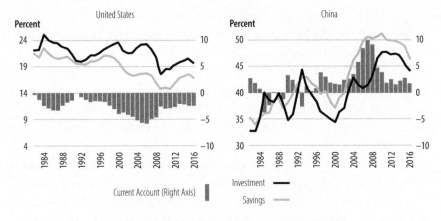

FIGURE 6-11 Current account balances and savings and investment rates (Source: World Bank WDI)

Since China's investment rate is deemed to be too high, it is argued that China needs to consume more (that is, save less), to drive down the country's current account surpluses.

China's high savings rates have been attributed to structural factors, including a rapidly aging population and weak financial and social security systems. In addition, urbanization has been driving up savings rates by encouraging urban residents to save more to buy apartments. This has been reinforced by the "repressed consumption" of migrant workers who lack formal urban residency rights and are discouraged from accessing the normal range of consumption and social services. Thus, China's trade imbalances could be moderated with reforms in residency policies and strengthened social welfare systems, as a rapidly aging population begins to consume out of its past savings.

China's "Unfair" Trade and Investment Practices

That America's trade deficits can be largely resolved by its own domestic policies has not detracted from a popular perception that the decline in U.S. manufacturing jobs and loss in competitiveness are due to China's "unfair" trade and foreign-investment policies.

U.S. Employment Concerns

A 2014 study by the Economic Policy Institute concluded that America's trade deficits with China between 2001 and 2013 "eliminated or displaced" 3.2 million U.S. jobs.[33] Another oft-cited study concludes that the decline in U.S. jobs accelerated given China's surging trade surpluses a decade ago.[34] But other studies have concluded that U.S. productivity increases have been the main reason for job losses, and that there is a natural structural shift from manufacturing to services jobs as countries get richer.[35]

What has made the process seem like a China issue is the speed and size of the loss in jobs coinciding with China becoming the center of the regional production network. Much of the perceived job loss, however, was a loss in competitiveness of American and European firms to their counterparts in Japan, South Korea, and Taiwan rather than to China's low-skilled assembly-type activities.[36] China's manufacturing labor force is now also declining as workers shift into services and away from manufacturing—as was the case with the other successful economies transitioning from middle- to high-income status.[37]

Unfair Practices Driven by State Interventions and Competitive Practices

Complaints that China has not been competing fairly have been around for decades. The concerns centered around the state providing support for export-oriented production. Most of the more obvious export subsidies have been phased out in response to WTO litigation, but complaints persist about SOEs benefiting from preferential credit allocations and access to cheap land. Another concern is that China's tariffs and nontariff barriers continue to play a major role in protecting Chinese firms. While China's tariffs are not as low as in the United States and the European Union, its structure and level are not unusual for a developing country at its per capita income level. The debate is whether China should continue to enjoy the flexibility accorded to developing countries or should now be held to developed country standards. This feeds into the debate about the prominent role played by its SOEs, as explored in Yasheng Huang's chapter.

The issue arises primarily because of China's size, which many see as giving it a degree of "monopoly" power in dealing with foreign companies seeking access to China's market and in influencing global commodity and product markets. Economic theory suggests that checking China's excessive power may require more stringent regulatory actions.

Such sentiments have intensified in recent years as foreign firms have become more vociferous in complaining about having been treated "unfairly" relative to domestic firms. Among the most heated accusations are complaints about foreign firms being "forced" to transfer technology to Chinese counterparts to secure the right to operate in China. As elaborated further in Xiaojun Li's chapter, the OECD's FDI regulatory restrictiveness index shows China as being the fourth most restrictive of the sixty-two countries surveyed.[38] China's protected services sector has a disproportionately more negative effect on the United States than Europe, since its strengths lie in higher-value services, notably in IT and finance.[39]

Unfair Practices—Technology Transfer and IPR Violations

As Barry Naughton's chapter points out, China intends to become a global innovation leader and reduce its dependence on the West for advanced technologies.[40] This was signaled in various development plans, most notably in the Made in China 2025 initiative, which came out in 2015. These programs include references to the highly contentious issue to promote "indigenous innovation," which reinforces the sense that China is not behaving fairly.

The Trump administration has highlighted these concerns in moving forward in the summer of 2018 with actions to restrict China's access to U.S. technology via foreign investments and licensing agreements. The White House also alleges that China is violating WTO rules by pressuring foreign firms to transfer their technology to Chinese firms as a condition for accessing China's domestic market. Beijing has responded that they do not discriminate against foreign firms, and at various occasions has altered some of its directives to allay such concerns. Nevertheless, complaints have persisted that many localities still adhere to restrictive practices even if Beijing no longer supports such policies.

The primary means for this to occur comes from requiring foreign companies to transfer technology to local firms as part of a joint venture arrangement, as a condition for entry, as discussed in Xiaojun Li's chapter. Many foreign firms do not like this condition, but have accepted it as part of the cost of doing business in China and therefore have incorporated these risks in their plans. From China's perspective, the transfer of technology is a business decision between the two firms, and the foreign company can always say no.

Differentiating between a deal that is merely "tough" and one that is "forced" may not be possible. Thus, some observers have commented that there may not be any valid examples of "forced transfer."[41] Even if there are such prohibitions, proving that this is happening may be difficult, since such intentions are unlikely to be put in writing.

Technology transfer usually occurs naturally through trade and foreign investment links between developing and developed countries. Nations have generally agreed that this kind of north-south technology transfer should be encouraged. WTO guidelines[42] reflect this view as indicated in its membership agreement that "requires developed country members to provide incentives for their companies to promote the transfer of technology to least-developed countries in order to enable them to create a sound and viable technological base."

Successful countries are those that have a greater capacity to "adopt" foreign technologies for domestic use, and China has done far better than other countries.[43] Most adoption comes from trade, licensing agreements, and from FDI, most of which is conducted in line with globally accepted norms. Thus, any international regulation that runs counter to the general sentiment of encouraging the transfer of technology to developing countries is often simply ignored.[44]

U.S. officials have argued that China is no longer a low-income country and its size and financial strengths disqualify it from being treated as a developing country, even if its per capita income would warrant such a status. Moreover, the economic consequences of technology theft are seen as especially damaging to the United States. Frequently cited is a 2013 report by the Commission on the Theft of American Intellectual Property, which estimated that global IPR theft costs the U.S. economy $300 billion, of which China accounted for 50 to 80 percent of the losses.[45] China has responded that such accusations are exaggerated and that it has taken many actions to curb such abuses.

Figure 6-12 shows how China compares with other successful Asian economies that have been cited for Section 301 violations during their progression to high-income status. Such patterns suggest that rapidly growing developing countries are prone to IPR violations but that this disappears once they reach higher income levels.[46]

China argues that it has been addressing these concerns and that IPR theft is also a problem for domestic Chinese firms. A commonly held view of experts is that as China's economy becomes more developed, it will naturally strengthen its IPR protection policies, since this is part of the process of becoming a more technologically sophisticated economy. As

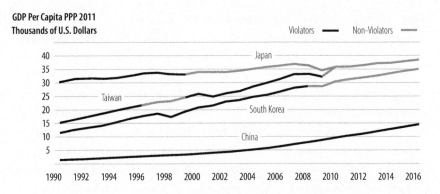

FIGURE 6-12 **Section 301 IPR violators** (Source: World Bank WDI; Federal Reserve Economic Data; USTR Special 301 Report)

more domestic firms end up bearing the costs of such violations relative to foreign companies, the environment to support IPR will naturally shift. This is already happening; for example, 96 percent of the respondents to the American Chamber of Commerce 2018 business survey said that IPR enforcement had improved in recent years, and 62 percent said that the transparency of the policy development process had increased compared with 9 percent saying it had gotten worse.[47]

WTO Compliance and Dealing with Unfair Practices
China's accession to WTO was seen at that time as a major step forward in integrating it into the global trading system and aligning its behavior with international norms. Much of the foreign criticism reflects concerns about the prominent role played by the state in China. The resulting controversies cannot be easily dealt with under the existing WTO framework.[48] As of late 2017, the United States had brought twenty-one dispute settlement cases against China (roughly half of the total number of cases). This formed part of the rationale for China filing a case against the United States for its continued treatment of China as a nonmarket economy in imposing such penalties.

China's Current Trade Objectives and Challenges

The levying of punitive tariffs by the United States and retaliation by China in 2018 has created the possibility of a prolonged trade war. Negotiations that would result in a temporary truce or a more formal agreement may bring periods of respite, but there is a high probability that these tensions will persist. The impasse comes from the wide chasm in perceptions about these issues and absence of any institutional framework for resolving the differences. Washington's demands fall into three categories reflecting three different constituents. The White House is fixated on America's huge bilateral trade deficits with China. The U.S. business community is more concerned about China's "unfair" investment practices and alleged forced transfer of technology. Geo-strategists are obsessed with China's intentions to become a major technological power, thereby threatening America's global dominance. Put all three concerns together, and it is easy to see why forging a sustainable solution will be difficult.

Beijing has stepped up its support for multilateralism and a strengthened WTO in response to the White House's strategy to denigrate these institutions and use punitive tariffs to force countries to address bilateral trade issues. From China's perspective, there are advantages in being recognized as a leader in supporting globalization. China will never be the pure market economy typical of the West, and its size and the power of the state to support collective actions has shown that it needs to be more sensitive to its global impact to lower trade tensions. The priority now is for China to strengthen its protection of intellectual property, dismantle the formal and informal barriers that restrict foreign investment, especially in services, and assure the global community of its commitment to further reforms.

For those seeking a stronger, rules-based international system to deal with the current economic tensions, one option is to strengthen and make better use of the WTO's dispute resolution arrangements. WTO guidelines have not evolved rapidly enough in line with global trade and investment trends, given the increasing importance of technology diffusion, e-commerce, and cross-border information flows. Some of America's specific foreign investment concerns involving China's unfair practices and the role of its state-owned enterprises, however, cannot be effectively dealt with within the WTO system, particularly if they relate to security or technology transfer concerns. As discussed in Xiaojun Li's chapter, moving forward with the bilateral investment treaty (BIT) that had been under negotiation during the Obama administration would provide the means to address these issues. A BIT in conjunction with a revitalized WTO would provide the necessary institutional arrangements to moderate global trade tensions—making it less likely that punitive tariffs would be used to promote negotiated agreements in the future.

Notes

1. These theories underpinned the Nobel Prizes awarded to W. Arthur Lewis in 1979 and Paul Krugman in 2008. See Yukon Huang, *Cracking the China Conundrum: Why Conventional Economic Wisdom Is Wrong* (New York, New York: Oxford University Press, 2017), chapter 3.

2. Agglomeration economies are the dynamic benefits coming from the interaction of firms, labor, and knowledge-related activities when economic agents are concentrated in a specific locality.

3. Nicholas Lardy, *China's Unfinished Economic Revolution* (Washington, DC: Brookings Institution Press, 2003).

4. Alan Smart and Jinn-Yuh Hsu, "The Chinese Diaspora, Foreign Investment and Economic Development in China," *Review of International Affairs*, vol. 3, no. 4, Summer 2004, 544–566.

5. See Yukon Huang, "Reinterpreting China's Success Through the New Economic Geography," CEIP, Asia Program Paper No 111, November 2010.

6. World Bank, *China 2020* (Washington, DC: World Bank, 1997), 10.

7. World Bank, *China Foreign Trade Reform: Meeting the Challenge of the 1990s* (Washington DC: World Bank, 1993).

8. Julia Ya Qing, "'WTO-Plus' Obligations and Their Implications for the World Trade Organization Legal System—An Appraisal of the China Accession Protocol," *Journal of World Trade*, vol. 37, no. 3 (2003), 483–522.

9. Wayne Morrison, "China and the World Trade Organization," U.S. Congressional Research Office, 2001.

10. This list draws on Wayne Morrison, "China–U.S. Trade Issues," U.S. Congressional Research Office, 2017.

11. Sheng Bin, "China's Trade Development Strategy and Trade Policy Reforms: Overview and Prospect," International Institute for Sustainable Development, April 2015.

12. Bin, "China's Trade Development."

13. Sheng Bin, "Political Economy of China's Trade Policy: The Evidence from Industrial Protection in the 1990s," *Frontiers of Economics in China*, vol. 3 (2006), 406–432.

14. L. G. Branstetter and R. Feenstra, "Trade and foreign direct investment in China: A political economy approach," *Journal of International Economics*, vol. 58, no. 2 (2002), 335–358.

15. Willem Thorbecke, "Measuring the Competitiveness of China's Processes Exports," *China and World Economy*, vol. 23, no. 1 (2015), 78–100.

16. R. Koopman, Z. Wang, and S. J. Wei, "How much of Chinese exports is really made in China?" *NBER Working Paper 14109*, National Bureau of Economic Research, 2008.

17. Prema-chandra Athukorala and Jayant Menon, "Global Production Sharing, Trade Patterns and Determinants of Trade Flows in East Asia," Asian Development Bank, January 2010.

18. Wayne Morrison, "China's Economic Rise, History, Trends, Challenges and Implications for the United States," U.S. Congressional Research Service, October 2015.

19. Yukon Huang, "In the Middle Kingdom's Shadow," *Wall Street Journal*, March 26, 2012.

20. A. Antkiewics and J. Whalley, "China's new regional trade agreements," *World Economy*, vol. 28 no. 10 (2005), 1539–1557. Also, see S. Y. Yang and I. Martinez-Zarzoso, "A panel data analysis of trade creation and trade diversion effects," *China Economic Review*, 29 (2014), 138–151.

21. Data are accessible through the UN Comtrade Database (https://comtrade.un.org/data/dev/portal/).

22. Hejin Chen and J. Whalley, "China's Service Trade," *Journal of Economic Surveys*, vol. 28, no. 4 (2014), 746–774.

23. Joong Shik Kang and Wei Liao, "Chinese Imports: What Is Behind the Slowdown?" *IMF Working Paper*, WP/16/106, 2016.

24. H. L. Kee and Heiwai Tang, "How did China move up the global value chains?" *VOX China*, August 30, 2017.

25. This is described in an October 2015 supplemental document referenced in the OECD-WTO Trade in Value Added database (https://www.oecd.org/sti/ind/tiva/CN_2015_China.pdf).

26. A 2014 U.S.-China Business Council Survey indicated that the primary objective of 91 percent of its respondents was to access the China market, up from 57 percent in 2006.

27. For a discussion of the source and nature of the poll results see Huang, *Cracking the China Conundrum*, chapter 2.

28. Chad Brown, "Steel, Aluminum, Lumber, Solar: Trump's Stealth Trade Protection," *Policy Brief 17–21* (Washington, DC: Peterson Institute for International Economics, 2017).

29. Robert Z. Lawrence, "Five Reasons Why the Focus on Trade Deficits Is Misleading," *PIIE Policy Brief*, March 2018.

30. See Wayne Morrison, "China-U.S. Trade Issues," U.S. Congressional Research Service, January 4, 2017.

31. OECD, "Measuring Trade in Value Added: An OECD-WTO joint initiative," 2015.

32. William Cline, "Renminbi Series Part 2: Is China's Currency Fairly Valued?" Peterson Institute for International Economics, *China Watch Series*, March 23, 2016.

33. EPI, *China Trade, Outsourcing and Jobs*, December 11, 2014.

34. David Autor, David Dorn, and Gordon Hanson, "The China Syndrome: Local Labour Market Effects of Import Competition in the United States," *American Economic Review*, 2013, 2121–2168.

35. Ball State University, *The Myth and the Reality of Manufacturing in America*, June 2015.

36. Yukon Huang, "America's Hammering China's RMB Makes Little Sense," *Forum Discussing International Affairs and Economics*, summer 2012.

37. Michael Schuman, "Is China Stealing Jobs? It May Be Losing Them, Instead," *New York Times*, July 22, 2016.

38. Data are accessible at the OECD FDI Regulatory Restrictiveness Index (https://www.oecd.org/investment/fdiindex.htm).

39. Huang, *Cracking the China Conundrum*, 144.

40. James McGregor, "China's Drive for 'Indigenous Innovation': A Web of Industrial Policies," United States Chamber of Commerce, July 28, 2010.

41. Wendy Wu, "US 'Lacks Evidence' for Forced Tech Transfers Claim against China at WTO," *South China Morning Post*, March 29, 2018.

42. WTO statement on IPR, "Intellectual Property: Protection and Enforcement" (https://www.wto.org/english/thewto_e/whatis_e/tif_e/agrm7_e.htm).

43. World Bank, *Global Development Horizons 2011: Multipolarity—The New Global Economy* (Washington, D.C.: World Bank, 2011).

44. Robert D. Atkinson, Hearing on "The Impact of International Transfer on American Research and Development," House Science Committee, December 5, 2012.

45. The Commission on the Theft of American Intellectual Property, *Report of the Commission on the Theft of Intellectual Property*, May 2013.

46. Huang, *Cracking the China Conundrum*, chapter 8.

47. Am Cham Business Survey 2018.

48. Joel P. Trachtman, "U.S.-Chinese Trade: Interface and Lawfare," EUI Working Papers, RSCAS 2017/11, 2017.

SEVEN

Regulating China's Inward FDI

Changes, Challenges, and the Future

XIAOJUN LI

On April 10, 1980, after over a year of painstaking negotiations that included Deng Xiaoping's famous remark on breadcrumbs, Beijing Air Catering (BAC), a joint venture between Maxim's Catering Limited—Hong Kong's largest catering group—and the Civil Aviation Administration of China was approved on the heels of the China–Foreign Equity Joint Venture Enterprise Law passed a year earlier. As the very first foreign-invested firm in China, and boasting the coveted "001" registration number with the State Administration for Industry and Commerce, BAC provides in-flight catering services that are up to international standards, putting an end to the days when flight attendants on some domestic flights reportedly dished out steamed buns, pickled vegetables, and Ma Ling luncheon meat in the same aluminum lunch boxes seen in factory canteens throughout China.

Over the next four decades of reform and opening up, with new laws and regulations progressively lowering the entry barriers to investment, foreign direct investment (FDI) poured into China at an average annual growth rate of 13.1 percent, unrivaled by any country in the developing world. In 2016, 27,900 new foreign-invested enterprises (FIEs) were established, spanning every province, including more than 840 with a total investment of more than $100 million. The investments have also become more diversified, with more than 70 percent of the new FDI going into

service industries, from real estate to banking. The total value of FDI inflows has reached $126 billion, making China the world's second-largest
recipient of FDI behind the United States and the largest destination
among developing countries.[1]

From an economic perspective, FDI as a form of international economic integration can bring substantial gains to both parties, according to
the principle of comparative advantage.[2] FDI inflows are particularly valuable for developing countries lacking technology and managerial skills.
Indeed, few would disagree that FDI should be credited as a major driving
force behind China's spectacular economic takeoff and its emergence as
the second-largest economy in the world over a mere forty years.[3] Through
most of the reform period, FDI contributed substantially to the country's
economic growth, productivity gains, trade expansion, domestic fixed investment, and employment.[4] The impact of FDI further ripples through
the FIEs' supply chains as well as the consumer spending of their employees and suppliers.[5] At their peak, FIEs employed 15.9 percent of the urban
workforce in 2010, generated 35.9 percent of China's industrial output in
2003, and accounted for 58.3 percent of Chinese exports and 59.7 percent
of imports in 2005.

With the rise of the private sector and large, powerful state-owned
enterprises (SOEs), FIEs now compose less than 3 percent of China's total
number of firms, according to numbers released by the Ministry of Commerce (MOC) in 2017. Nevertheless, they continue to play an outsized
role in the Chinese economy, accounting for nearly half of the country's
foreign trade, more than one-fourth of reported industrial profits, and one-
fifth of tax revenue.[6] In fact, as China's economy enters a period of "new
normal," with Chinese leaders determined to move the economy toward a
more balanced, sustainable, and inclusive growth path, as outlined in the
Thirteenth Five-Year Plan, it is all the more important for China to attract
FDI, which will bring in much-needed technology and skills in the service
industry and high-end manufacturing that are critical for Made in China
2025, Internet Plus, and several other ambitious initiatives.

There have been signs of worry, however. Between 2011 and 2015, the
annual growth rate of FDI has dipped to 3 percent from 13.3 percent
over the previous five-year period. In 2016, when China's outbound FDI
exceeded inbound FDI for the first time, inward FDI growth faltered
further, dropping sharply from 5.5 percent in the previous year to −0.2
percent.[7] On the ground, foreign investors were pulling out of the Chi-

nese market. Early in 2017, for example, hard-disk manufacturer Seagate abruptly announced that it would shut down its plant in Suzhou and lay off more than two thousand employees, joining a slew of multinational corporations such as Best Buy, Home Depot, Microsoft, Marks & Spencer, National, Oracle, L'Oréal, Panasonic, Philips, Revlon, and Sony, which since 2015 have either downsized their operations in China or shuttered them altogether.[8]

In an effort to reverse this alarming new trend, the Chinese government rolled out a series of regulatory changes aimed at simplifying the administrative procedures and improving the business environment for foreign investors. Major revisions to the laws and regulations governing inward FDI were implemented in June 2016, including the promulgation of the revised Foreign Investment Industrial Guidance Catalogue and the long-anticipated National Negative List. In July 2017, Premier Li Keqiang hosted a State Council Executive Meeting, which led to the "Notice on Several Measures of Promoting Foreign Investment Growth (Circular No. 39)."[9] The notice urged the government to build a legal, international, and convenient environment for foreign businesses by introducing new measures to enhance market access for FIEs in the services, manufacturing, mining, and infrastructure sectors.

However, the changes to the regulatory framework do not seem to have shored up confidence among foreign investors. According to the 2018 annual China Business Climate Survey, conducted by the American Chamber of Commerce in Shanghai, an astounding 75 percent of members feel increasingly unwelcome in China. Close to half of respondents indicate they are treated unfairly by industrial policies that favor SOEs in the form of innovation incentives, subsidies, and government procurement, as well as the inconsistencies and abrupt changes in these policies. Nearly a quarter of the firms report that they have moved or plan to move their business out of China.[10]

What contributes to the growing pessimism among foreign investors, despite positive changes in China's foreign investment regulatory framework? What can Beijing do to keep attracting FDI in an era of significant domestic and global economic shifts? These are the two central questions addressed in this chapter. The first section, "China's Inward FDI Over the Past Four Decades," examines the data on China's inward FDI over time, both at the aggregate level and in terms of their geographical and sectoral compositions. The next section, "China's Evolving FDI Regulatory Regime," provides a brief overview of the evolution of China's FDI regulatory regime. China's challenges in maintaining its attractiveness for foreign investment and possible solutions to these challenges are discussed in the section titled "Challenges in Maintaining China's Attractiveness for FDI." The penultimate section proposes bilateral investment treaties as a potential new driver for FDI. The chapter concludes with a discussion of some policy suggestions.

China's Inward FDI Over the Past Four Decades

In chapter 6, David Dollar presents a general overview of China's inward FDI during the reform era. In this section, I dive deeper into the data to provide a more fine-grained account of the evolution of inward FDI, both at the aggregate level and in terms of its geographical and sectoral distributions as well as its home countries and corporate structures. In doing so, I draw primarily on data provided by the National Bureau of Statistics (NBS), available in the annual statistical yearbooks.[11] It is worth noting that prior to 2007, NBS reported two types of data on inward FDI: contractual value (that is, the amount foreign investors put down in the investment application approved by the government) and realized amount, which is not bound by the contractual amount and is typically much smaller.[12] For practical purposes, therefore, we should always use the realized amount, which is the economically more meaningful measure.

Figure 7-1 plots China's annual inward FDI and the number of newly established FIEs from 1979 to 2016. Between 1979 and 1988, FDI inflow grew moderately but steadily from $30 billion to $102 billion.[13] This trend was broken in 1989, when protests in Tiananmen Square spooked foreign investors. In 1992, after Deng Xiaoping made his famous southern tour to reaffirm China's commitment to the opening-up policy and market reforms, FDI once again surged into the country. In that year, 48,858 FIEs were established with a realized amount reaching nearly $200 billion. The following year saw a record 83,595 new FIEs, and the realized amount more than doubled. Over the next four years, while the number of new FIEs declined, the value of investments continued to grow at double-digit rates, establishing China as the largest FDI destination in the developing world.

The Asian Financial Crisis in 1997 put another brake on the upward trajectory, as investments from major sources such as Hong Kong, Taiwan,

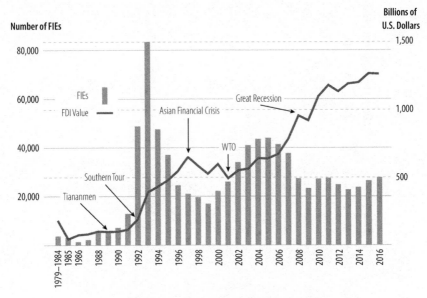

FIGURE 7-1 China's annual inward FDI and FIEs,
1979–2016 (Source: *China Statistical Yearbook*)

Japan, and South Korea declined. Both the number of FIEs and the amount of investment experienced negative growth, dropping to 1995 levels by the time of China's accession to the WTO in 2001, which necessitated that Beijing further liberalize its investment regime, particularly with respect to intellectual property rights (IPRs) and trade-related investment measures (TRIMs). Between 2001 and 2011, inward FDI grew at about 12 percent per year, dipping slightly in 2009 after the global financial crisis, but it quickly rebounded a year later. Since then, the number of new FIEs and the FDI values seem to have stalled.

With the dramatic rise in FDI over time, the Chinese government has also become increasingly good at keeping track of the FDI statistics. Starting in 1997, the NBS began to systematically release more disaggregated data on the sectoral, geographical, and ownership composition of FIEs and FDIs. Table 7-1 presents FDI values and number of FIEs from 1997 to 2016, tabulated by their ownership structures, sectors, and sources. A closer examination of these data reveals a number of patterns.

In terms of ownership structure, FIEs established in China can be broadly divided into four types: equity joint ventures, cooperative joint ventures, wholly foreign-owned, and others. Before 1985, setting up an

Year	Total		Investment Mode (Value and Number of FIEs)								Sector (Value)				Origin by Continent (Value)					
	Value	FIEs	Equity JV		Coop JV		Wholly owned		Others		Agri	Mine	Manu	Serv	AF	EU	LA	NA	OC	AS
1997	64.4	21,138	19.5	9,001	8.9	2,373	16.2	9,602	0.3	6	0.6	0.9	28.1	12.3	0.1	4.4	2.0	3.7	0.6	34.3
1998	58.6	19,850	18.3	8,107	9.7	2,003	16.5	9,673	0.7	9	0.6	0.6	25.6	16.2	0.2	4.3	4.6	4.3	0.5	31.3
1999	52.7	17,002	15.8	7,050	8.2	1,656	15.5	8,201	0.3	3	0.7	0.6	22.6	11.9	0.2	4.8	3.2	4.6	0.5	26.8
2000	59.4	22,347	14.3	8,378	6.6	1,757	19.3	12,196	0.1	8	0.7	0.6	25.8	11.1	0.3	4.8	4.6	4.8	0.7	25.5
2001	49.7	26,140	15.7	8,893	6.2	1,589	23.9	15,643	0.5	11	0.9	0.8	30.9	9.2	0.3	4.5	6.3	5.1	1.0	29.6
2002	55.0	34,171	15.0	10,380	5.1	1,595	31.7	22,173	0.7	19	1.0	0.6	36.8	8.8	0.6	4.0	14.9	1.4	1.0	32.6
2003	56.1	41,081	15.4	12,521	3.8	1,547	33.4	26,943	0.3	37	1.0	0.3	36.9	8.2	0.6	4.3	6.9	5.2	1.7	34.1
2004	64.1	43,664	16.4	11,570	3.1	1,343	40.2	30,708	0.8	43	N/A	N/A	N/A	N/A	0.8	4.8	9.0	5.0	2.0	37.6
2005	63.8	44,001	14.6	10,480	1.8	1,166	43.0	32,308	0.9	47	0.7	0.4	42.5	16.8	1.1	5.6	11.3	3.7	2.0	35.7
2006	67.1	41,473	14.4	10,223	1.9	1,036	46.3	30,164	0.4	50	0.6	0.5	40.1	21.9	1.2	5.7	14.2	3.7	2.3	35.1
2007	78.3	37,871	15.6	7,649	1.4	641	57.3	29,543	0.5	38	0.9	0.5	40.9	32.5	1.5	4.4	20.1	3.4	2.7	42.1
2008	95.3	27,514	17.3	4,612	1.9	468	72.3	22,396	0.9	38	1.2	0.6	49.9	40.7	1.7	5.5	20.9	4.0	3.2	56.3
2009	91.8	23,435	17.3	4,283	2.0	390	68.7	18,741	2.0	21	1.4	0.5	46.8	41.3	1.3	5.5	14.7	3.7	2.5	60.6

Year	Total		Investment Mode (Value and Number of FIEs)								Sector (Value)				Origin by Continent (Value)					
	Value	FIEs	Equity JV		Coop JV		Wholly owned		Others		Agri	Mine	Manu	Serv	AF	EU	LA	NA	OC	AS
2010	108.8	27,406	22.5	4,970	1.6	300	81.0	22,085	0.6	51	1.9	0.7	49.6	53.5	1.3	5.9	13.5	4.0	2.3	77.6
2011	117.7	27,712	21.4	5,005	1.8	284	91.2	22,388	1.6	35	2.0	0.6	52.1	61.3	1.6	5.9	12.5	3.6	2.6	89.5
2012	113.3	24,925	21.7	4,355	2.3	166	86.1	20,352	1.6	52	2.1	0.8	48.9	60.0	1.4	6.3	10.2	3.8	2.3	86.7
2013	118.7	22,773	23.8	4,476	1.9	142	89.6	18,125	2.3	30	1.8	0.4	45.6	69.9	1.4	6.9	8.2	4.1	2.3	94.7
2014	119.7	23,778	21.0	4,824	1.6	104	94.7	18,809	2.2	41	1.5	0.6	39.9	77.5	1.0	6.7	7.7	3.3	1.9	98.6
2015	126.3	26,575	25.9	5,989	1.8	110	95.3	20,398	3.3	78	1.5	0.2	39.5	84.9	0.6	6.9	9.1	3.0	2.4	104.2
2016	126.0	27,900	30.2	6,662	0.8	126	86.1	21,024	8.8	6	1.9	0.1	35.5	88.5	1.1	9.4	12.2	3.1	1.3	98.8

Notes: Inward FDI values and number of FIEs are tabulated by mode of investment (equity joint venture, foreign wholly owned, cooperative joint venture, and others), sector (agriculture, mining, manufacturing, and service), and home country by continent (Africa, Europe, Latin America, North America, Oceania, and Asia). Values are in billion US dollars. No data are available for sectoral investment in 2004. Source: *China Statistical Yearbook*.

TABLE 7-1   China's Inward FDI, 1997–2016.

equity joint venture with a Chinese partner was the only possible option
for foreigners hoping to invest in China. The share of equity joint ventures in both the number of firms and investments began to decline when
the other options became available in the mid-1980s; by the turn of the
century, wholly foreign-owned enterprises had become the most popular
option, accounting for 47.2 percent of total investment and 54.5 percent of
newly established FIEs in 2000 (figure 7-2a and 7-2b). This trend, driven
largely by joint ventures' stagnant performance and concerns about technology transfer, continued until 2009, when the share of equity joint ventures rose again.[14]

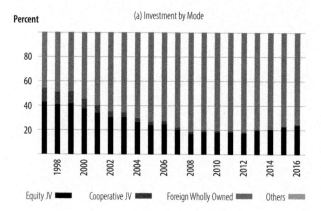

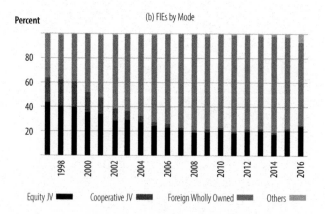

FIGURE 7-2   **Share of FDI by investment mode, sector, and home
country, 1997–2016** (Source: *China Statistical Yearbook*)

Moving on to sectoral distribution, we can see that the proportion of foreign investment in the primary sectors of agriculture and mining has remained low, hovering between 3 percent and 5 percent, largely because these industries have a long production cycle and a slow return on investment (figure 7-2c). On the other hand, the manufacturing sector absorbed the lion's share of China's FDI, peaking at 65.7 percent in 2003, until being overtaken in 2010 by the service sector, which has increased dramatically following China's accession to the WTO. In 2016, more than 70 percent of China's $126 billion FDI was in the service sector, with the top five industries—real estate, leasing and business services, retail and

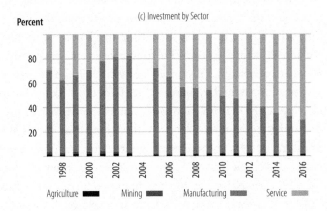

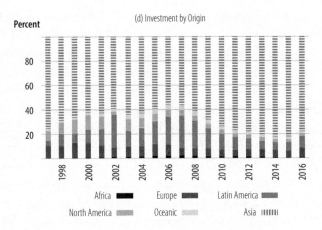

wholesale, financial services, and information technology—accounting for 79 percent of total investment in the service sector. The rise of service FDI may also explain the increase of equity joint ventures described above, as wholly foreign-owned firms in these industries are still off-limits. Within the manufacturing sector, while some traditional industries such as textile and consumer products have seen declining foreign investments, high-tech manufacturing industries such as pharmaceutical instruments and devices have flourished in recent years. All in all, the pattern is consistent with China's gradual shift from industrial and manufacturing to a service-based economy and its upward move in the global value chain.

By region, the vast majority of China's use of foreign capital comes from countries and economies in Asia, such as Hong Kong, Japan, and Taiwan, accounting for nearly 80 percent of all inward FDI before the Asian Financial Crisis, but then dwindling to 57 percent in 2007 (figure 7-2d). During the same period, FDI from other continents, except North America, all experienced substantial growth. Foreign investment from Latin America, in particular, increased tenfold, most likely due to the rise in round-tripping FDI from countries such as the British Virgin Islands, Bermuda, and the Cayman Islands.[15] This trend was reversed in 2008, when China revised its corporate income tax law, unifying the tax rates for domestic and foreign firms.[16] The result was an even greater concentration of FDIs. In 2016, the top ten home countries accounted for 94 percent of China's total inward FDI, an increase of 0.4 percent from a year earlier.[17]

Finally, the geographical distributions of FDIs within China have also been changing; these are visualized in figure 7-3 using year-end FDI stock in four snapshot years. In 1997, FDI was concentrated in the coastal provinces, thanks to their higher level of economic development, more developed transportation system, and high level of industrial aggregation. With its proximity to Hong Kong, Guangdong led the pack with $271 billion in FDI stock, followed by Shanghai, Jiangsu, Fujian, Shandong, and Liaoning. Over time, however, the central and western regions were gradually catching up, and by 2016, their share of FDI stock had reached more than 20 percent. Chongqing, in particular, has become a major destination for foreign investment, jumping from number 22 to 12 from 2001 to 2016. In contrast, FDI in the northeast provinces, concentrated in heavy industries and manufacturing, stagnated, with Liaoning falling out of the top five at some point between 2008 and 2016. These changing patterns are broadly

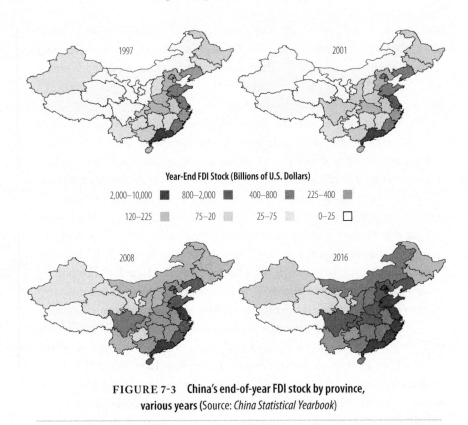

FIGURE 7-3   China's end-of-year FDI stock by province,
various years (Source: *China Statistical Yearbook*)

consistent with China's Western Development Strategy, begun in 2010, and the sectoral shift in the composition of FDI over time, as discussed earlier.

China's Evolving FDI Regulatory Regime

Recognition of the economic benefits of FDI does not necessarily mean that countries always embrace them with open arms. On the contrary, host countries often worry about loss of national sovereignty and other possible adverse consequences of inviting foreign investors. The surge of Japanese FDI in the United States during the 1980s, for example, gave rise to widespread public concerns about excessive foreign control and adverse effects on national security, which eventually led to the Exon-Florio Provision of the 1988 Omnibus Trade Act, giving the U.S. president authority to block foreign investment for national security reasons.[18] Similarly, as we will see in Chapter 8 by Tom Miller, the growing wave of Chinese investments going into every corner of the globe has also raised concerns and even fear in host countries, from U.S. regulators scuttling deals made by Chinese investors in American tech start-ups to the United Kingdom's review of a proposed Chinese-funded nuclear plant.

In developing countries, there are additional fears of adverse economic and political effects that include balance-of-payments deficits, reduced domestic research and development, diminished competition, the crowding out of domestic firms, and depressed labor and environmental standards. These fears can be elevated when combined with heightened nationalism during foreign policy crises. For instance, Japan's direct investments in China experienced a sharp decline of 20 percent in 2013, largely in response to the widespread demonstrations that broke out in China over Japan's decision to nationalize the Diaoyu/Senkaku Islands.[19] For policy-makers, therefore, the challenge is to balance the potential economic cost of restricting FDI against the need to address noneconomic considerations.

Indeed, the debate over the trade-off between economic efficiency and national sovereignty was front and center during the drafting of the China–Foreign Equity Joint Venture Enterprise Law in 1979.[20] Lawmakers led by Peng Zhen initially considered putting a 49 percent cap on foreign shares and a two-thirds supermajority rule for major decisions in joint ventures. The business community, however, worried that such terms would significantly reduce the attractiveness of China as a destination for FDI. In the end, it was Deng Xiaoping who made the call to remove both limits, demonstrating to the world that China would open up to foreign investments.[21]

In April 1982, at the Twenty-third Session of the Fifth National People's Congress, foreign investment was officially added to the Constitution of the People's Republic of China, establishing the legal status of FIEs in China. Specifically, Article 18 of the Constitution stipulates that "foreign enterprises and other economic organizations or individuals are allowed to invest in China in accordance with the laws and regulations of the People's Republic of China and carry out various forms of economic cooperation with Chinese enterprises or other economic organizations." Furthermore, "the legal rights and interests of foreign companies and other foreign economic organizations within China are protected by the laws of the People's Republic of China."[22]

The Foreign-Invested Enterprise Law and the Foreign Cooperative

Joint Venture Enterprise Law were subsequently issued in 1986 and 1988. Along with the Foreign Equity Joint Venture Enterprise Law, these three central laws, colloquially known as *"sanzi qiye fa* (三资企业法)," as well as their corresponding implementation provisions promulgated by the State Council, form the foundation of China's foreign investment regulatory regime.

In addition to the three central laws, there are more than a thousand rules and regulatory documents related to foreign investment in China, issued by various government ministries. Among them is the Foreign Investment Industrial Guidance Catalogue (the Catalogue), first issued in 1995 jointly by the State Planning Commission, the State Economic and Trade Commission, and the Ministry of Foreign Trade and Economic Cooperation. The Catalogue consists of three categories (encouraged, restricted, and prohibited), with the unpublished fourth category (permitted) deemed to include all sectors not in the other three. As such, the Catalogue identifies industries in which foreign investors are allowed to invest and, in many cases, sets limits on how those investments can be structured in the case of joint ventures.

Throughout the reform period, Chinese regulators have continuously refined the laws and regulations to relax controls on foreign investment, though the scope and pace of liberalization have been uneven across sectors and issues.[23] A major round of revision occurred during China's entry into the WTO, when all three central laws were substantially amended between 2000 and 2001, including the removal of restrictions that allowed wholly owned FIEs only if they adopted advanced technology or exported the majority of their products. Furthermore, many service sectors were moved from the prohibited to the restricted category in the 2002 revised Catalogue, in accordance with China's WTO commitment to open up these sectors within five years of China's accession in December 2001.

Following the Eighteenth Party Congress in November 2012, the Chinese Communist Party launched one of the largest and most ambitious economic reform programs since 1978, calling for, among other things, the broadening of foreign investment access in China. A year later, the pilot Shanghai Free Trade Zone (FTZ) was officially launched as a testing ground to attract foreign investment by reducing restrictions, including a negative list created by the State Council, which permitted all investments except those in the list. The number of restrictive measures in the FTZ negative list continued to shrink in the following years, from 190 in

2013 to 139 in 2014, when three more FTZs were established in Fujian, Guangdong, and Tianjin, and to 93 in 2017, when an additional seven FTZs opened up in Chongqing, Liaoning, Henan, Hubei, Shaanxi, Sichuan, and Zhejiang.

Building on the experience gained in the FTZs, the National Development and Reform Commission (NDRC) and the Ministry of Commerce (MOFCOM) released a new version of the Catalogue in 2017, establishing the first nationwide negative list system. This means that only those industries mentioned in the list require pre-approval from MOFCOM, while the rest can proceed directly into the registration process. Previously, even projects that fell into the "encouraged" category could be subject to pre-approval. For foreign investors, the new system means more clarity and, in some cases, simpler procedures. Furthermore, the Catalogue reduces the number of "restricted" and "prohibited" items from 93 to 63 and adds new sectors to the "encouraged" category.

As noted in Chapter 6, many industries in China are still partially or completely closed to foreign investors, including sectors reserved for domestic companies due to their political, strategic, economic, or cultural importance. In the most recent OECD's FDI regulatory restrictiveness index, released in 2016, China was ranked the fourth most restrictive country against FDI out of sixty-two countries, behind the Philippines,

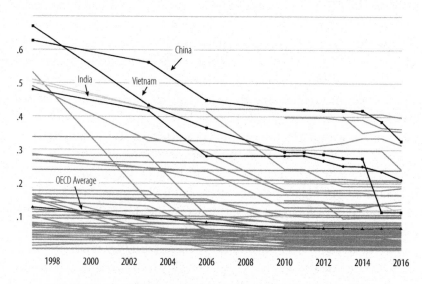

FIGURE 7-4   **OECD FDI restrictiveness index, 1997–2016** (Source: OECD)

Saudi Arabia, and Myanmar.[24] However, this ranking obscures the fact that China is one of the few countries to have significantly liberalized their statutory restrictions on international investment over a short space of only twenty years (figure 7-4).

The improvement in FDI restrictiveness is more apparent if we unpack the overall index (figure 7-5). While the vast majority of sectors and industries were restricted in 1997, by 2016, architecture, engineering, forestry, hotels and restaurants, electric and electronic instruments, chemicals, and food are almost completely open. The most heavily restricted sectors, such as telecommunications, air and maritime transport, finance, public utilities, and media, are not much different from the lists in the OECD countries twenty years ago, which similarly covered industries highly sensitive to national security or national sovereignty considerations.[25]

Challenges in Maintaining China's Attractiveness for FDI

On paper, China's FDI regulatory regime has been moving toward more relaxation. However, problems arise when it comes to implementing and enforcing these rules and regulations, due to the lack of capacity or accountability of local agents in charge of enforcement, whose own interests may not align with those of policy-makers. Scholars in the China field have extensively documented the gaps between the central government's official national policies and their problematic implementation at local levels.[26] Foreign investment is no exception.

While the central government and agencies have set the ground rules for FDI, local governments in China have substantial discretion in enacting their own regulations and rules to manage foreign investments in their areas, ostensibly in accordance with national laws and policies. Under this complex regulatory system, foreign investors often are required to go through extensive review and approval processes by multiple government agencies, including relevant industry regulators if the investment will be going into industries the Catalogue deems restricted. Separate approval processes also exist when it comes to land use and other administrative areas.

To make things even more complicated, the regulatory agencies often have overlapping authorities that can change overnight, making it hard for investors to know exactly what to do. A recent example involves the China International Economic and Trade Arbitration Commission (CIETAC),

FIGURE 7-5 China's FDI restrictiveness by sector, 1997 and 2016 (Source: OECD)

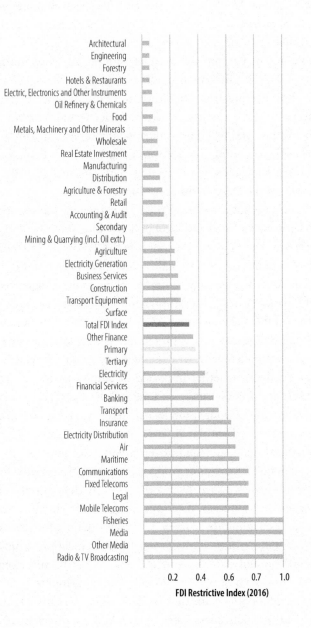

Architectural
Engineering
Forestry
Hotels & Restaurants
Electric, Electronics and Other Instruments
Oil Refinery & Chemicals
Food
Metals, Machinery and Other Minerals
Wholesale
Real Estate Investment
Manufacturing
Distribution
Agriculture & Forestry
Retail
Accounting & Audit
Secondary
Mining & Quarrying (incl. Oil extr.)
Agriculture
Electricity Generation
Business Services
Construction
Transport Equipment
Surface
Total FDI Index
Other Finance
Primary
Tertiary
Electricity
Financial Services
Banking
Transport
Insurance
Electricity Distribution
Air
Maritime
Communications
Fixed Telecoms
Legal
Mobile Telecoms
Fisheries
Media
Other Media
Radio & TV Broadcasting

0.2   0.4   0.6 0.7   1.0

FDI Restrictive Index (2016)

the most widely utilized arbitral body for disputes involving foreign investment in China. In 2012, two of CIETAC's sub-commissions in Shanghai and Shenzhen declared their independence, changed their names, and
issued their own rules in anticipation of revenue loss after the CIETAC
headquarter in Beijing was granted significantly more authority. In response, CIETAC Beijing disqualified CIETAC Shanghai and Shenzhen
from administering arbitration disputes. For a long time, therefore, it was
unclear whether the newly created agencies would have the legal authority to arbitrate and whether a court would enforce an arbitral decision by
either of those bodies. The split-up debacle was particularly troublesome
for foreign companies with existing contracts that identify Shanghai or
Shenzhen as the location for arbitration.[27]

The decentralized nature of the FDI regulatory framework also leads to
a gap between national and local policies. One prominent example of this
is China's industrial policy, specifically the Trial Administrative Measures
on the Accreditation of National Indigenous Innovation Products promulgated in 2006 by three key central-level government agencies: the Ministry of Finance (MOF), the Ministry of Science and Technology (MOST),
and the NDRC. The measures provisionally set criteria for evaluating and
certifying indigenous innovation products that would receive government
procurement preferences, which effectively ruled out qualification of any
foreign products, whether imported or made in China.[28] Due to strong
criticisms and complaints from foreign businesses and governments, the
compilation of a national product catalogue was soon tabled, and the measures were revoked entirely in 2011. Nevertheless, a considerable number
of provincial and municipal governments have gone on to release their
own indigenous innovation product catalogues. In seventy-four such sub-
central catalogues issued by February 2011, the majority of these local
catalogues were found to "discriminate against foreign invested enterprises
products," according to a survey by the U.S.-China Business Council.[29]

When taking into consideration the aforementioned problems in implementation and enforcement, one should not be surprised to see that
China is not the best place to do business compared to most other developed and developing countries. In 1997, when the OECD released its first
global FDI restrictiveness index, which looks at discriminatory screening
or approval mechanisms as part of the measure, China was the second
most restrictive country after Vietnam. Similarly, the China Business Climate Survey conducted in the same year found American firms' top two

concerns about doing business in China to be "lack of transparency of rules and regulations" and "inconsistent enforcement of rules and regulations."[30]

Strikingly, these same concerns remain twenty years later. In the 2018 Business Climate Survey, 60 percent of the surveyed managers referred to "inconsistent regulation and enforcement" as their top concern about doing business in China. Uneven enforcement, according to the managers, has become a subtler version of protectionism, with foreign companies bearing more than their share of the government's heavy hand. Nearly half (46 percent) believed they were treated unfairly compared to local companies, with some claiming to have undergone tax audits or reviews of work permits more frequently than their domestic counterparts. Similarly, firms in the Canada-China Business Survey in 2014 identified "inconsistent interpretation of regulations and laws and lack of transparency" as the top major obstacle to doing business in China.[31] For global companies in China, "operating by the book often seems to involve a book still being written."[32]

Despite its highly restrictive investment rules, investors flocked to China during the earlier period of reform for a number of reasons. First and foremost, the consensus in the FDI literature is that host countries with larger market size, faster economic growth, and a higher degree of economic development will provide more and better opportunities for these industries to exploit their ownership advantages.[33] The size of China's market and the rate of economic growth are therefore ideal for foreign investors seeking overseas consumers for their products as well as those who engage primarily in export-oriented FDI. Furthermore, with the world's largest population, China has rich supplies of labor, and workers' average salaries are lower than in most other developing countries. Last but not least, local governments looking for foreign investment to promote economic growth and bolster employment often compete with each other by offering a range of incentives that include but are not limited to tax breaks and land supply.[34] Consequently, foreign investors have enough incentives to justify making the trip to China despite the restrictive and uneven implementation of the FDI rules.

Most of these favorable conditions have dissipated in the last decade, however. After nearly thirty years of double-digit growth, China's economy has slowed down since the 2008 global financial crisis. In 2016, the annual GDP growth rate dipped to 6.7 percent, the lowest in a decade. Chinese factory workers are now getting paid more than ever, a combined result of rising living standards and a broader demographic shift. In 2016, China's average hourly wage reached $3.60, more than five times India's. Preferential policies previously doled out to foreign investors have also started to dry up. The revised corporate income tax mentioned above, for example, effectively removed the tax benefits that foreign investors had enjoyed for decades. Some of the new government-backed initiatives, such as Made in China 2025, aimed at securing China's advantage in hi-tech industries, have further contributed to a heightened sense of unease and alarm among foreign investors and governments alike.

Now more than ever, navigating the obstacle course that is China's FDI regulatory regime, which is fraught with pitfalls and unexpected twists and turns, seems increasingly unpalatable for foreign investors, especially with other markets in the developing world quickly catching up. This can be seen in the substantial improvements of the FDI index in countries like India and Vietnam (figure 7-4). In fact, in the annual survey on Business Conditions of Japanese Companies in Asia and Oceania, conducted by the Japan External Trade Organization (JETRO), Southeast Asia has consistently beat China since 2012 as the location where firms would be most likely to expand.[35] Similarly, a 2019 survey of 630 Japanese companies in East Asia, Southeast Asia, India, and Australia shows that Vietnam is seen as the most promising economy for investment (35.7 percent), followed by India (17.8 percent) and China (7.9 percent), down from 12.6 percent the year before.[36]

To maintain itself as an attractive destination for investment, therefore, China needs to increase regulatory "fairness, predictability, and transparency"—factors firms have cited as important steps that would have the greatest impact on their investment decisions in China.[37] The proposed new foreign investment law (FIL) suggests that policy-makers in Beijing are well aware of the challenges and are moving in the right direction. Released by MOFCOM in a draft version in January 2015 for public consultation, the FIL represents China's most ambitious endeavor to overhaul the FDI regulatory regime that has been in place for decades. If enacted, the FIL would unify the three central FDI laws and their implementing rules, as well as applicable provisions scattered throughout numerous other laws, regulations, and departmental rules. Furthermore, the FIL would adopt a reporting mechanism to replace MOFCOM's approvals system, thereby reducing investor uncertainty from transactions currently subject to discretionary approvals at both central and local levels.[38]

Bilateral Investment Treaties as New Drivers for FDI

In addition to reforming the FDI regulatory framework domestically, China can also use bilateral investment treaties (BITs) to attract foreign investment. BITs are legally binding agreements that set up rules of the road for foreign investment in the signatory countries, giving investors better access to foreign markets—and on fairer terms.[39] By entering into a BIT, countries agree that foreign investors shall not be treated any worse than national investors (national treatment) and that privileges granted to one foreign investor must be granted to all foreign investors (most-favored nation, or MFN). They also agree to guarantee fair and equitable treatment for foreign investors in accordance with international standards after the investment has taken place. Finally, BITs usually include some provisions on investor-state dispute settlement (ISDS).

First appearing at the end of the 1950s, BITs worldwide increased exponentially in the 1990s, and according to the United Nations Conference on Trade and Development (UNCTAD), 2,947 BITs have been signed to date and 2,364 are currently in force. BITs are especially popular among developing countries, which face a dynamic inconsistency problem in attracting FDI. The dynamic inconsistency problem refers to the fact that even though host countries can promise fair and equitable treatment beforehand, once the investments are made, the host country can freely renege on those promises and, in some cases, expropriate the investments altogether. By entering into a legally binding bilateral treaty, host countries can use the BIT as a commitment to business-friendly policies, a signal aimed at quelling investor concerns over fair treatment post-investment.

The most important aspect of a BIT is the binding ISDS provision.[40] This "breakthrough" in investment law endows private investors with the right to challenge host governments on virtually any policies involving foreign investment without having to exhaust often onerous domestic legal systems, instead going straight to international arbitration.[41] As such, BITs provide foreign investors with a rare and important instrument of protection for which there are currently few legal alternatives.[42] Empirical research has demonstrated that signing BITs indeed boosts FDI inflow.[43]

China signed its first BIT with Sweden on March 29, 1982. Since then, more than 120 BITs have been concluded between China and a wide variety of countries on every inhabited continent (figure 7-6). However, not all BITs are equal. In the 1980s, most of the BITs signed by China were with Euro-

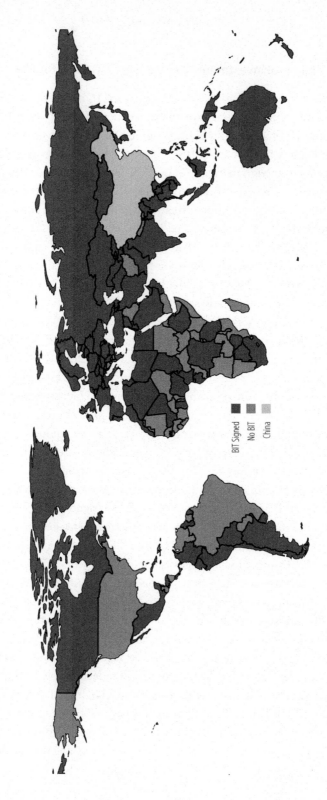

BIT Signed
No BIT
China

FIGURE 7-6 China's bilateral investment treaties (Source: UNCTAD Investment Policy Hub [http://investmentpolicyhub.unctad.org/])

pean capital-exporting countries and poor developing countries. These early BITs included basic provisions on fair and equitable treatment, MFN treatment, restrictions on expropriation, and capital convertibility, but missed the important ISDS and national treatment provisions.[44]

As China itself gradually started exporting capital in the 1990s, mostly to other developing countries, it adopted a more liberal approach to BITs, opting for stronger legal protections for its own foreign investments. The 1998 China-Barbados BIT for the first time included provisions on international arbitration for investor-state disputes, which became a standard practice in nearly all of China's subsequent BITs in the 2000s.[45] In the meantime, Chinese BITs also increasingly included national treatment provisions, though most of them were incorporating vague, openended language and only applied to the post-establishment stage of the investment.

Since the 2008 global financial crisis, China has been making more progress toward higher standards in some of its more recent investment treaties, such as the 2012 Canada-China Foreign Investment Protection Agreement (FIPA) and the China-Japan–Republic of Korea Agreement for Promotion, Facilitation and Protection of Investment. In the ongoing China–United States BIT negotiations, in particular, China is looking toward breaking away from its traditional BIT model in at least two aspects. First, China has signaled its willingness to allow nondiscriminatory access to its market at all stages of investment. This would protect pre-investment activities and is expected to open the Chinese market and afford greater certainty for investments in various sectors. Second, China has agreed that it will negotiate on the basis of a negative list, allowing foreign investment in a much broader range of industries and sectors of its economy.[46]

Committing to more rigorous market-opening conditions in negotiating these high-standard BITs can help address three interrelated challenges facing the Chinese government. One is that as China becomes a net capital exporter and its outbound investment continues to grow, the principle of reciprocity embodied in the BITs can help lower the barriers that Chinese firms face in host nations, especially in traditional capital-exporting countries such as the United States. A second is that China can leverage BITs as a counterbalance against several megaregional FTAs under negotiation that would exclude China, including the (Comprehensive and Progressive) Agreement for Trans-Pacific Partnership and the Transatlantic Trade and

Investment Partnership. The third and most important for Chinese leaders is that BITs can help them push forward reform of the domestic FDI regulatory regime by committing to external obligations, a strategy that proved effective during China's bid for its accession to the WTO, which stimulated reforms in SOEs and the government system.

Evidence of foreign investors being reassured by the BITs can be seen in the changing attitudes of Canadian firms in China after FIPA went into effect. The top two concerns in 2014, "inconsistent interpretation of regulations/laws" and "weak dispute settlement mechanism," were down to thirteenth and twenty-fifth place, respectively, according to CCBC's latest survey. Furthermore, "protection of and enforcement of intellectual property rights" was viewed as very important by only 36 percent of the survey participants in 2016, down from 46 percent in 2014.[47] Overall, more than 50 percent of the Canadian firms that are aware of FIPA said that the investment treaty has helped their business by "imposing discipline on conduct by Chinese officials at different levels of government" and "protecting investor rights through the arbitration process."[48]

Conclusion

During the Boao Forum for Asia on April 11, 2018, President Xi Jinping announced that China's doors would only open "wider and wider" to foreign investment, promising to remove foreign equity stake caps for banks, securities firms, and insurance by the end of 2018.[49] Xi further assured foreign investors that China would prioritize protecting intellectual property rights and tweak its domestic regulations to comply with international economic and trade rules.[50] Xi's speech reaffirmed the central government's determination to further liberalize the FDI regulatory framework in an attempt to maintain China's position as a top destination for foreign investors.

Skeptics may point out that past similar promises to open up usually fell short due to poor implementation and uneven enforcement at the local level, in spite of the central leaders' good intentions. Yet there is reason to believe that having consolidated power through a sweeping bureaucratic reshuffle as well as constitutional amendments that removed term limits, President Xi, for the first time since Deng Xiaoping, will be able to deliver on his promises and push forward liberalization without much opposition from the ruling elites and local agents. A clear demonstration of the government's resolve would be the ratification *and* enforcement of the proposed new FIL, especially if it improves the "transparency, predictability, and fairness of the regulatory environment," factors cited by firms in the China Business Climate Survey as the most significant for increasing their investment levels in China.[51]

China would also be able to lock in domestic reforms by committing to high-standard BITs, several of which, including the China–United States and China–European Union BITs, are currently under negotiation. For their part, Chinese regulators could use international pressure as an opportunity to build transparency and equity into their rules and enforcement. Those steps would improve confidence in the market and unlock increased foreign investment. Having a BIT with China would provide foreign investors with fair treatment both pre- and post-establishment, as well as expanded access to the second-largest market in the world.

Indeed, one-quarter of American firms in the 2018 China Business Climate Survey singled out an investment treaty between the United States and China as the most valuable step the U.S. government could take to improve their ability to operate in China.[52] What these firms can do is proactively work to identify and prioritize the existing laws, regulations, and administrative practices that restrict or otherwise impede their operations in China and seek opportunities to share that information with the government, which can, in turn, put pressure on the Chinese government. They can also apply pressure directly by "voting with their feet" (that is, relocating their businesses to other markets), a threat that now is more credible, given the rising cost of labor in China. As demonstrated by the case of the indigenous innovation policy, the Chinese government *can* be pressured into making policy changes.

Finally, there is now a new group of allies within China, which can potentially be mobilized to lobby for a better FDI regulatory environment. As more and more Chinese firms, both state and privately owned, venture abroad to invest in developing and developed countries, they are now calling for Beijing to strengthen its protection of their investment by negotiating high-standard agreements with host nations. It is, therefore, in the interest of both China and its partner countries to conclude the best possible agreements, which hopefully can set the FDI ground rules for years to come.

Notes

1. "FDI Grew by 4.1% in 2016," *Xinhua News*, January 13, 2017.

2. Hans Christiansen, *Foreign Direct Investment for Development: Maximising Benefits, Minimising Costs* (Paris, France: OCED, 2002).

3. For a comprehensive overview of the broad impact of FDI on China's economy, see Michael J. Enright, *Developing China: The Remarkable Impact of Foreign Direct Investment* (Abingdon, United Kingdom: Taylor & Francis, 2016).

4. On economic growth, see John Whalley and Xian Xin, "China's FDI and Non-FDI Economies and the Sustainability of Future High Chinese Growth," *China Economic Review*, vol. 21, no. 1 (2010), 123–135; Shiyong Zhao, "Privatization, FDI Inflow and Economic Growth: Evidence from China's Provinces, 1978–2008," *Applied Economics*, vol. 45, no. 15 (2013), 2127–2139. On productivity, see Eunsuk Hong and Sun Laixiang, "Foreign Direct Investment and Total Factor Productivity in China: A Spatial Dynamic Panel Analysis," *Oxford Bulletin of Economics and Statistics*, vol. 73, no. 6 (2011), 771–791. On trade, see Kevin Honglin Zhang, "What Drives Export Competitiveness? The Role of FDI in Chinese Manufacturing," *Contemporary Economic Policy*, vol. 33, no. 3 (2015), 499–512. On investment, see Guoxin Wu, Yu Sun, and Zhuning Li, "The Crowding-in and Crowding-out Effects of FDI on Domestic Investment in the Yangtze Delta Region," *China: An International Journal*, vol. 10, no. 2 (2012), 119–133. On employment, see Sune Karlsson, Nannan Lundin, Fredrik Sjöholm, and Ping He, "Foreign Firms and Chinese Employment," *World Economy*, vol. 32, no. 1 (2009), 178–201; Qing Liu, Ruosi Lu, and Chao Zhang, "The Labor Market Effect of Foreign Acquisitions: Evidence from Chinese Manufacturing Firms," *China Economic Review*, vol. 32 (2015), 110–120.

5. Hao Xu, Difang Wan, and Ying Sun, "Technology Spillovers of Foreign Direct Investment in Coastal Regions of East China: A Perspective on Technology Absorptive Capacity," *Emerging Markets Finance and Trade*, vol. 50, sup. 1 (2014), 96–106; Lingyun Huang, Xiaming Liu, and Lei Xu, "Regional Innovation and Spillover Effects of Foreign Direct Investment in China: A Threshold Approach," *Regional Studies*, vol. 46, no. 5 (2012), 583–596; Chunlai Chen, Yu Sheng, and Christopher Findlay, "Export Spillovers of FDI on China's Domestic Firms," *Review of International Economics*, vol. 21, no. 5 (2013), 841–856.

6. "FDI Reaches Record Level in 2017," *Xinhua News*, January 16, 2018.

7. I use the estimates provided by the National Bureau of Statistics (NBS) to calculate this rate (see table 7-1 and figure 7-1). In contrast, the Ministry of Commerce has reported a positive, albeit very small, increase in FDI, presumably using its own estimates, ostensibly to paint a bright picture. Such discrepancy is not uncommon when it comes to Chinese statistics. See, for example, Jeremy L. Wallace, "Juking the Stats? Authoritarian Information Problems in China," *British Journal of Political Science*, vol. 46, no. 1 (2016), 11–29. For consistency, I use the NBS estimates throughout this chapter.

8. Jane Li, "Why Foreign Companies Are Shutting Shop in China," *South China Morning Post*, February 2, 2017.

9. State Council Circular No. 39, "Notice of the State Council on Several Measures to Promote Foreign Investment Growth," State Council of China, August 16, 2017.

10. AmCham China (American Chamber of Commerce in China), "2018 China Business Climate Survey Report," January 29, 2018.

11. Another commonly used source of Chinese FDI is the United Nations Conference on Trade and Development (UNCTAD) FDI data; these are slightly different from the NBS data, which are restricted to nonfinancial FDI. I use the NBS data because they provide more disaggregated information on the geographical and sectoral composition of inward FDI.

12. Indeed, it had been found that local officials often inflate the reported contractual amount to impress the upper level; see Shang-Jin Wei, "Foreign Direct Investment in China: Sources and Consequences," in Takatoshi Ito and Anne O. Krueger, eds., *Financial Deregulation and Integration in East Asia* (Chicago, Illinois: University of Chicago Press, 1996), 77–105.

13. Annual FID data are not available between 1979 and 1984, only in the aggregate.

14. The underperformance of joint ventures is not unique in China; see J. Michael Geringer and Louis Hebert, "Measuring Performance of International Joint Ventures," *Journal of International Business Studies*, vol. 22, no. 2 (1991), 249–263.

15. Geng Xiao, *People's Republic of China's Round-tripping FDI: Scale, Causes and Implications*, ADB Institute Discussion Papers No. 7 (Tokyo, Japan: Asian Development Bank Institute, 2004).

16. Before the income tax integration, the average effective tax rates for domestic and foreign firms were 25 percent and 13 percent, respectively.

17. The top ten countries/economies are Hong Kong ($87.18 billion), Singapore ($6.18 billion), South Korea ($4.75 billion), the United States ($3.83 billion), Taiwan Province ($3.62 billion), Macao ($3.48 billion), Japan ($3.11 billion), Germany ($2.71 billion), the United Kingdom ($2.21 billion), and Luxembourg ($1.39 billion).

18. Stephen S. Golub, "Measures of Restrictions on Inward Foreign Direct Investment for OECD Countries," *OECD Economic Studies*, vol. 1, no. 1 (2013), 88–122.

19. Xiaojun Li and Ka Zeng, "Individual Preferences for FDI in Developing Countries: Experimental Evidence from China," *Journal of Experimental Political Science*, vol. 4, no. 3 (2017), 195–205.

20. Margaret M. Pearson, *Joint Ventures in the People's Republic of China: The Control of Foreign Direct Investment Under Socialism* (Princeton, New Jersey: Princeton University Press, 1992).

21. Shi Guangsheng, *A History of China's Foreign Trade Reform and Development* [中国对外经济贸易改革和发展史] (Beijing, China: People's Press, 2013).

22. The Constitution of the People's Republic of China.

23. Margaret M. Pearson, "The Erosion of Controls over Foreign Capital in

China, 1979–1988: Having Their Cake and Eating It Too?" *Modern China*, vol. 17, no. 1 (1991), 112–150.

24. The OECD FDI Regulatory Restrictiveness Index is based on four main indicators of restrictions against foreign investments: foreign equity restrictions; discriminatory screening or approval mechanisms; restrictions on key foreign personnel; and other operational restrictions (such as limits on purchase of land or on repatriation of profits and capital).

25. Golub, "Measures of Restrictions."

26. See, for example, Kenneth Lieberthal and Michel Oksenberg, *Policy Making in China: Leaders, Structures, and Processes* (Princeton, New Jersey: Princeton University Press, 1990); Melanie Manion, "Policy Implementation in the People's Republic of China: Authoritative Decisions Versus Individual Interests," *Journal of Asian Studies*, vol. 50, no. 2 (1991), 253–279; Kevin J. O'Brien and Lianjiang Li, "Selective Policy Implementation in Rural China," *Comparative Politics*, vol. 31, no. 2 (1999), 167–186; Sarah Eaton and Genia Kostka, "Authoritarian Environmentalism Undermined? Local Leaders' Time Horizons and Environmental Policy Implementation in China," *China Quarterly*, vol. 218 (2014), 359–380.

27. "*Shewai Zhongcai Nao Fenzhi: Zhengyi Beihou Shenfen Chengmi* (CIETAC Split Drama: The Mystery behind the Controversy)," *Yicai*, May 4, 2012.

28. AmCham China, "2007 China Business Climate Survey Report."

29. Stanley Lubman, "Changes to China's 'Indigenous Innovation' Policy: Don't Get Too Excited," *Wall Street Journal*, July 22, 2011.

30. AmCham China, "1997 China Business Climate Survey Report."

31. "Canada China Business Survey," Canada–China Business Council (CCBC), April 25, 2017.

32. AmCham China, "2018 China Business Climate Survey Report."

33. John H. Dunning, *Explaining International Production* (London, United Kingdom: Unwin Hyman, 1988); John H. Dunning, *Multinational Enterprises and the Global Economy* (Reading, Massachusetts: Addison-Wesley, 1993); Edward Graham, "The (Not Wholly Satisfactory) State of the Theory of Foreign Direct Investment and the Multinational Enterprise," in Jerome L. Stein, ed., *The Globalization of Markets: Capital Flows, Exchange Rates and Trade Regimes* (Berlin, Germany: Springer-Verlag, 1997), 99–122; Nathan Jensen, Glen Biglaiser, Quan Li, Edmund Malesky, Pablo Pinto, Santiago Pinto, and Joseph Staats, *Politics and Foreign Direct Investment* (Ann Arbor, Michigan: University of Michigan Press, 2012).

34. Ling Chen, *Manipulating Globalization: The Influence of Bureaucrats on Business in China* (Palo Alto, California: Stanford University Press, 2018.)

35. "2017 JETRO Survey on Business Conditions of Japanese Companies in Asia and Oceania," Japan External Trade Organization (JETRO).

36. NNA Japan, "Japanese Firms Pick Vietnam as Asia's Top Investment Spot, with India a Distant Second," *Japan Times*, January 10, 2019.

37. AmCham China, "2018 China Business Climate Survey Report."

38. The draft FIL revealed on December 23, 2018, states that forced technology transfer through administrative measures is prohibited and technology cooperation should be based on voluntarily agreed terms and business practices.

39. UNCTAD, *Bilateral Investment Treaties in the Mid-1990s* (New York and Geneva: United Nations, 1998).

40. Susan D. Franck, "Foreign Direct Investment, Investment Treaty Arbitration, and the Rule of Law," *Pacific McGeorge Global Business & Development Law Journal*, vol. 19 (2006), 337.

41. Zachary Elkins, Andrew Guzman, and Beth Simmons, "Competing for Capital: The Diffusion of Bilateral Investment Treaties, 1960–2000," *International Organization*, vol. 60 (2006), 811–846.

42. Only a few regional free-trade agreements contain investment protection provisions, such as the North American Free Trade Agreement (NAFTA) and the proposed Trans-Pacific Partnership. The TRIMs Agreement under the WTO imposes rudimentary discipline on the regulation of foreign investment but nowhere near as comprehensive as the provisions contained in many BITs.

43. See, for example, Eric Neumayer and Laura Spess, "Do Bilateral Investment Treaties Increase Foreign Direct Investment to Developing Countries?" *World Development*, vol. 33, no. 10 (2005), 1567–1585; Andrew Kerner, "Why Should I Believe You? The Costs and Consequences of Bilateral Investment Treaties," *International Studies Quarterly*, vol. 53, no. 1 (2009), 73–102; Matthias Busse, Jens Königer, and Peter Nunnenkamp, "FDI Promotion through Bilateral Investment Treaties: More Than a Bit?" *Review of World Economics*, vol. 146, no. 1 (2010), 147–177.

44. Axel Berger, "China's New Bilateral Investment Treaty Program: Substance, Rationale and Implications for International Investment Law Making," German Development Institute, November 2008.

45. Berger, "China's New Bilateral Investment Treaty Program."

46. Yong Wang, "China's BIT Progress and Implications for China-Canada FTA Talks," Centre for International Governance Innovation Policy Brief, No. 104, 2017.

47. CCBC, "Canada–China Business Survey."

48. CCBC, "Canada–China Business Survey."

49. Sidney Leng, Liu Zhen, Sarah Zheng, and Wendy Wu, "Chinese President Xi Jinping Stands Up for Globalisation and Free Trade at Asia's Davos," *South China Morning Post*, April 10, 2018,

50. Leng, Zhen, Zheng, and Wu, "Chinese President Xi Jinping Stands Up for Globalisation and Free Trade."

51. AmCham China, "2018 China Business Climate Survey Report."

52. AmCham China, "2018 China Business Climate Survey Report."

EIGHT

Great Leap Outward

Chinese ODI and the Belt and Road Initiative

TOM MILLER

Introduction[1]

China has been a major destination for *inbound* investment for some twenty-five years, but has only been a significant source of *outbound* investment for the past decade. Foreign capital began to trickle into Chinese factories, real estate, and infrastructure in the mid-1980s, a few years after the launch of Reform and Opening. By the late 1990s, that trickle had turned into a flood, and over the following ten years China's stock of foreign direct investment (FDI) rapidly surged past $1 trillion. Today, forty years after China began to open to the world, a staggering $3 trillion of foreign investment has washed up on Chinese shores.[2]

China's outward direct investment (ODI) started much more tentatively. In the first two decades of the reform period, Chinese enterprises invested about $30 billion abroad—just one-tenth of the total that flowed in during the same period. That began to change in 1999, when former president Jiang Zemin launched the Go Out policy, encouraging state-owned enterprises (SOEs) to buy assets overseas. ODI flows accelerated in the mid-2000s, as rising export profits swelled China's foreign exchange reserves, and then ramped up as firms took advantage of the international fire sale sparked by the global financial crisis. For the first time, private companies joined their state-owned counterparts as big outward investors.

In recent years, Xi Jinping's forceful and nationalistic leadership has seen a step-change in China's ambitions overseas and a commensurate rise in Chinese ODI. Xi is attempting to harness the power of the state to realize one overriding goal: the "Chinese Dream" of national greatness.[3] He is not the first modern Chinese leader to promise "the great rejuvenation of the Chinese nation," but he is the first to set a target date: 2049, the centenary of the founding of the People's Republic of China. By mid-century, Xi says, China must be "wealthy and strong," both at home and abroad.[4] All policy, including the regulation of outward investment flows, is crafted with the goal of national glory in mind.

Since Xi took power in late 2012, the total stock of Chinese ODI has trebled and the state has begun to play a bigger role in directing where it goes. Chinese investment is increasingly a tool to project state power: individual companies can and do pursue their own commercial interests, yet state support is reserved for investments that are deemed to further national industrial or strategic policies, whether made by SOEs or private firms. China is using investments and economic activity overseas to strengthen national competitiveness and build geopolitical leverage, with the aim of reshaping the world in its interests.

Broadly, the strategy has two prongs. First, to acquire the foreign technology needed to upgrade the nation's manufacturing capabilities, so that Chinese industry can compete at the top of the global value chain. This requires purchasing technology firms and intellectual property in developed economies, especially the United States and Europe. Second, to assert China's economic leadership across the developing world, bolstering its position as the only serious rival to the United States. This is the strategic underpinning of Xi's signature foreign policy, the Belt and Road Initiative (BRI)—the main focus of this chapter. Both prongs are designed to ensure that China realizes its long-term goal of becoming a dominant global power.

A Brief History of Outbound Investment

China's swift economic rise on the international stage has come in two main phases. The first phase was founded on trade: after joining the World Trade Organization in 2001, China moved from the margins of the global trading system to become the world's largest exporter in 2009. The second phase, which began in earnest in the late 2000s, saw China's surge as an international investor. In 2008, China's annual outward investment breached $50 billion for the first time, more than double the figure in 2007. By 2016, it had ballooned to at least $170 billion, or as high as $196 billion, depending on which metric we use.[5] China now vies with Japan as the world's second-biggest source of outward direct investment, behind only the United States.

Jiang Zemin's Go Out strategy encouraged state-backed firms to buy up not only natural resources, but also foreign technology, brands, and distribution channels. The aim was to increase their competitiveness, transforming the most successful into multinational companies. Some deals were driven by a desire for prestige; others by a desire to strengthen the acquirer's position back home. In 2005, for example, Lenovo Group bought IBM's personal computer division, including its valuable ThinkPad brand—shocking observers who had never imagined that an obscure Chinese firm could buy such a venerable name. Nevertheless, the vast majority of acquisitions continued to be made by state firms in natural resources, mainly in the developing world. To this day, a large chunk of China's stock of ODI is concentrated in oil and gas, high-grade coal mines, metal ores, and hydropower.

The direction of investment flows began to change with the global financial crisis of 2007–2008. At first, the commodity-price crash gave mining and energy companies such as state oil major CNPC an added incentive to snaffle further resource assets on the cheap. The single biggest deal was state-owned Chinalco's $14 billion investment in Anglo-Australian miner Rio Tinto in 2008. But Chinese firms also took the opportunity to diversify their investments, acquiring newly available assets in nonresource sectors in developed markets. They targeted technology, consumer goods and services, agriculture, and real estate—seeking foreign brands and know-how for use at home, or access to new markets abroad. A notable example was Geely Auto's $2.7 billion purchase of Swedish automaker Volvo in 2010.

As Chinese ODI became more driven by the private sector, capital naturally flowed to economies with large markets, stable investment regimes, and strong consumer and technology assets. By 2012, the trend suggested that Chinese ODI was becoming more "normal" and less frightening than it had previously seemed, when scaremongers suggested that unstoppable state firms, backed by a bottomless treasury, had embarked on a mad quest to "lock up" scarce natural resources. The private real-estate conglomerate Dalian Wanda bought AMC Entertainment, owner of America's biggest chain of movie theaters, for $2.6 billion. And WH Group, a meat processor based in Henan province, lifted the bar for private acquisitions with its $7.1 billion takeover of Smithfield Foods, the largest pork producer in the United States.

The expanding footprint of private firms in rich-world economies continued for another three or four years. From 2014, Beijing made it easier for firms to make foreign acquisitions, scrapping pre-approvals for deals below $1 billion and requiring companies to register only their planned transactions rather than seek central permission. With a $4 trillion pile of foreign exchange reserves, Beijing sought to loosen its tight capital controls while enabling private firms to become more competitive in the international market. This released pent-up demand from Chinese enterprises seeking to diversify abroad, with private investors snapping up European soccer clubs, golf courses, tourism companies, and hotel chains. As ODI values doubled between 2012 and 2016, it seemed self-evident that China, long one of the world's biggest destinations for foreign investment, was on the road to becoming a net exporter of capital.

Yet, in late 2016, the regulatory pendulum swung back.[6] Uneasy about the flood of capital pouring overseas into often dubious-looking investments in nonstrategic industries, the leadership instructed Chinese regulators to become more stringent. With the rising U.S. dollar placing huge downward pressure on the renminbi, the State Administration of Foreign Exchange (SAFE) acted to prevent capital leaving the country. Unofficially, it ordered banks to stop processing outward investments of more than $50 million without approval. Several government agencies announced they would closely monitor specific types of outbound investment, including purchases of real estate, hotels, cinemas, and sports clubs.[7] In January 2017, the State-owned Assets Supervision and Administrative Commission (SASAC) issued new rules on overseas investments, in principle banning large SOEs from venturing outside their core businesses.[8]

Zhou Xiaochuan, the central bank governor, stepped into the fray. "Some investments do not meet our industrial policy requirements for outward investment," he said in March 2017. "Therefore we think a certain degree of policy guidance is necessary and effective."[9] That summer, banks were ordered to examine their exposure to a group of acquisitive private firms, including property-to-entertainment giant Dalian Wanda, insurance and investment conglomerate Fosun International, and travel group HNA.[10] The biggest headlines were reserved for the Beijing-based conglomerate Anbang Insurance Group, which had raised eyebrows by purchasing New York's iconic Waldorf Astoria hotel for $2 billion. After regulators announced a new ODI regime based on lists of "encouraged," "restricted," and "prohibited" investments,[11] the central government arrested Anbang's flamboyant chairman for "economic crimes" and summarily took control of his company.[12]

Guojin mintui: The State Advances, the Private Sector Retreats

Measuring China's ODI flows is tricky: the Ministry of Commerce (Mofcom) and SAFE publish different figures that do not line up. Mofcom's numbers track every sizable "nonfinancial" investment made overseas; SAFE's numbers track the broader balance of payments, including all financial outflows. Mofcom's ODI statistics are most widely quoted, but some critics believe they suffer from political manipulation.[13] One way to crosscheck the official data is to use independent estimates of Chinese ODI built on counts of cross-border deals. The most comprehensive public data-set is the China Global Investment Tracker (CGIT), maintained by the American Enterprise Institute, which lists every recorded transaction more than $100 million from 2005 onward.[14] Another useful series is published by the Rhodium Group, a New York–based consultancy, although it only records transactions in the United States.[15]

Mofcom's data suggest that the crackdown, which began in late 2016, worked: ODI fell to $120 billion in 2017, a significant drop from the year before. There is some disagreement over the extent of the investment slowdown, but ODI outflows would have been significantly higher without government restrictions.[16] The most dramatic fall occurred in the United States, where total investments halved to below $25 billion, according to the CGIT. The Rhodium Group's China Investment Monitor recorded a similar decline: transactions slipped to $29 billion, down 35 percent from the figure in 2016, with the biggest falls in entertainment, consumer products and services, real estate, and hospitality. The real fall was even more precipitous, as 60 percent of the transaction value made by Chinese firms in 2017 stemmed from the completion of deals announced in 2016.[17]

In the United States, much of the decline was directly attributable to Beijing's crackdown on "irrational" investments in nonstrategic sectors: it is no coincidence that transaction values remained stable or even grew in areas regarded as important by the state, such as biotech, IT, transportation, and infrastructure. But higher regulatory hurdles in Washington were also an important factor. After broadening its definition of national security risks, the Committee on Foreign Investment in the United States (CFIUS) delayed or refused to approve many more deals in 2017 than in previous years. The stricter approvals process targeted acquisitions of companies deemed to have strategic value, as well as those with access to sensitive U.S. consumer data.

CFIUS's crackdown reflected deepening concern about Chinese state-led investments and unfair commercial practices. In both the United States and Europe, Chinese firms regularly make cross-border acquisitions that foreign firms would never be permitted to make in China. The lack of "investment reciprocity" is particularly stark in Europe: Chinese foreign investment into the European Union nearly doubled to $40 billion in 2016, from $22 billion in 2015, while European investment in China declined to a paltry $8 billion.[18] According to the OECD's FDI Restrictiveness Index, China has, by a wide margin, the most stringent limits on foreign investors among major economies.[19] Many sectors are off-limits to foreign investors altogether, and others restricted to minority shareholdings or joint ventures. These restrictions are especially pervasive in China's fast-growing service sectors, which is also where developed countries tend to have the greatest comparative advantage.

Since the policy shift that began in late 2016, China's overseas investment regime has been tilted heavily in favor of SOEs and enterprises operating in strategic sectors. In 2017, the private share of ODI fell to 36 percent, down from 46 percent in 2016.[20] Restrictions on outward investment by private firms eased a little in the second half of 2017, but banks and companies still routinely consult regulators before making outbound deals, according to investment bankers and M&A lawyers.[21] Priority is given to investments that comply with national economic and strategic objectives, such as deals in high-tech sectors like semiconductors. Acquisitions by state firms looking to advance national policy goals, notably the flagship Made in China 2025 industrial policy and the Belt and Road Initiative, are much more likely to gain official approval. That means that private firms risk losing out—with the possible exception of politically canny tech companies like Tencent, Alibaba, and Huawei, which are willing to pursue deals that benefit China Inc.

No doubt this state-driven investment model once made perfect sense within the government's walled compound of Zhongnanhai, but it has backfired abroad. In both the United States and Europe, opposition has hardened against Chinese acquisitions that threaten Western leadership in critical technologies. In the United States, private firms accounted for about 90 percent of Chinese transactions by value in 2017, as regulators blocked investments by SOEs on national security grounds. President Trump's administration is determined to protect strategic industries further, ordering an investigation of China's unfair commercial practices under Section 301 of the U.S. Trade Act. In a detailed report published in March 2018, the Office of the U.S. Trade Representative (USTR) accused the Chinese government of facilitating "the systematic investment in, and acquisition of, American companies and assets by Chinese entities, to obtain cutting-edge technologies and intellectual property and generate large-scale technology transfer in industries deemed important by state industrial plans."[22] In response, the USTR said it would prepare to impose punitive tariffs on Chinese imports, targeting strategic sectors included in the Made in China 2025 plan, such as advanced IT products, robotics, aerospace, high-speed rail equipment, and electric vehicles. In addition, it proposed imposing investment restrictions independently of those made by CFIUS. Trade hawks within the U.S. administration even pushed for employing the International Emergency Economic Powers Act of 1977, which would give the president considerable authority to curb Chinese investments.[23]

In the event, the White House slapped tariffs that summer on Chinese imports worth approximately $50 billion. These were followed by broader tariffs, initially set at 10 percent, on $200 billion of Chinese imports. Far from targeting only strategic sectors, the tariff list contained nearly six thousand product lines, from frozen cuts of pork to plastic furniture.[24] The administration stepped back from using a national-emergency law to penalize China, instead persuading Congress to pass the Foreign Investment Risk Review Modernization Act, which beefs up CFIUS's ability to review and block foreign investments in a wide swath of technological fields.[25] Finally, it imposed tougher export restrictions on U.S. firms selling or licensing technological products or services abroad—a policy clearly directed at China.[26]

Europe, too, has begun to take a tougher stance. A shift in sentiment occurred in January 2017 with Chinese appliance maker Midea's $5.2 billion acquisition of Kuka, a German advanced robotics firm. Two months later, the European Union Chamber of Commerce in China issued a report on Chinese industrial policy, concluding that there had been an "unprecedented wave of outbound investments" under the Made in China 2025 push.[27] In February 2018, the Berlin-based Global Public Policy Institute and Mercator Institute for Chinese Studies jointly published a hard-hitting and influential report arguing that China was using investment as a tool for its "authoritarian advance" in Europe. "The EU and its members need to bolster a flexible set of investment screening tools," it concluded, adding that "Europe must be able to stop state-driven takeovers of companies that are of significant public interest."[28] In December 2018, the EU Parliament's Committee on International Trade agreed to establish a framework for screening FDI, while Germany expanded the range of transactions that can be reviewed on national security concerns.[29]

As the United States and Europe both erect higher regulatory barriers, China's strategic investment push in the developed world is at risk of foundering.

What Is the Belt and Road Initiative?

The story is quite different in the developing world, where Chinese firms have a longer history of economic activity, notably in building infrastructure. China has deep roots in Africa especially, where several aid and construction projects even predated Reform and Opening. By 1975, China had aid programs in more African countries than did the United States. In the 1980s, construction companies sent over to build aid projects stayed on in their host countries, scooping up private contracts. And by 1999, Chinese investors had oil fields in Sudan, copper mines in Zambia, and farms in half a dozen countries.[30]

This century, China's economic activity has spread rapidly: it is hard to think of a single developing country where Chinese firms and investors are not already ensconced or sniffing for business. Until recently, investments and construction projects were carried out on a largely ad hoc basis, often within the broad remit of the Go Out policy. But that has begun to change under Xi Jinping's leadership, as many Chinese investments have been channeled through the Belt and Road Initiative, his signature foreign policy. Often this is little more than a branding exercise, but investments that are officially accepted as Belt and Road projects are much more likely to benefit from government support, such as access to cheap financing.

The BRI takes its inspiration from the ancient Silk Road that ran from China to Europe via central Asia. Stretching from the South China Sea across the Eurasian landmass, it envisages building roads, railways, and industrial corridors over some of the wildest terrain on earth, and linking these to upgraded ports in Asia, Africa, the Middle East, and Europe. Beijing claims that more than one hundred countries belong to the initiative, but the list continues to grow and there appear to be few geographical restraints on membership.[31] With no clear definition, the BRI has become government shorthand for Chinese financing, investment, and construction across much, if not most, of the developing world.

The initiative runs under a confusion of different monikers. Xi first proposed building a Silk Road Economic Belt, a land route through Central Asia and the Middle East to Europe, during a speech in Kazakhstan in September 2013.[32] A month later, in a speech to the Indonesian parliament, he proposed creating a Twenty-first Century Maritime Silk Road, a web of sea lanes through the South China Sea and Indian Ocean.[33] First called the New Silk Road, the scheme was later dubbed One Belt, One Road (*yidai yilu*), which sounds less clunky in Chinese than in English. After much internal debate, it was officially renamed the Belt and Road Initiative in 2015. Beijing is adamant that the BRI should not be called a *plan* or a *strategy*, lest it be interpreted as a ruse to build a vast economic empire. China claims no ownership over the initiative, which it says is about "interconnected development" and "international coordination"— though, in reality, it is very much a Chinese project.

The BRI is the most ambitious piece of outward investment policy of Xi Jinping's "New Era."[34] Yet, although the initiative has enjoyed a huge propaganda push, Beijing has done a poor job of explaining its intentions. Officially, the BRI targets five vague goals: policy coordination, facilities connectivity, unimpeded trade, financial integration, and people-to-people contacts.[35] It is less a coherent plan involving a clear list of projects than a series of wide-ranging policy aims. It is designed to bring a more strategic approach to overseas infrastructure construction than in the past, but many of the projects now included under its banner have been planned for years.

Transport connectivity is at the heart of the initiative. Six distinct "economic corridors" are associated with it, but there are few clear transport routes.[36] In reality, Chinese firms will help to lay new roads and railway tracks, linking them to new or upgraded ports, wherever they find willing partners. Their success will rely on the vagaries of diplomatic negotiations, corporate deal-making, project management, and economic demand. Some routes, such as the rail lines that lead from China to Europe via Kazakhstan and Russia, already exist; others are on the drawing table and may never leave it. Much like the ancient Silk Road, the Belt and Road will form a network of trading routes influenced by the competing demands of geography, commerce, and geopolitics.

The BRI is motivated by a number of sweeping goals that go far beyond the usual motivations for foreign investment. In the first place, it aims to protect national security. China wants to create a network of economic dependency that will consolidate its regional leadership and enable it to hedge against the United States' alliance structure in Asia. Beijing has few genuine friends, but it is serious about buying influence. This is a departure from the past, when it did not try to cultivate close diplomatic relations, other than with the rogue states of North Korea and Myanmar. Above all, China expects its partners to respect its "core interests," especially its territorial claims in Taiwan, Tibet, Xinjiang, and the South China Sea. Simply put, Beijing is offering economic benefits in exchange for political support. This is a crucial aspect of what it really means by "win-win" diplomacy.[37]

Equally important are economic motivations. At home, Beijing calculates that better connectivity will help its landlocked border regions become viable trade zones, bringing much-needed development. Abroad, Beijing hopes that state engineering firms, commodity producers, and capital goods makers will find lucrative new markets. Envisaging a regional production chain centered on China's own advanced manufacturing, it is subsidizing SOEs to export technology and industrial goods, which it hopes will lead to the widespread adoption of Chinese standards. Demand for Chinese construction services and capital goods will, in turn, be driven by state banks financing Chinese firms to build high-speed railways, pipelines, power grids, and telecoms networks.

Finally, there are financial considerations. Beijing is pushing for greater financial cooperation and integration of cross-border markets, including an increased use of the renminbi for trade settlement. This would serve the long-term ambition of making the renminbi an international currency, taking its place alongside the dollar and the euro. In addition, it wants to nurture an alternative investment channel for China's mountain of foreign exchange reserves.

Building and Financing Foreign Infrastructure: Loans and Aid

The BRI has generated excitable headlines about how vast Chinese "investments" will reshape the Eurasian continent. Chinese enterprises are certainly pushing huge amounts of capital into projects, but most are not truly Chinese investments, as they do not involve owning assets. Chinese acquisitions in Belt and Road countries are actually relatively small—only around 10 percent of annual ODI flows. In reality, the BRI is more often an opportunity for state construction enterprises to rake in billions of dollars from contracts abroad, often funded by loans from Chinese state-owned banks to host governments.

Mofcom's data show that Chinese firms invested $44 billion in sixty-odd countries along the Belt and Road in the three years from 2015 to 2017—almost exactly what China National Chemical Corporation paid in a single deal for Swiss agro-tech giant Syngenta in 2017. That year, official BRI investments amounted to a little more than $14 billion.[38] In March 2017, the head of the National Development and Reform Commission said that "more than $50 billion" had been invested since the launch of the initiative in late 2013, without giving details. These are significant sums, but only a fraction of total outward investment.

Chinese enterprises receive far more income from construction and engineering contracts than they spend on foreign assets. The value of overseas construction contracts and revenues has risen quickly, even as ODI along the Belt and Road flatlined in 2015–2017. Mofcom reports that sixty-one Belt and Road countries generated new construction contracts worth $126 billion and actual revenues of $76 billion in 2016, accounting for about half of China's total of both. In 2017, the value of contracts rose to $144 billion for 7,217 projects in sixty-one countries, up 15 percent. Actual project revenues received amounted to $86 billion, 51 percent of China's global total.[39]

Construction is dominated by large SOEs, which enjoy huge financial backing from state banks.[40] Bank of China, for example, has said it would lend $100 billion in 2016–2018 on BRI projects; CITIC Bank pledged total lending of $113 billion over an unspecified time frame.[41] Not all of these loans will truly go to BRI projects, as any number of loans may be labeled "Belt and Road" by savvy executives looking to impress their political masters. But there is no doubt that plenty of state-sponsored funding is available for enterprises engaged in projects that tick the requisite boxes.

By far the most significant financiers are China's two policy banks: China Development Bank (CDB) and the Export-Import Bank of China (Exim). In May 2017, Xi Jinping announced at the Belt and Road Forum—a bloated and costly international public relations exercise held in Beijing—that an extra $55 billion would be injected into China's policy banks to help bankroll BRI projects. Some of this cash will go to supporting SOEs' foreign operations; the bulk will probably be loaned to foreign governments that cannot afford to pay their Chinese constructors upfront. For several years, CDB and Exim have lent more in Asia than the World Bank and ADB combined.

CDB's original mandate was to support domestic infrastructure, but since 2008 it has also funded foreign resource acquisitions by state-owned firms. In addition to financing China's push across Africa, it helped grease big state-to-state oil deals with Venezuela, Russia, and Brazil. Its portfolio of international loans rose from nearly zero in 2007 to $187 billion in 2013, though its net lending fell back a little in 2014.[42] Its average annual net international lending exceeded any of the multilateral development banks in 2008–2014. CDB claimed to have lent $180 billion for BRI projects by the end of 2017.[43]

China Exim Bank, for its part, was traditionally a supplier of trade credits to facilitate exports and imports. But since 2010, it has also become a major financier overseas: in 2014 alone, it disbursed $151 billion, equivalent to the entire GDP of Bangladesh. Its accounts are rather opaque, but in 2014 its total non–trade related disbursements amounted to $80 billion—more than the combined lending of all the seven major multilateral development banks. Some of this was channeled to Chinese engineering firms and materials companies selling goods and services abroad, but Exim Bank probably ranks as the world's single biggest financier of overseas development.[44] It claimed to have lent $110 billion for BRI projects by the end of 2016.[45]

Over the past decade, China has become the world's most important source of development finance, but most loans issued by Chinese banks to foreign states and companies are still made on broadly commercial terms. The policy banks borrow in international capital markets at market prices, so they cannot afford to give money away at concessional rates. If borrowing countries default, the Chinese state will book the final loss. For this reason, the BRI and other economic activity overseas are not handouts: China's interests come first.

The BRI is, therefore, quite unlike the Marshall Plan, to which it is sometimes compared. According to economic historians, the United States gifted 90 percent of the $13 billion it plowed into Europe's war-ravaged economies between April 1948 and the summer of 1951—equivalent to $130 billion today, based on U.S. consumer-price inflation.[46] China is likely to provide far higher sums, but on much less generous terms. The caveat is that the Chinese government accepts that loans made for strategic rather than commercial reasons may never be repaid. Government officials privately admit they expect to lose up to 80 percent of their investment in Pakistan, 50 percent in Myanmar, and 30 percent in Central Asia.[47] That is a price worth paying, Beijing evidently believes, to secure geopolitical influence and/or greater border security.

Most Chinese financing comes in the form of export credits and loans made at market or close-to-market interest rates. In risky parts of the world, where other investors and financiers fear to tread, Chinese banks can even afford to charge much higher rates. This development finance generally comes with few—if any—strings attached, allowing rogue countries to pocket funds without making the kinds of economic or political reforms demanded by traditional aid donors.

Take Sri Lanka, to which China made a series of high-interest loans under the corrupt regime of the former president Mahinda Rajapaksa. The high rates charged by Chinese banks became a bone of contention when a new government took power in 2015, especially when it became apparent that funds had been siphoned off as kickbacks to Rajapaksa's cronies.[48] "The Chinese are not providing gifts," Ravi Karunanayake, Sri Lanka's then–finance minister told me that spring. "They've lent us $5 billion on very, very commercial terms. Most of the loans are at about 6 percent, but the highest is 8.8 percent."[49] By comparison, multilateral development banks typically charge well under 2 percent. In 2016, a Sri Lankan minister informed reporters that a Chinese lender, presumably China Exim Bank, had agreed to issue a large loan at an interest rate of 2 percent to enable Sri Lanka to pay off previous loans taken out at 6.9 percent.[50]

Beijing, then, is sometimes willing to renegotiate the terms of loans. In the right circumstances, it is also willing to provide grants and aid loans at minimal interest rates. In addition to the $8 billion lent to Sri Lanka at market rates, for example, Chinese banks made concessionary loans worth around $3 billion.[51] China does not regularly release statistics on its foreign aid, but it provided approximately 400 billion renminbi (about $60 billion) in development aid to 166 countries and international organizations between 1956 and 2016, according to a government white paper.[52] In 2013, it disbursed $7 billion in aid globally, ranking sixth, according to the OECD.[53] It is certainly by far the largest aid donor among developing countries.

A database compiled at the College of William & Mary suggests that China's aid program is actually more generous.[54] It estimates that Beijing committed to disbursing $354 billion of aid and development finance between 2000 and 2014. Well over $200 billion of this was loaned on nonconcessional terms for commercially oriented projects; but China also provided at least $80 billion of genuine development aid, in which 25 percent or more of the funds were given as free grants. Since a further $60 billion of Chinese financing was too opaque to be classified as either "nonconcessional" or "development aid," China's actual aid disbursement could easily have topped $100 billion. By comparison, the United States donated $366 billion of development aid during the same period.

Beijing's next task is to manage its aid programs more effectively. At the 2018 annual meeting of the National People's Congress, it was announced that a new International Development Cooperation Agency would be established to utilize foreign aid as "an important instrument for great power diplomacy." The new agency merges offices under the ministries of commerce and foreign affairs, which have typically handed out funds to client states or friendly foreign leaders.[55] As China grows richer and more confident, it is set to behave more like other rich economies, doling out aid across a broader range of developing countries in an attempt to win international goodwill.

Mixed Progress Along the Belt and the Road

China's ODI and development finance is designed to benefit the state by bringing both economic and diplomatic rewards. The Belt and Road Initiative is the most important piece of this effort, but it is too early to assess whether it is a success. China's diplomatic efforts to win friends across the developing world are ongoing, while building infrastructure and fostering new trade flows will take years. Much of the construction associated with the BRI was planned or already underway before Xi Jinping repackaged it under his grand initiative, so it is impossible to unravel many recent developments from preexisting projects and trends. At this early stage, it is fair to say only that the vastly increased political support offered since the BRI was announced has added considerable financial and diplomatic momentum to China's economic activity overseas.

The impact is most obvious in Pakistan, where the China-Pakistan Economic Corridor (CPEC)—an estimated $62 billion package of infrastructure, power, and agriculture projects that includes a highway linking landlocked western China to the Arabian Sea—was launched in 2015. Gwadar Port, the gateway to the corridor, opened in 2016 after upgrades worth $1.6 billion. China actually began work there as far back as 2002, completing the first phase of a deep-water port in 2007, but the BRI has provided extra cash and linked the project to the more ambitious economic corridor. China Overseas Port Holding Company plans to spend $4.5 billion on roads, power, hotels, and other infrastructure in Gwadar's industrial zone. Inland, several coal- and wind-power projects have been completed ahead of schedule, meaning that Pakistan is on course to eliminate a power shortage that has cost it an estimated 4–6 percent of GDP per year.[56]

In Central Asia, the New Eurasian Land Bridge—a series of roads and railway lines between China and Europe—has also made progress. Kazakhstan began building a railway linking China to Russia back in 2004, and the first rail services to Duisburg in Germany launched in 2012, a full year before Xi Jinping first spoke of building a new Silk Road. But freight traffic only really began to take off in 2015 and is accelerating rapidly. More than two thousand direct freight trains ran between China and Europe in 2017, nearly three times the total in 2015, connecting roughly thirty-five Chinese cities with twelve European countries, in as little as ten to fourteen days.[57] Sinotrans, the largest state-owned logistics firm, forecasts the number of trains will rise to five thousand in 2020.[58]

Projects to improve connectivity across Southeast Asia are also developing. One example is an alliance between ten Chinese ports and six Malaysian ports, which are working together to reduce bottlenecks and boost trade; China is investing $10 billion in a deep-sea port and commercial marina in Malacca. Up the coast, China Communications Construction Company has begun work on a 620-km rail line from Kuala Lumpur to the Thai border, financed by a $12 billion loan from China Exim Bank. In late 2017, construction began in northeast Thailand on a section of line that will link to a $7.2 billion railway across Laos, which Chinese engineers are busy carving through the jungle.[59] If all goes according to plan, these sections will eventually join up to form a 3,900-km railway from Kunming to Singapore.

Beyond Asia, Chinese engineers have upgraded the railway line from Nairobi to the port of Mombasa on Africa's east coast. A new Chinese-built and -operated railway also runs from Ethiopia to Djibouti, where China opened its first overseas military base in 2017. In the Mediterranean, China Ocean Shipping Company (COSCO) has invested at least 4.3 billion euros in Greece's Piraeus Port, which it acquired in 2016. Container throughput nearly quadrupled under its management between 2010 and 2015, with Huawei, ZTE, Samsung, HP, and Sony using Piraeus as their gateway to Europe. COSCO has committed to investing a further 700 million euros over the coming decade as it aims to make Piraeus the biggest commercial container port in the Mediterranean, eventually competing with the northern European hubs of Hamburg, Rotterdam, and Antwerp.[60]

Yet, despite these successes, doubts hang over the viability of many Belt and Road projects, for a variety of reasons. One issue is the lack of security in politically volatile states. An obvious example is Pakistan, which has reportedly deployed 14,500 security personnel to ensure the safety of some 7,000 Chinese nationals working on CPEC. The danger was evident in May 2017, when two Chinese-language teachers were kidnapped by armed men in Quetta, a remote but important section of the corridor. One of Beijing's motives in Pakistan is to prevent violent extremism seeping over the border into Xinjiang, where Beijing is brutally attempting to keep a lid on ethnic tensions between the native Muslim populace and Han Chinese immigrants. Far from being a commercial venture, "this massive investment is actually a form of bribe" to persuade Islamabad to get a grip on terrorism, says one Beijing-based expert.[61] But further trouble is almost inevitable.

The biggest challenge for many recipients of Chinese loans and aid is that their growing dependence risks turning them into vassal states. Here the prime test case is, again, Pakistan. When plans for CPEC were announced in April 2015, they were greeted with wild public enthusiasm. Yet public support has weakened since May 2017, when the *Dawn* newspaper got its hands on the original CPEC master plan.[62] Drawn up by CDB, which is financing much of the scheme, it lays out China's goals to 2030. It envisages a broad and deep penetration of Pakistan's agriculture, industry, and society, including leasing out thousands of acres of rural land to Chinese enterprises and building a twenty-four-hour surveillance system in cities from Peshawar to Karachi.

Critics fear that the hugely expensive initiative will leave Pakistan bankrupt and economically shackled to China. CDB's own appraisal of Pakistan's financial position is hardly encouraging: based on assessments made by the IMF, World Bank, and the ADB, it estimated in the report that Pakistan's economy could not absorb FDI much above $2 billion per year. "It is recommended that China's maximum annual direct investment in Pakistan should be around $1 billion," it concluded. Yet CDB alone lent $7.9 billion in 2006–2017,[63] while Industrial and Commercial Bank of China signed deals worth more than $4.5 billion in 2015.[64] The World Bank records that Chinese banks disbursed nearly $4 billion to Pakistan in the fiscal year ending June 30, 2017.[65]

Pakistan issued a $2.5 billion sovereign bond in late 2017, its largest ever, partly to pay for surging machinery imports associated with CPEC. It came after the national trade deficit widened to a worryingly high 8.7 percent of GDP, raising the prospect of an IMF bailout. The government in Islamabad remains a firm proponent of CPEC, but it is looking more carefully at the financial sustainability of individual projects. In November 2017, it withdrew a proposed $14 billion dam after concluding that Beijing's strict monetary conditions would damage its national interests.[66]

Criticism of the BRI is also deepening elsewhere in the developing world, where skeptics have begun to refer to "One Belt, One Trap." Skeptics fear that new railways in Southeast Asia will not deliver the economic benefits Beijing promises. The Laos section of the Kunming-to-Singapore line alone is projected to cost the equivalent of half the national annual economic output, while a much-hyped high-speed rail line between Bandung and Jakarta in Indonesia has suffered from expensive delays and may never be built. Meanwhile, the Malaysian government that took power in May 2018 immediately suspended more than $20 billion worth of "unequal treaties" made with Chinese firms. These included the East Coast Rail Link, China's biggest project in Southeast Asia, part of the network of railways it is building between southwest China and Singapore. "We do not want a situation where there is a new version of colonialism because poor countries are unable to compete with rich countries," Malaysian prime minister Mahathir Mohamed combatively told a press conference in Beijing in August 2018.[67]

China's image has been especially damaged by its actions in Sri Lanka, which is struggling to extricate itself from high-interest infrastructure loans negotiated under its corrupt former president. When I interviewed government ministers in March 2015, they stressed how determined they were to attract financing and investment from alternative sources. When they failed to do so, they had little option but to offer Chinese firms debt-for-equity swaps in Chinese-financed projects.[68] In December 2017, Colombo pocketed $1.1 billion in return for handing over the strategically located port of Hambantota to China Merchants Port Holdings on a ninety-nine-year lease. The deal came despite violent protests over the land around the port becoming a "Chinese colony."[69] In a tweet, the Xinhua News agency blithely called it "another milestone" along the Belt and Road.[70]

China has only grown more entrenched in Sri Lanka since criticism of its influence there became widespread. In the three years after the fall of Rajapaksa's government, Chinese firms invested $2.4 billion and won construction contracts worth $2.3 billion.[71] In January 2018, a minister confirmed that a consortium led by the state-run China Harbour Engineering Company, Ltd. would plow $1 billion into building office towers on reclaimed land in Colombo port.[72] Sri Lanka anticipates investing $13 billion in housing, marinas, health facilities, schools, and other facilities there over the next thirty years. A large chunk will almost certainly be financed by Chinese banks.

Sri Lanka owes China in the region of $8 billion, about 10 percent of its GDP. But it is far from being China's most vulnerable partner. A report by the Center for Global Development, a U.S. think tank, analyzed sixty-eight countries hosting BRI projects.[73] It found twenty-three at risk of debt distress, including eight at high risk: Pakistan, Djibouti, the Maldives, Laos, Mongolia, Montenegro, Tajikistan, and Kyrgyzstan. It predicts all eight countries could default on their sovereign debt if planned BRI projects go ahead. In addition, the IMF and World Bank's Debt Sustainability Framework for Low-income Countries rates Laos and the Maldives as already on the threshold of debt distress.[74]

Some of the most virulent criticisms of the BRI come from China's strategic competitors, not from the indebted countries themselves. Opponents in India argue that China's true goal is to advance its geopolitical interests. Its suspicions were first aroused when a People's Liberation Army Navy submarine docked at a Chinese-owned container port in Colombo in 2014, seeming to confirm its fears about China's ambitions to wrest control of the Indian Ocean. India has only grown more agitated by the progress of CPEC, which not only runs through disputed territory in

Kashmir and Gilgit-Baltistan, but also gives China a potential naval base at Gwadar in the Arabian Sea. Military chiefs view China's port-building in the Indian Ocean as a "string of pearls" threatening to choke Mother India. While some of these fears are overblown, China's financial muscle-flexing does threaten to weaken India's traditional grip in South Asia.

Another example is the Himalayan kingdom of Nepal, where a pro-China, communist government took power in March 2018. India has long and deep roots in its much smaller northeast neighbor, but China has exploited Nepali resentment of India to its advantage. With Beijing pledging $8.3 billion to build roads and hydropower plants as part of the BRI, Nepal's leaders have vowed to break away from New Delhi's "microman-agement." Beijing is even talking of building an $8 billion railway linking Kathmandu and Lhasa, the capital of Tibet.[75]

A similar story appeared to be playing out three thousand km south, in the Maldives, under its staunchly pro-Beijing president Abdullah Yameen. China Communications Construction Company was contracted to build a 1.3km "friendship bridge" linking the airport island to Malé, the capi-tal, and to expand the airport, build roads, and erect a twenty-five-story hospital.[76] In November 2017, Yameen rushed a controversial free-trade deal with China through parliament in just one hour, despite angry pro-tests from the opposition. There was much speculation in New Delhi that Yameen, who had been strongly backing the Maritime Silk Road, would allow China to set up a naval base on the palm-covered island of Gaadhoo in the heart of the Indian Ocean. But the president's cozying up to Beijing eventually backfired: in September 2018, he was deposed by a rival who pledged to loosen ties with China and restore relations with India.

Discontent with the BRI has even spread to Europe, where crit-ics accuse China of strategically building stocks of influence.[77] Its sway is strongest in Central and Eastern Europe, where the 16+1 framework has sown division within the European Union. In June 2017, not long after Cosco took control of Piraeus Port, Athens shot down a joint Euro-pean Union resolution condemning China's human rights abuses.[78] And in Hungary, where China Railway International Corporation is building a 3.2 billion euro high-speed railway from Budapest to Belgrade, Prime Minister Viktor Orbán has played the China card to put pressure on his EU partners. "Central Europe needs capital to build new roads and pipe-lines," Mr. Orbán said in Berlin in early 2018. "If the EU is unable to provide enough capital, we will just collect it in China." To help matters along, Hungary has worked to prevent a strong EU stance against China's territorial advances in the South China Sea.[79]

As elsewhere, China's economic influence in Greece and Hungary shows the efficacy of its strategy to use loans and investment to buy diplomatic leverage. But Beijing needs to beware negative political repercussions: if it is seen to be interfering in Europe, then the momentum for greater investment protections and other retaliatory measures will only strengthen. It does not help that Chinese-sponsored investments bring so few opportunities for local firms. Foreign firms are struggling to benefit commercially from the BRI, despite Beijing's protestations that it is open to all. According to a report by CSIS, a full 89 percent of contractors on BRI projects tracked by its database were Chinese, while just 3 percent of contracts were won by third parties.[80] If the initiative brings strife without opportunity, international support will wane.

The risk of blowback is even stronger in Asia, where fear of China and resentment of its influence runs deep. Populist resistance to Chinese investments is a hazard for Chinese firms, especially in fragile states run by authoritarian governments, where regime change can see dramatic shifts in the political winds. China has bitter experience of this in Myanmar, where it rapidly lost its grip after spending more than two decades cultivating close ties with the military junta. When the regime crumbled in 2011, political liberalization gave ordinary people a voice to protest against China's presence, forcing the government to postpone or cancel Chinese investments worth many billions of dollars. Bilateral relations have improved since 2016, mainly thanks to China's support of Aung San Suu Kyi's government during the Rohingya refugee crisis. But the events in Myanmar could be echoed in other countries where China's presence breeds ill will.

To be sure, the Belt and Road Initiative has the potential to bring useful infrastructure, new trade routes, and better connectivity across underdeveloped parts of the world—even if it does deliver some costly boondoggles along the way. Yet few of China's potential partners wholeheartedly believe that its infrastructure diplomacy is really designed to deliver win-win development: more often, it is presumed to mean a double-win for China. Much of the success of the BRI will depend on Beijing's ability to persuade its partner countries that working closely with it is really in their best interests.

Conclusion

Only a decade ago, China was largely a passive player in the game of global investment flows: as a relatively undeveloped economy, it received ever-growing investments at home, but its own investments abroad were both small and limited to the acquisition of natural resources. Today, a much wealthier China is one of the world's biggest investors, with an ODI stock approaching $1.5 trillion.[81] At least twenty countries have received Chinese investment or construction worth $20 billion or more.[82] Yet China's investments and economic activity overseas are under scrutiny as never before. In the rich world, the state-backed acquisition of foreign technology is stoking protectionism. In the developing world, where the Belt and Road Initiative promises to bring much-needed infrastructure, the greater fear is one of economic—and growing political—dependence.

China will not retreat from high-profile industrial policies that cause particular concern, such as the Made in China 2025 plan or its strategy to develop a world-class semiconductor industry. These are central to Xi's vision of an economically powerful China and are not open for negotiation. But the onus may have to switch to developing these industries domestically if the United States and Europe block purchases of high technology on national security grounds. In 2015 alone, Chinese companies announced takeovers of foreign semiconductor firms worth $35 billion. Since then, several other proposed acquisitions of semiconductor firms have been derailed by CFIUS. The Trump administration is toughening scrutiny on all Chinese technology investments, while political support for restrictions on Chinese investment is also calcifying in Europe.

Meanwhile, the Belt and Road Initiative will continue to elicit both hope and fear. The challenge for China's partner countries is how to extract as much economic benefit from it as they can without losing economic or political sovereignty. This is a precarious balancing act. Almost all states in China's immediate vicinity are putting in place hedging strategies to ensure they do not become appendages of the Chinese giant next door. Vietnam, for example, has moved markedly closer to the United States in recent years. Nevertheless, the weakest states will struggle to remain truly independent.

That may be an acceptable trade-off for some countries desperately seeking economic development. That is their choice: Beijing cannot force anyone to accept its money. Canny governments are also happy to play China off against other states or multilateral lenders—especially in Southeast Asia, where Japan is doling out cheap funds to maintain its traditional influence in the face of Chinese competition.

Instead, the greater danger may actually be to the state banks financing Chinese investments and projects overseas. If their foreign partners cannot service their debts, they will eventually seek debt relief from Beijing. This will be painful—as Chinese banks have already found to their great cost in Venezuela, a bankrupt state to which they have loaned more than $60 billion. In time, China may come to regret burdening itself with desperate client states that cannot repay.

Yet that is a risk that the Chinese government seems willing to bear. The role of the state in enabling and directing the stream of Chinese capital overseas has ebbed and flowed over the years, but there is little doubt about the priorities of the current leadership. State firms, whether buying semiconductors or building bridges, are expected to be profitable in the pursuit of national strategic objectives—but Beijing will bail them out if they lose money on foreign adventures taken at the behest of the state. It will also support private firms in realizing their overseas ambitions, but only insofar as their investments and activities overseas are deemed beneficial to China Inc.

Forty years after it began to open up to the world, China has developed into one of the biggest sources of global investment. If the world lets it—and China is politically vulnerable, despite its economic leverage—it has the potential to dominate global capital flows for the next forty years. That was unimaginable only a few decades ago.

Notes

1. Much of this chapter is based on my most recent book, which I do not reference elsewhere. See Tom Miller, *China's Asian Dream: Empire Building Along the New Silk Road* (London, United Kingdom: Zed Books, 2017).

2. Here I am using balance-of-payments data rather than aggregated investment data. See the World Bank, "Foreign direct investment, net inflows (BoP, current US$), 1982–2016" (https://data.worldbank.org/indicator/BX.KLT.DINV.CD.WD?end=2016&locations=CN&start=1982&view=chart).

3. Xi Jinping made his first public comments on the "Chinese Dream," also translated as "China Dream," when he visited "The Road Toward Renewal" exhibition at the National Museum of China on November 29, 2012.

4. For a useful roundup of Xi's speeches on the "Chinese Dream," in which he talks about China becoming "wealthy and strong" (fuqiang), see *"Xí Jìnpíng zŏng shūjì 15 piān jiǎnghuà xìtŏng chǎnshù 'zhōngguó mèng"* [General Secretary Xi Jinping's 15 speeches expound the "Chinese Dream"], People's Daily Online, June 19, 2013.

5. The lower number comes from the Ministry of Commerce, which records individual investments. The higher number is from the State Administration of Foreign Exchange, which calculates the balance of payments and includes financial investments and reinvested earnings. See the chart on p. 4 of the 2016 official ODI report, *"2016 Niándù zhōng guó duìwài zhíjiē tóuzī tŏngjì gōngbào"* [2016 China Statistical Bulletin on Foreign Direct Investment], Ministry of Commerce, November 2017.

6. See Yanmei Xie, "Rebooting China Inc.," Gavekal Dragonomics, September 15, 2017.

7. *"Fāzhăn găigé wěi děng sì bùmén jiù dāngqián duìwài tóuzī xíngshì xià jiāqiáng duìwài tóuzī jiānguǎn dá jìzhě wèn"* [The National Development and Reform Commission and four other departments answered questions on strengthening foreign investment supervision under the current foreign investment situation], National Development and Reform Commission, December 6, 2016.

8. *"Zhōngyāng qǐyè jìngwài tóuzī jiāndū guǎnlǐ bànfǎ"* [Measures for the Supervision and Administration of Overseas Investment by Central Enterprises], State-owned Assets Supervision and Administration Commission of the State Council, January 18, 2017.

9. *"Zhōngguó rénmíng yínháng xíng zhǎng zhōu xiǎochuān jiù jīnróng găigé yǔ fāzhăn dá jìzhě wèn"* [Zhou Xiaochuan, Governor of the People's Bank of China, answered questions on financial reform and development], National People's Congress (transcript), March 10, 2017.

10. Lucy Hornby et al., "Big China companies targeted over 'systematic risk'," *Financial Times*, June 23, 2017.

11. See Thilo Hanemann et al., "Chinese FDI in the US in 2017: A Double Policy Punch," Rhodium Group, January 17, 2018.

12. Tom Hancock et al., "China seizes Anbang in latest move to curb dealmakers," *Financial Times*, February 23, 2018.

13. See, e.g., Derek Scissors, "Private Data, Not Private Firms: The Real Issues in Chinese Investment," AEI, January 10, 2018.

14. AEI, China Global Investment Tracker (www.aei.org/china-global-investment-tracker/).

15. Rhodium Group, China Investment Monitor: Capturing Chinese Foreign Investment Data in Real Time (https://rhg.com/interactive/china-investment-monitor).

16. The CGIT's record of individual transactions shows that ODI actually rose by 9 percent to $181 billion in 2017. Derek Scissors, who manages the CGIT, suggests that the bulk of ChemChina's record $43 billion acquisition of Swiss agrotech giant Syngenta does not seem to have been counted. Still, he concedes that

the number of transactions fell, as did volume in many countries and sectors. Scissors, "Private Data, Not Private Firms: The Real Issues in Chinese Investment."

17. Hanemann, "Chinese FDI in the US in 2017: A Double Policy Punch."

18. See Thilo Hanemann et al., *Record Flows and Growing Imbalances: Chinese Investment in Europe in 2016*," Merics Papers on China, January 2017.

19. OECD Data, "FDI Restrictiveness" (https://data.oecd.org/fdi/fdi-restrictiveness.htm).

20. Scissors, "Private Data, Not Private Firms: The Real Issues in Chinese Investment."

21. Xie, "Rebooting China Inc."

22. *Findings of the Investigation into China's Acts, Policies, and Practices Related to Technology Transfer, Intellectual Property, and Innovation Under Section 301 of the Trade Act of 1974*, Office of the United States Trade Representative, March 22, 2018.

23. Saleha Mohsin et al., "Trump Decides Against Harshest Measures on China Investments," Bloomberg, June 27, 2018.

24. "Tariff List—September 17, 2018," Office of the United States Trade Representative (https://ustr.gov/sites/default/files/enforcement/301Investigations/Tariff%20List-09.17.18.pdf).

25. David McLaughlin et al., "Congress Toughens Foreign Deal Reviews with China in Crosshairs," Bloomberg, August 1, 2018.

26. Charlene Barshefsky et al., "The US Tightens Export Controls, Targeting China," WilmerHale, August 2, 2018.

27. "China Manufacturing 2025: Putting Industrial Policy Ahead of Market Forces," European Union Chamber of Commerce in China, March 2017.

28. See Thorsten Benner et al., *Authoritarian Advance: Responding to China's Growing Political Influence in Europe*, GPPI and Merics, February 2018.

29. Naboth van den Broek et al., "EU and Germany Move to Further Tighten FDI Screening Process," WilmerHale, December 20, 2018.

30. See Deborah Brautigam, "China in Africa: Investors, not Infesters," *China Economic Quarterly*, Gavekal Dragonomics, September 2012.

31. A list of member countries is available on the official Belt and Road Portal, Office of the Leading Group for the Belt and Road Initiative, State Information Center (https://eng.yidaiyilu.gov.cn/info/iList.jsp?cat_id=10076&cur_page=1).

32. "President Xi Jinping Delivers Important Speech and Proposes to Build a Silk Road Economic Belt with Central Asian Countries," Ministry of Foreign Affairs (transcript), September 7, 2013.

33. "Speech by Chinese President Xi Jinping to Indonesian Parliament," ASEAN-China Center, October 2, 2013.

34. Just how ambitious is a subject of much debate. The BRI is often referred to as $1 trillion project; sometimes even higher figures are quoted. The truth is that there is no official number, and we can only guess how much capital will be plowed into BRI projects over the coming decade and beyond.

35. "Vision and Actions on Jointly Building Silk Road Economic Belt and

21st-Century Maritime Silk Road," National Development and Reform Commission et al., March 28, 2015.

36. The six corridors are: (1) New Eurasian Land Bridge from China to Europe; (2) China-Mongolia-Russia Corridor; (3) China-Central Asia-West Asia Corridor to Turkey; (4) China-Indochina Peninsula Corridor; (5) Bangladesh-China-Myanmar-India Economic Corridor; (6) China-Pakistan Economic Corridor.

37. One good example of the power of economic incentives came in October 2016, when China secured an unexpected diplomatic coup with the Philippines. Just three months after Manila won its international arbitration appeal against China's maritime claims in the South China Sea, Philippines president Rodrigo Duterte returned home from Beijing with a trade and investment package worth $24 billion. Since then, territorial tensions between the two countries have cooled considerably.

38. "*2017 Nián wǒ duì 'yīdài yīlù' yánxiàn guójiā tóuzī hézuò qíngkuàng*" [Overview of investment and cooperation with countries along the Belt and Road in 2017], Ministry of Commerce, January 16, 2018 (http://fec.mofcom.gov.cn/article/fwydyl/tjsj/201801/20180102699450.shtml).

39. "*2017 Nián wǒ duì 'yīdài yīlù' yánxiàn guójiā tóuzī hézuò qíngkuàng*" Ministry of Commerce.

40. The "Belt and Road Big Data Report 2017," published by the State Council Information Center, lists the top ten Chinese enterprises taking part in BRI projects. Eight are state-owned: State Grid Corporation of China, State Power Investment Corporation, China National Petroleum Corporation, Sinopec Corporation, China Railway Construction Corporation Limited, CRRC Corporation Limited, Bank of China, and China Mobile Communications Corporation. The two private firms are Alibaba Group and Huawei Technologies Co., Ltd. See "B&R by the Numbers: Enterprises need to be prepared for B&R projects," Office of the Leading Group for the Belt and Road Initiative, State Information Center, December 21, 2017.

41. Arthur Kroeber, "Financing China's global dreams," *China Economic Quarterly*, Gavekal Dragonomics, November 2015.

42. See Henry Sanderson and Michael Forsythe, *China's Superbank: Debt, Oil and Influence—How China Development Bank Is Rewriting the Rules of Finance* (Singapore: Wiley, 2013).

43. "Will China's Belt and Road Initiative Outdo the Marshall Plan?" *Economist*, March 8, 2017.

44. Kroeber, "Financing China's global dreams."

45. "Will China's Belt and Road Initiative Outdo the Marshall Plan?"

46. "Will China's Belt and Road Initiative Outdo the Marshall Plan?"

47. Author interview with Sun Yun in Washington, DC, October 2, 2015.

48. Author interviews with government ministers in Colombo, March 13, 2015.

49. Author interview, March 13, 2015.

50. See Kalinga Seneviratne, "Sri Lanka Turning Anew Into a Geopoliti-

cal Battle Ground—Analysis," *Eurasia Review*, January 30, 2016. A smaller loan was granted by Exim Bank later that year: see "Cabinet approves fresh loan from China EXIM Bank," June 9, 2016.

51. AIDData, a Reseach Lab at William & Mary, "China's Global Development Footprint" (http://aiddata.org/china).

52. "China provides world with 58 bln USD in development aid in six decades: white paper," *Xinhua*, December 1, 2016.

53. See Naohiro Kitano et al., *Estimating China's Foreign Aid 2001–2013*, JICA Research Institute, June 2014. Further information can be found in the *White Paper on China's Foreign Aid (2014)*, State Council, July 10, 2014.

54. AIDData, "China's Global Development Footprint."

55. See Yanmei Xie, "A New Organization Chart," Gavekal Dragonomics, March 14, 2018.

56. Arif Rafiq, "The China-Pakistan Economic Corridor: Three Years Later," *Reconnecting Asia*, February 12, 2018.

57. Jonathan Hillman, "The Rise of China-Europe Railways," Center for Strategic and International Studies, March 6, 2018.

58. "Introduction of Rail Transportation Business," Sinotrans Limited, June 2, 2017.

59. Luke Hunt, "Construction of Thailand-China Railway Finally Gets Underway," *Diplomat*, December 28, 2017.

60. David Glass, "Cosco reveals $620m Piraeus development plan," *Seatrade Maritime News*, January 29, 2018.

61. Author interview in Beijing, June 19, 2015.

62. Khurram Husain, "Exclusive: CPEC master plan revealed," *Dawn*, June 21, 2017.

63. *"Bājīsītǎn zhōng diàn hú bù 2×66 wàn qiānwǎ rán méi diànzhàn róngzī qiānyuē yíshì jǔxíng"* [Signing ceremony for the financing of two 660,000 KW coal-fired power stations in Pakistan], Xinhua, October 24, 2017.

64. Ismail Dilawar, "Chinese-Led Infrastructure Boom Mostly Bypasses Pakistan's Banks," Bloomberg, 26 October 2017.

65. "Pakistan Development Update: Managing Risks for Sustained Growth," World Bank, November 2017.

66. Shahbaz Rana, "Pakistan stops bid to include Diamer-Bhasha Dam in CPEC," *Tribune*, 15 November 2017.

67. Philip Wen, "Mahathir says China will sympathize with Malaysia's problems," Reuters, August 20, 2018.

68. Ben Blanchard, "Sri Lanka requests equity swap for some of its $8 bln China debt," Reuters, April 9, 2016.

69. "Protest over Hambantota port deal turns violent," Al Jazeera, January 7, 2017.

70. China Xinhua News tweeted this on December 9, 2017.

71. AEI, China Global Investment Tracker.

72. Shihar Aneez, "China Harbour Engineering to invest $1 billion in Sri

Lanka's Port City: minister," Reuters, January 2, 2018.

73. John Hurley et al., "Examining the Debt Implications of the Belt and Road Initiative from a Policy Perspective," CGD Policy Paper 121, March 2018.

74. IMF, List of LIC DSAs for PRGT-Eligible Countries, January 31, 2019 (https://www.imf.org/external/pubs/ft/dsa/dsalist.pdf).

75. See, e.g., Debasish Roy Chowdhury, "Driven by India into China's Arms, Is Nepal the New Sri Lanka?," *South China Morning Post*, February 25, 2018.

76. See, e.g., "In South Asia, Chinese infrastructure brings debt and antagonism," *Economist*, March 18, 2018.

77. Benner et al., *Authoritarian Advance.*

78. Robin Emmott et al., "Greece blocks EU statement on China human rights at U.N.," Reuters, June 18, 2017.

79. Thorsten Benner and Kristin Shi-Kupfer, "Europe needs to step up vigilance on China's influence," *Financial Times*, February 16, 2018.

80. Hillman, "The Rise of China-Europe Railways."

81. *"2016 Niándù zhōng guó duìwài zhíjiē tóuzī tǒngjì gōngbào"* [2016 China Statistical Bulletin on Foreign Direct Investment], Ministry of Commerce.

82. Scissors, "Private Data, Not Private Firms: The Real Issues in Chinese Investment."

ACKNOWLEDGMENTS

The chapters in this book are based on papers initially presented at the sixth annual conference of the Center for the Study of Contemporary China at the University of Pennsylvania. We are grateful to distinguished discussants at the conference whose comments and suggestions provided valuable guidance as the authors prepared their chapters. The discussants include Ling Chen, Hanming Fang, Yue Hou, Devesh Kapur, Margaret Pearson, Joel Trachtman, Juan Wang, and Minyuan Zhao.

We thank all of the conference participants for their helpful advice, as well as the anonymous reviewer whose comments improved this book. We are also very grateful to Bill Finan, Elliott Beard, and Cecilia González at Brookings Institution Press, who facilitated the preparation of this volume.

We thank Jamie Seah for her assistance in running the conference. We are especially grateful to Dr. Yuanyuan Zeng, Associate Director of the Center for the Study of Contemporary China, whose distinctive combination of substantive expertise and administrative skills are vital to the success of the center's program, of which this book is a part.

This volume would not have been possible without the financial support of the Center for the Study of Contemporary China, whose funding is provided by the University of Pennsylvania's provost, as well as Penn's School of Arts and Sciences, Law School, Annenberg School for Communications, and Wharton School.

CONTRIBUTORS

JACQUES DELISLE, is the Stephen A. Cozen Professor of Law and Professor of Political Science, Director of the Center for East Asian Studies, Co-Director of the Center for Asian Law, and Deputy Director of the Center for the Study of Contemporary China at the University of Pennsylvania. He is also Director of the Asia Program at the Foreign Policy Research Institute. His research focuses on Chinese law and politics, including China's engagement with the international legal order, Taiwan's international status, domestic legal reform in China, and comparative law in East Asia. His books include *China's Global Engagement: Cooperation, Competition, and Influence in the 21st Century* (2017, co-edited with Avery Goldstein), *The Internet, Social Media, and a Changing China* (2015, co-edited with Avery Goldstein and Guobin Yang), and *Political Changes in Taiwan under Ma Ying-jeou* (2014, co-edited with Jean-Pierre Cabestan). His writings have appeared in *Orbis, Journal of Contemporary China*, and many law reviews and edited volumes.

AVERY GOLDSTEIN, is the David M. Knott Professor of Global Politics and International Relations in the Political Science Department, Director of Center for the Study of Contemporary China, and Associate Director of the Christopher H. Browne Center for International Politics at the University of Pennsylvania. His research focuses on international relations, security studies, and Chinese politics. Goldstein's books include *Rising to the Challenge: China's Grand Strategy and International Security* (2005), *China's Global Engagement: Cooperation, Competition, and Influence in the 21st Century* (2017, co-edited with Jacques deLisle), and *The Nexus of Economics, Security, and International Relations in East Asia* (2012, co-edited with Edward D. Mansfield). His articles have appeared in *International Security, Foreign Affairs, International Organization,* the *Journal of Strategic Studies, China Quarterly, Asian Survey, Comparative Politics, Orbis,* and *Security Studies.*

DAVID DOLLAR is a senior fellow in the John L. Thornton China Center at the Brookings Institution. From 2009 to 2013, Dollar was the U.S. Treasury's economic and financial emissary to China, based in Beijing. Prior to joining Treasury, Dollar worked twenty years for the World Bank, serving as country director for China and Mongolia, based in Beijing (2004–2009). His other World Bank assignments focused on Asian economies. Dollar also worked in the World Bank's research department, focusing on economic reform in China, globalization, and economic growth. He also taught economics at UCLA and spent a semester in Beijing at the Graduate School of the Chinese Academy of Social Sciences in 1986. He has a doctorate in economics from New York University and a bachelor's in Chinese history and language from Dartmouth College.

YASHENG HUANG is Epoch Foundation Professor of International Management at MIT Sloan School of Management and served as an associate dean between 2013 and 2017. He is currently involved in three research areas: (1) a book project on the nature of the Chinese state, (2) collaborating with researchers at Tsinghua University to construct databases on historical inventions in China, and (3) a co-PI in a multidisciplinary research team at MIT on food safety (supported by the FDA between 2013 and 2016 and by the Walmart Foundation since 2016). He has published eleven books in English and in Chinese and many papers in academic journals.

YUKON HUANG is a senior fellow at the Carnegie Endowment in Washington, DC. He was formerly the World Bank's country director for China and, earlier, Russia. His research focuses on China's economy and its global impact. Dr. Huang has published widely on development issues in professional journals and the public media, including the *Financial Times,* the *Wall Street Journal,* the *New York Times,* and *Foreign Affairs.* His latest book, *Cracking the China Conundrum: Why Conventional Economic Wisdom Is Wrong,* was published in 2017 by Oxford University Press. He has a PhD in economics from Princeton University and a BA from Yale University.

XIAOJUN LI is an assistant professor of political science at the University of British Columbia and a former Princeton-Harvard China and the World Postdoctoral Fellow at Harvard University's Fairbank Center for Chinese Studies. He holds a PhD in political science from Stanford University. His research explores the domestic origins of foreign economic policies with a focus on China's trade and investment policies. His work has appeared in the *Journal of Politics, International Studies Quarterly,* the *Canadian Journal of Political Science,* the *Journal of Experimental Political Science, Foreign Policy Analysis, International Relations of the Asia-Pacific,* and the *Journal of Contemporary China,* among other peer-reviewed journals.

TOM MILLER is a senior analyst at Gavekal Dragonomics, where he edited the *China Economic Quarterly* from 2008 until 2017. A former journalist, he has reported from a dozen countries in Asia. His most recent book, *China's Asian Dream: Empire Building Along the New Silk Road* (2017), has been translated into five languages. His first book, *China's Urban Billion: The Story Behind the Biggest Migration in Human History* (2012), was translated into Chinese. Tom studied English literature at Oxford, Chinese history and politics at the School of Oriental and African Studies (SOAS) in London, and the Chinese language in Beijing.

BARRY NAUGHTON is the So Kwanlok Professor, School of Global Policy and Strategy, University of California, San Diego. Naughton's work on the Chinese economy focuses on market transition, industry and technology, foreign trade, and political economy. His first book, *Growing Out of the Plan,* won the Ohira Prize in 1996, and a new edition of his popular survey and textbook, *The Chinese Economy: Adaptation and Growth,* appeared in 2018. Naughton received his PhD in Economics from Yale University in 1986.

JEAN C. OI is the William Haas Professor of Chinese Politics in the Department of Political Science and a Senior Fellow of the Freeman Spogli

Institute for International Studies at Stanford University. She directs the China Program at the Walter H. Shorenstein Asia-Pacific Research Center and is the Lee Shau Kee Director of the Stanford Center at Peking University. Oi has published extensively on China's reforms. Her recent books include *Zouping Revisited: Adaptive Governance in a Chinese County*, co-edited with Steven Goldstein (2018), and *Challenges in the Process of China's Urbanization*, co-edited with Karen Eggleston and Yiming Wang (2017). Her current research is on fiscal reform and local government debt as well as continuing SOE reforms.

VICTOR C. SHIH is associate professor at the School of Global Policy and Strategy at the University of California, San Diego, specializing in China. He is the author of a book published by the Cambridge University Press, titled *Factions and Finance in China: Elite Conflict and Inflation*. He is also the author of numerous articles appearing in academic and business journals, including the *American Political Science Review, Comparative Political Studies,* the *Journal of Politics,* and the *Wall Street Journal.* Shih served as principal in The Carlyle Group's global market strategy group and continues to advise the financial community on China-related issues. He is currently working on a book on elite coalition strategies under Mao and Xi, as well as several papers using quantitative data to analyze the Chinese political elite.

INDEX